day trips® series

day trip
kansas city

sixteenth edition

 getaway ideas for the local traveler

diana lambdin meyer

gpp®

travel

Guilford, Connecticut

All the information in this guidebook is subject to change. We recommend that you call ahead to obtain current information before traveling.

Maps: XNR Productions Inc. © **Rowman & Littlefield**
Spot photography throughout © Trevor Goodwin/licensed by Shutterstock.com

ISSN 1538-4993
ISBN 978-0-7627-7934-5

Printed in the United States of America

contents

southwest

day trip 01

day trip 02

day trip 03

west

day trip 01

day trip 02

day trip 03

day trip 04

day trip 05

day trip 06

northwest

day trip 01

day trip 02

day trip 03

day trip 04

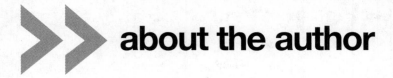

about the author

Diana Lambdin Meyer of Parkville has contributed to dozens of travel guidebooks and written thousands of articles for newspapers, magazines, and websites during her freelance writing career that spans three decades. She is an award-winning member of the Midwest Travel Writers Association and the Society of American Travel Writers. She and her husband, Bruce, a professional photographer, travel the world in search of stories, education, and adventure, but the Midwest remains their home and their heart in all professional pursuits.

day trips from kansas city

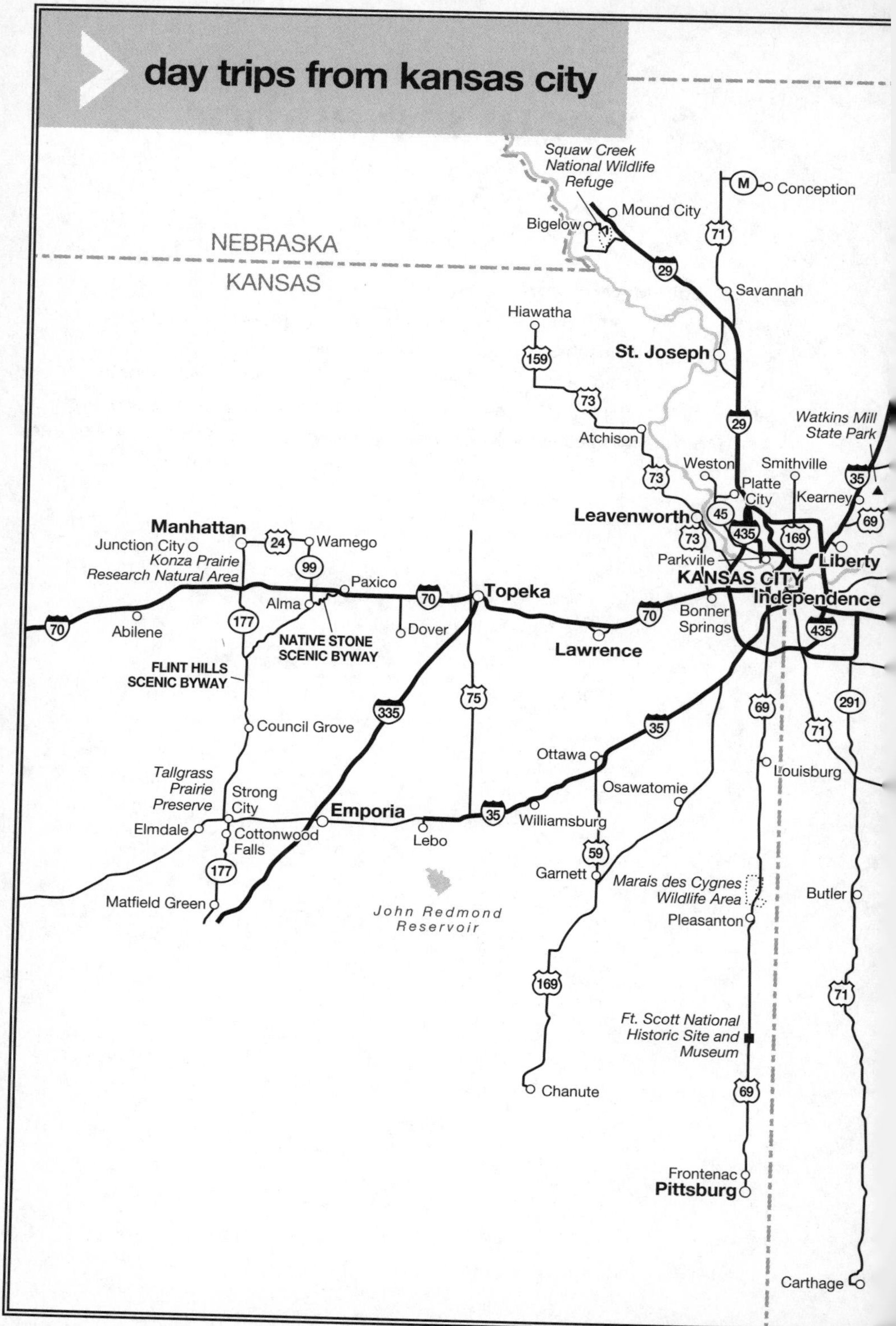

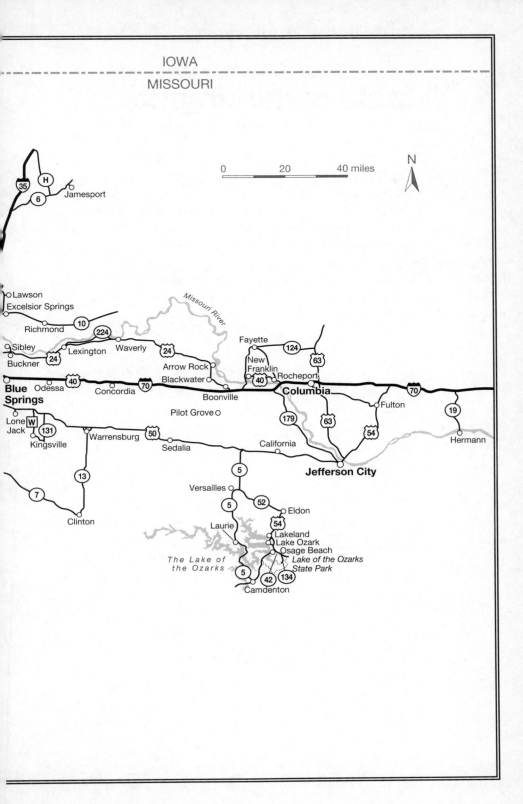

acknowledgments

I knew the name and the work of Shifra Stein long before I knew her cackling laugh, her energetic wit, and the warmth of her friendship. Although I didn't know it, my life became much richer and much more complex the day she and I met for the first time for lunch in the River Market. I don't even remember the day or the year. She and her husband/ photographer, Bob Barrett, became a meaningful force in my life and that of my husband/ photographer, Bruce. Although I worked with Shifra behind the scenes on several editions of *Day Trips* before this, the 16th edition on which my name appears solo, this is and always will be Shifra Stein's *Day Trips from Kansas City*.

introduction

Day Trips from Kansas City has had a long and happy life. It was first published in 1980, the year I graduated from college, having been written on an old electric typewriter. The Internet was limited to molasses-in-January-like communication among a few scholarly communities. Cordless telephones were rare indeed and the concept of cellular phones was all but unknown. Global Positioning Systems (GPS) were high-tech pieces of equipment costing thousands of dollars that helped airline pilots arrive at their assigned destinations.

That was the environment in which *Day Trips* was born, a world much different from that which we experience today. But one thing has not changed—a desire to throw off the shackles of the everyday and get away to refresh our spirits, if just for a few hours. Otherwise, we become stale, monotonous, and boring company.

During its lifetime, *Day Trips* has been updated and revised every couple of years, incorporating numerous suggestions from readers and travelers who excel in exploration far from the madding crowds, a destination first identified by the poet Thomas Gray in 1751. Even then, the peace and quiet and change of pace were valued among sensitive souls.

That's where this *Day Trips* takes you—to places where the whippoorwill calls and the tall grass prairie whispers from its untouched pastures. Wrapped in these pages are lessons in history and tutorials in human nature, inspirational locations that will stir your creative spirit, and quirky places that should make you smile.

We're uniquely fortunate here in America's heartland that so much of the world has traveled here before us, albeit in covered wagons, steamboats, and coal-fired locomotives. However, it's time you make your own trail. This copy of *Day Trips from Kansas City* will hopefully help you find your way.

But perhaps you'll seek your own road to places you've never been before. Having seen them, please let us know. We're always open for new places to call our own.

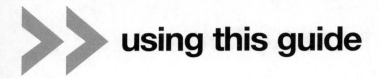

using this guide

Day Trips from Kansas City is organized by general direction from the downtown area: northeast, east, southeast, south, southwest, west, and northwest. It by no means purports to cover every worthy destination, but offers 22 complete trips that will appeal to couples, families, friends, and fellow travelers.

hours & prices

In the interest of accuracy and because they frequently change, hours of operation and attraction prices are given in general terms. (***Note:*** Most attraction listings mention only that there is an admission fee.) Always remember to call ahead to get the most up-to-date information, as websites are not always reliable. If you have questions, contact the establishments for specifics.

pricing key

The price codes for accommodations and restaurants are represented as a scale of one to three dollar signs ($). You can assume all establishments listed accept major credit cards unless otherwise noted. For details, contact the locations directly.

accommodations

The price code reflects the average cost of a double-occupancy room during the peak price period (not including tax or extras). Please also note that during peak season in some areas, a 2-night stay (or more) is required. Always check online or call to find out if any special discounts are available.

$	Less than $100
$$	$100 to $175
$$$	More than $175

restaurants

The price code reflects the average price of dinner entrees for two (excluding cocktails, wine, appetizers, desserts, tax, and tip). You should usually expect to pay less for lunch and/or breakfast, when applicable.

$	$10 to $20
$$	$20 to $40
$$$	More than $40

Wheelchair accessibility: The designation is provided only for those wildlife areas and historic sites that provide amenities for the physically challenged.

Lewis and Clark Trail: The designation is provided to highlight sites associated with the Corps of Discovery journey through this region in 1804–06.

where to get more information

Day Trips attempts to cover a variety of bases and interests, but if you're looking for additional material, plenty is out there. Most states and cities, and even some smaller towns, have their own tourism bureaus, so for most trips, they are listed as a first "Where to Go" location. They are a good place to start, often offering comprehensive websites and welcoming calls, e-mails, or requests for printed visitor guides, brochures, and maps. In addition to the resources in this book, some additional sources of information include:

kansas

Kansas Department of Wildlife, Parks and Tourism
512 SE Twenty-fifth Ave.
Pratt, KS 67124
(620) 672-5911
www.kdwp.state.ks.us

The Kansas Historical Society
6425 SW Sixth Ave.
Topeka, KS 66615
(785) 272-8681
www.kshs.org

Kansas Travel and Tourism
1020 S. Kansas Ave., #200
Topeka, KS 66612
(785) 296-2009
www.travelks.com

missouri

Missouri Department of Conservation
PO Box 180
Jefferson City, MO 65102-0180
(573) 751-4115

Kansas City Office
8616 E. Sixty-third St.
Kansas City, MO 64133
(816) 356-2280
www.conservation.state.mo.us

Missouri Department of Natural Resources
Division of State Parks
PO Box 176
Jefferson City, MO 65102
(800) 334-6946
www.mostateparks.com

Missouri Department of Tourism
PO Box 1055
Jefferson City, MO 65102
(573) 751-4133 or (800) 519-2100
www.visitmo.com

Missouri Historical Society
PO Box 11940
St. Louis, MO 63112
(314) 746-4599
www.mohistory.org

Platte County Convention and Visitors Bureau
11724 NW Plaza Circle, #200
Kansas City, MO 64153
(816) 270-3979 or (888) 875-2883
www.visitplatte.com

Kansas City District Corps of Engineers
700 Federal Building
Kansas City, MO 64106
(816) 983-3632
Campers 62 or older may purchase Golden Age Passports for a modest cost and get half off on all camping fees in US Army Corps of Engineers parks.

Kansas City Regional Destination Alliance
www.kcdestinations.com

Lewis and Clark Trail
www.nps.gov/lecl

northeast

day trip 01

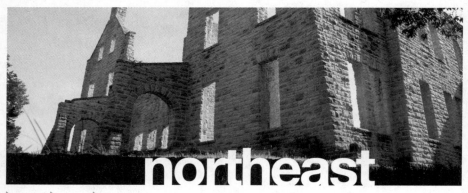

northeast

city by the lake:
smithville, mo

smithville, mo

Humphrey Smith came to Clay County in 1822 and built the first grain mill north of the Missouri River on the Little Platte River. The town that developed was known as Smith's Fork but later was incorporated as Smith's Mill. At some point, the town became Smithville, which it remains today.

Most people envision Smithville Lake when they think of this community about 20 minutes north of downtown Kansas City. The lake was created in the late 1970s and is managed by the US Army Corps of Engineers. Many flights coming into Kansas City International Airport circle over the lake to get a perfect view of this long, narrow body of water that stretches 18 miles north of Smithville.

The focal point of most community activities is the downtown square, which is lined with a variety of antiques and gift shops and a few thrift stores that are always worthy of investigation. A farmers' market operates here Sat morning from May through Oct, and a number of special events keep the square lively throughout the year.

getting there

From downtown Kansas City, take the Broadway Bridge, aka US 169, and head straight north for about 25 minutes, depending on how fast you drive.

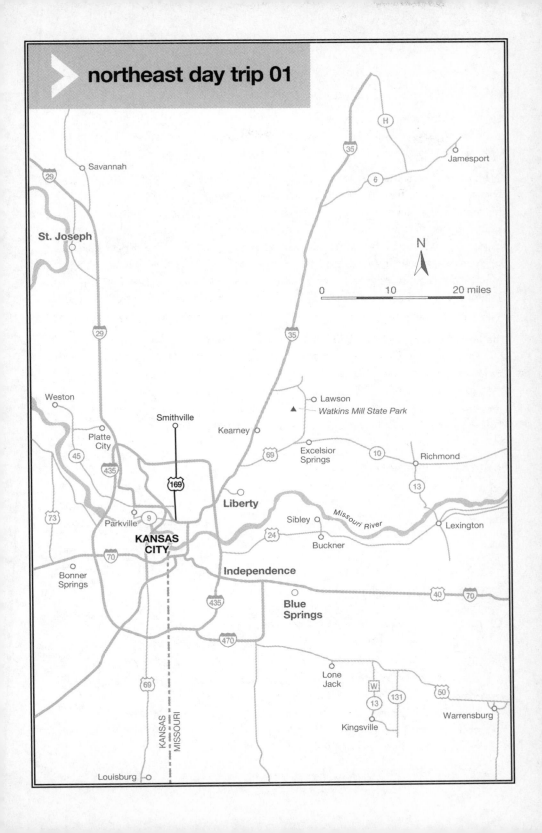

northeast day trip 01

where to go

Smithville Chamber of Commerce. 105 W. Main St.; (816) 532-0946; www.smithville chamber.org. The office is open only in the morning hours Mon through Fri, so come early for the latest information on happenings in Smithville.

Comanche Acres Iris Gardens. 12421 SE MO 116, Gower; (816) 424-6436; www .comancheacresiris.com. Travel about 4 miles north of Smithville on US 169, then turn left on MO 16 to the beautiful 17 acres of Comanche Acres Iris Gardens. Before the land was flooded to form Smithville Lake, Jim and Lamoyne Hedgecock scoured the old homesteads for iris rhizomes, which they replanted. They've bred nearly 2,500 new types of flowers, which they sell around the world through a catalog company—and to anyone who happens by. Their irises have won dozens of awards around the world. Spring is the most impressive time for a visit. You can wander through the flowers without charge and enjoy the guinea hens, turkeys, and ducks that eat the bugs from the blooms, but please don't bring your dog.

The Jerry L. Litton Visitor Center. SR 92 east from Kearney or US 169 north from Kansas City to 16311 Hwy. DD (south end of dam), PO Box 428; (816) 532-0174; www.nwk .usace.army.mil/sm. The visitor center is named after the late sixth district congressman; it offers exhibits and artifacts concerning the Missouri Valley and the Native Americans who inhabited it. There's information about the lake and dam and on the life of Litton. The center also has nature films, and you can schedule tours of the dam control tower. Free. Open 8 a.m. to 4 p.m., Mon through Sat.

Shatto Milk Company. 9406 N. MO 33, Osborn; (816) 930-3862; www.shattomilkcompany .com. Head north out of Smithville on US 169 and turn right on MO 116, following signs to the Shatto Milk Company. This century-old family-owned dairy produces hormone-free milk bottled in glass bottles, as well as cheese curds, butter, and ice cream. Enjoy a fresh-baked

beauty & remembrance

The downtown square of Smithville, the location of many community activities, is a spacious plaza-style setting with picnic tables, benches, potted plants, and grand shade trees. The focal point, however, is the public stage. It is dedicated to the memory of Allie Kemp, a Leawood teenager who was tragically murdered in 2003. Kemp's father is a native of Smithville, and her grandparents live here today. The family business, Diversified Metal Fabricators, created the beautiful accent pieces that adorn the stage. As one local businessperson said, "It's a beautiful place in memory of a beautiful young woman."

chocolate-chip cookie and a glass of cold milk at the end of your tour. Open daily. There is a fee for the tour, for which reservations are required, but you can watch the bottling operation from the store without a charge. Check the website for special events, such as Easter egg hunts and family fun days at the farm.

Smithville Lake and Clay County Parks (Camp Branch, Little Platte Park, and Crow's Creek Area). Two miles east of US 169 on NE 180th Street; (816) 407-3400; www.clay countymo.gov. Located amid rolling hills and grassland, the 7,200-acre lake is just 20 miles from downtown Kansas City and is surrounded by 27 miles horseback-riding trails along with 24 miles of walking/biking trails and a new 11-mile mountain biking trail. Clay County operates recreation areas on the lake, leasing nearly 5,500 acres from the US Army Corps of Engineers. The recreation areas include more than 777 campsites for tents and RVs, 2 swimming beaches, 200 picnic sites, 11 shelter houses, and 2 full-service marinas. Three disc golf courses were added in 2011. Favorites with anglers are bass, walleye, crappie, and catfish.

Golfers are offered challenging play on two par-72, award-winning 18-hole championship golf courses. The Lake House Grille, located in Little Platte Park, is open from May through Sept (816-820-6740).

The Kansas City Trapshooters Association offers the public a chance to do some of the finest trap and skeet shooting in the Midwest. This well-equipped facility includes 12 trapshooting pads, 2 skeet houses, 5-man sporting clays, and a clubhouse. In addition to all campground restrooms, Crow's Creek Area offers a wheelchair-accessible fishing dock and picnic shelter. Most of the walking trails have been paved in recent years. Admission fee.

Woodhenge. (816) 407-3400. Located on the west side of Smithville Lake in Little Platte Park, this is a working replica of the only known square prehistoric Native American solar calendar. The original site was flooded when Smithville Lake was created in the late 1970s. It's an interesting place to visit if you're already at the lake. Open year-round. Free with admission to the park.

where to eat

Justus Drugstore. 106 W. Main St.; (816) 532-2300; www.drugstorerestaurant.com. Jonathon Justus is the genius in the kitchen of this little spot that was indeed a drugstore not so many years ago. Using the farm-to-table, locally grown concept, Justus does something just a little different every week. The Berkshire Pork 2 Ways is a constant on the menu, as is the American Kobe Rib-eye. The wine list includes 300 labels. Reservations required for dinner only Wed through Sun. $$$.

Lowman's Cafe. 505 S. US 169; (816) 532-9000. This is where the locals come for a cup of coffee and to catch up on the latest gossip. You can count on a great selection of cream pies and the Lowman's special-recipe barbecue sauce on the ham and beef sandwiches served 7 days a week. $ (no cards).

day trip 02

northeast

jesse james country:
liberty, mo; kearney, mo; excelsior springs, mo; richmond, mo

liberty, mo

One of the most famous robberies attributed to the notorious James Gang was the daylight holdup of Clay County Savings in Liberty back in 1866. The robbers took $60,000 in gold and currency, and none of the money was ever recovered. Others who put Liberty on the map are Joseph Smith, the Mormon prophet who was jailed here, and Alexander Doniphan, who took up the practice of law in Liberty in 1833. During his residence of 30 years, he became a leading citizen, orator, jurist, statesman, and soldier, eventually leading his famous expedition to Old Mexico in 1846–47, the longest military march ever made.

By 1820 Clay County was formed and named in honor of Henry Clay, the famed senator. Liberty, selected as the county seat, was established that same year. Two years later a college grew under the supervision of Dr. William Jewell, and today the lovely campus is still a fine center of higher learning. For more information: Liberty Area Chamber of Commerce, 1170 W. Kansas St., # H, Liberty; (816) 781-5200; www.libertychamber.com.

getting there

From downtown, take I-35 north toward Des Moines. Travel 16 miles and exit right on MO 152. Follow Kansas Street to the historic square.

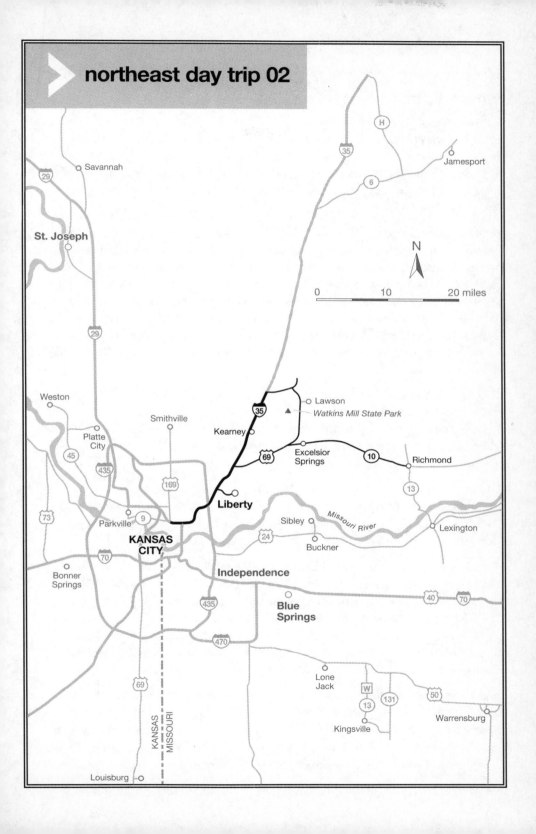

where to go

Belvoir Winery. 1325 Odd Fellows Rd.; (816) 200-1811; www.belvoirwinery.com. The old Odd Fellows Complex, built in the 1900s, has always held one of the most spectacular settings in the Northland. But when Dr. and Mrs. John Bean began planting grapevines and working on turning this property into a winery and event center, it became even more spectacular. In addition to wine tasting, you may enjoy ice cream and deli snacks on site. Belvoir is open 7 days a week.

Bratcher Cooperage. 109 S. Water St.; (816) 781-3988. Stop in this fun shop, a former gas station, to see one of the nation's top craft artisans at work. Doug Bratcher has been handcrafting barrels, buckets, kegs, and churns in the traditional style for more than 30 years. If he's not in the shop when you come by, it's because he is at Silver Dollar City, where he is a featured craft artisan. You'll also find his work in many state and national parks, at Civil War re-enactments, and in lots of movies, such as *Far and Away* with Tom Cruise and Nicole Kidman. You'll enjoy a visit with Doug's wife, Jan, who runs the gift shop filled with "Made in the USA" gifts, cards, and accessories. Open 10 a.m. to 5:30 p.m., Mon through Sat. Closed Sun.

Clay County Museum and Historical Society. 14 N. Main St.; (816) 792-1849. Housed in an 1877 drugstore, the museum collection focuses on Clay County history. It features a restored doctor's office, prehistoric Native American relics, toys, tools, arrowheads, and artifacts relating to the operation of a 19th-century drugstore. Open Mon through Sat, afternoons. Closed in Jan. Admission fee.

Corbin Theatre Co. 15 N. Water St.; (816) 529-4988; www.corbintheatre.org. Once the site of all entertainment in Liberty, this historic, circa-1880s theater was renovated in 2007. Theatrical productions are offered 4 to 6 times a season, in addition to jazz performances every Monday night. Visit the website for more entertaining events.

Historic Liberty Jail and Visitors Center (Mormon Jail). 216 N. Main St.; (816) 781-3188. Mormon leader Joseph Smith was imprisoned here in 1838–39 for his beliefs. Built in 1833, the limestone jail eventually crumbled but was reconstructed by the Church of Jesus Christ of Latter-day Saints in 1963. The jail has cutaway walls so that visitors can see what conditions were like nearly 175 years ago. The center also teaches about the unfairness of persecuting those of different faiths. Guided tours include historical highlights, exhibits, artwork, and interactive video displays. Open daily 9 a.m. to 9 p.m. Free.

Jesse James Bank Museum. 103 N. Water St. (the northeast corner of Courthouse Square); (816) 781-4458. Frank and Jesse James were responsible for the first successful daylight bank robbery during peacetime. The James boys made a bank "withdrawal" of $60,000 from the Clay County Savings Association on February 13, 1866. A William Jewell College student who witnessed the event was shot and killed. No one was ever convicted.

Today you can take a glimpse into the workings of a 19th-century bank and view a number of artifacts related to Jesse James. The original bank vault and a rare Seth Thomas calendar clock are part of the tour. The building is listed on the National Register of Historic Places. Closed Sun. Admission fee.

Martha Lafite Thompson Nature Sanctuary. 407 N. LaFrenz Rd. (0.5 mile southeast of William Jewell College); (816) 781-8598; www.naturesanctuary.com. This 100-acre sanctuary is filled with wildlife that inhabits prairies, woodlands, meadows, and marshes. White-tailed deer, raccoons, foxes, squirrels, birds, and butterflies delight the eyes. The visitor center features educational exhibits for children and has organized activities such as wildflower and full-moon hikes. There are also 2 geocaches on site. The visitor center is closed Sun and Mon, but the 4 miles of hiking trails are open daily from 8:30 a.m. to sunset. Admission fee.

Wynbrick Wellness Center. 1701 Wynbrick Dr.; (816) 792-4325; www.wynbrickcenter .com. This 1930s-era home has become a location for wellness and fellowship, according to Alice Brink, whose family started the center because of an interest in caring for others. The center is popular for small gatherings, such as teas and bridal showers; has fitness and educational programs; and offers spa services.

where to shop

Catfish and Tater. 12 N. Main St.; (816) 820-3791; www.catfishandtater.com. Are you looking for a dress, a handbag, or jewelry like no one else has? You'll find it in Heather Chaney's intimate boutique on the square. Or if you would like some clothing to match your latest tattoo, you can find that here as well. Heather's husband is a tattoo artist and transfers many of his designs to her clothing and home decor items. Or if you simply prefer clothing that comes from recycled and sustainable resources, you'll find that here as well.

Classy Chocolate. 18 W. Kansas St.; (816) 781-2260; www.classychocolate.com. You know you've entered a special place when the outdoor sign reads EXPERTS IN DECADENCE. Come in to satisfy your craving for chocolate-dipped strawberries or grapes or cashews or cookies. You name it, they dip it in chocolate here. Cupcakes, cheesecakes, wedding cakes, brownies. You get the idea. This is the place to blow your diet, increase you cholesterol levels, and enjoy life just a little more.

where to eat

Crepes on the Square. 4 N. Main St.; (816) 792-3200; www.crepesonthesquare.com. If you think crepes are just for breakfast, then plan a visit during lunch or dinner to this fun little shop on Liberty's historic square. While they certainly serve a healthy selection of breakfast crepes and many that are sweet and fruity, you'll also find combinations of turkey, brie, and cranberry, or other selections with peanut butter and bananas. If you're not sure about these ultra-thin French pancakes, you can also enjoy paninis and salads throughout the day. A variety of coffees and other drinks makes this a popular gathering spot at any time of the day. $.

Los Compas Mexican Restaurant. 5 E. Kansas St.; (816) 415-0244. For more than 100 years, this historic building on the downtown square was home to either a hardware store or a restaurant of the same name. Today it is a very popular Mexican restaurant, but the original tin ceilings, brick walls, and hardware cabinets are reminders of the building's place in Liberty history. Try one of the house specials—Chile Colorado and Chalupa Especial. $.

where to stay

The Stone-Yancey House. 421 N. Lightburne St.; (816) 415-1811; www.stoneyancey house.com. If you struggle with high cholesterol, you'll enjoy the breakfast Carolyn Hatcher serves her guests—a hot toddy oatmeal featuring a healthful dose of demara whiskey. But you'll also enjoy her fresh-baked cookies and evening desserts, plus the magnificent antiques and stained-glass windows in this 1889-era home. Carolyn and her husband, Steve, are only the fourth owners, and they have tastefully decorated the 3 bedrooms with period antiques. Carolyn's own wedding dress adorns the entryway. $$.

kearney, mo

Kearney is best known as the birthplace and burial place of outlaw Jesse James. A festival each September celebrates the city's most renowned resident (www.jessejamesfestival .com). But the community has more to offer than bad guys and bank robbers. The first thing to know about the community is that it's pronounced "Karn-knee", not "Ker-knee." Many assume the town was named after Kearney, Nebraska, and there's some evidence to support that. However, more likely is that it was named for Charles Esmond Kearney, an Irish immigrant who lived a colorful life after coming to the New World. Among his business ventures was a railroad partnership with Joseph Van Horn and Kersey Coates, names etched into Kansas City's history. A railroad stop was needed to ship the many cattle raised in this part of Clay County and since Charles Esmond Kearney was president of the company, that's probably how the town got its name. For more information, contact the Kearney Chamber of Commerce, (816) 628-4229; www.kearneychamber.org.

getting there

It's a quick 10-minute drive from Liberty to Kearney. The easiest route is straight up I-35 to exit 26. Or for a more scenic route, drive the back roads along MO 33. Leave downtown on Kansas Avenue and just follow the signs.

where to go

Jesse James Farm and Museum. 21216 James Farm Rd. (3 miles east of Kearney on MO 92); (816) 736-8500; www.jessejamesmuseum.org. This is the birthplace of Jesse James, where he and his brother Frank grew up during the mid-1800s. The house has been authentically restored, and the museum features the world's largest collection of James family artifacts, including guns, saddles, and boots. The quilt, handmade by Frank's wife, Annie, remains on the bed in which he died. Open year-round. Admission fee.

Jesse James Grave. Mount Olivet Cemetery, west end of MO 92 on the way out of Kearney. Jesse's grave is located between two small evergreen trees on the cemetery's west side. Originally he was buried on the front lawn of the farm so that his family could protect his remains from grave robbers and curiosity seekers. For years Jesse's mother, Zerelda, sold pebbles off the grave to tourists. Later his body was moved to Mount Olivet. A relatively small marker identifies the grave as that of Jesse James and his wife, Zerelda. Jesse's marker reads: BORN: SEPTEMBER 5, 1847. ASSASSINATED: APRIL 3, 1882. To the left and right of Jesse's grave stand taller monuments inscribed SAMUEL, where the outlaw's mother and stepfather are buried. Also nearby is the grave of young Archie Samuel, Jesse's half-brother who was killed when Pinkerton detectives bombed the James farm in January 1875. Open daily. Free.

Kearney Amphitheatre. Sixth and Jefferson Streets; (816) 903-4730; www.kearney amphitheater.com. A beautiful addition to the city in 2007, this amphitheatre in Jesse James Park is the place to be for Fourth of July celebrations, but check the website often to see the latest celebrity or community performance scheduled for this stage.

Kearney Museum. 101 S. Jefferson St.; (816) 628-4229. This small museum strives to compile a history of the community. Perhaps of greatest interest to those from outside the area is a bank vault that was not robbed by the James brothers, but instead contained the cremated ashes of Frank James for almost 30 years before they were interred beside his wife in an Independence, Missouri, cemetery. Open Thurs through Sat, 10 a.m. to 2 p.m. Admission fee.

Mount Gilead Church and School. 15918 Plattsburg Rd.; (816) 736-8500. This was the only school west of the Mississippi River to remain open during the Civil War. Third- and fourth-grade students are invited to take a class trip back to the 1800s, where they can experience an old-fashioned education. Lessons in history, reading, arithmetic, and spelling are taught by a schoolteacher in period attire. Experiencing school life in this one-room schoolhouse offers children a unique and unforgettable history lesson. The church is also available for weddings. Admission fee. Reservations required.

Tryst Falls Park. Located 5 miles east of Kearney on MO 92; (816) 407-3400. The Clay County Parks and Recreation Department runs this 40-acre park, which includes the area's only waterfall open to the public. It's a great place to picnic because of the many shelters and grills and the modern playground. Jesse James's father, a Baptist minister, baptized Walthus Watkins, owner of Watkins Mill, at Tryst Falls. Swimming is dangerous and not allowed here because of the rocks. Fishing is not allowed. The park makes a sightseeing stop in your tour of Jesse James Farm or Watkins Mill State Park. Open daily.

Watkins Woolen Mill State Historic Site and Park. Located 6.5 miles north of Excelsior Springs and 7 miles east of Kearney, off MO 92 at Highway RA, Lawson; (816) 580-3387; www.mostateparks.com. This is the last 19th-century woolen mill in America with original equipment. The mill heralds the beginning of the industrial age and still contains 60 of the original machines and a steam engine. The Watkins home, smokehouse, summer kitchen, and fruit dry house, along with an octagonal school and a church, add interest. The original farm was 3,550 acres, but the park is now 1,500 acres and includes the original sawmill, gristmill, and brick kiln built by the Watkins family.

The state park features picnicking, camping, hiking, fishing, and swimming in the lake. Bring your bike along and enjoy the 3.5-mile bike/hike trail around the shoreline. Bring food and drink; there are no concessions here and water is turned off from Nov 1 to Apr 1. Open daily. Free (admission fee for historic site).

where to stay

Stonehaven Guesthouse. 16421 Plattsburg Rd.; (816) 628-4647; www.stonehavenguest house.com. Surrounded by nearly 200 acres of grassland, this delightful getaway has been a family home since the 1880s. Made of local limestone, it is now a comfortable 3-bedroom, 2-bath guesthouse, complete with kitchen and laundry, located on property owned by Dave and Jo Fulton. If you're looking for peace and quiet, long walks, perhaps some fishing in the pond, or star-gazing at night, this is it. No credit cards. $$.

excelsior springs, mo

Long revered as a haven of health, Excelsior Springs has attracted thousands of people to its mineral waters since 1881 and still offers historical insight into the healing powers of the waters. A summer festival celebrates the influence of the waters in this town. For more information: Excelsior Springs Chamber of Commerce, 461 S. Thompson Ave.; (816) 630-6161; www.exspgschamber.com.

getting there

A 12-mile drive north on US 69 takes you to historic Excelsior Springs in about 20 minutes.

where to go

Historic Hall of Waters. 201 E. Broadway; (816) 631-2811. The Historic Hall of Waters was the central dispersal site of the five mineral waters found here and focused on the development of equipment for the use of water in therapeutic treatment. Siloam Springs remains today as the only natural supply of iron manganese mineral water in the country and is one of five recognized in existence worldwide. Here, you can belly up to the longest mineral-water bar in the world and sample the natural calcium mineral water or take home a bottle to drink. Bring your camera to photograph the beautiful Mayan Indian and art deco architectural designs. Admission fee.

where to stay

The Elms Resort and Spa. Regent Street and Elms Boulevard; (800) 843-3567; www .elmsresort.com. The Elms Resort has once again undergone a major renovation, thus maintaining its status a premiere retreat and conference center in the Kansas City area. Casual and fine dining options, indoor and outdoor swimming, and hiking and biking trails are all amenities above and beyond the well-appointed guest rooms and spa. $$$.

The Inn on Crescent Lake. 1261 St. Louis Ave.; (816) 630-6745; www.crescentlake.com. This country inn makes a great romantic getaway or a pleasant alternative for businesspeople tired of the motel shuffle. The 3-story Georgian colonial mansion is nestled on 22 acres and surrounded by 2 ponds and a lawn designed for strolling and relaxing. A full breakfast might include quiche, scones, waffles, French toast, and other delights.

Each of the 10 guest rooms has a private bath, including a whirlpool or claw-foot tub. The downstairs guest room is wheelchair-accessible, with its own separate entrance, and is adjacent to the kitchen. The ballroom-size third floor can be reserved as a honeymoon suite. It features a king-size bed, a separate sitting area, and a whirlpool bath and custom marble shower big enough for two.

If that's not enough, there's an outdoor swimming pool where you can practice your backstroke on warm summer days. The ponds are stocked with bass and catfish, and the inn will supply a boat. The inn is available for private parties, weddings, and corporate retreats, with enough meeting space to accommodate up to 50 people. $$$.

richmond, mo

Located 11 miles north of Lexington on MO 13, Richmond, MO, touts itself as "the Mushroom Capital of the World." Time your trip so that it coincides with Richmond's annual mushroom festival the first weekend in May. This is when those hard-to-find morel mushrooms pop up, begging to be sautéed in butter and wine. The mushrooms are plentiful enough around here for a celebration in their honor. Richmond hosts a parade, plenty of food and craft booths, a model train show, a carnival, a beer garden, and other activities.

Richmond folks will sell you some morels to take back home, but they won't reveal their secret mushroom spots. If you want to go searching in the woods, you're on your own.

Fans of Jesse James lore come to Richmond to visit the grave of Robert Ford, the man who shot the outlaw in the back. Ford was the subject of a 2007 movie (starring Missouri native Brad Pitt) called *The Assassination of Jesse James by the Coward Robert Ford.* Bob Ford and his brother Charley, who was in on the plan to shoot James, are buried in the Sunnyslope Cemetery. Also buried here is Joseph Smith, the founder and First Prophet of the Church of Jesus Christ of Latter-day Saints. For more information: Richmond Chamber of Commerce, 104 N. Main St.; (816) 776-6919; www.richmondchamber.org.

getting there

It will take about 30 minutes to reach Richmond from Excelsior Springs, but it is a pleasant 15-mile drive in the country along MO 10.

where to go

The Farris Theatre. 301 W. Main St.; (816) 776-6684; www.farristheatre.com. Look closely at this structure and see if it reminds you of the Folly Theatre in downtown Kansas City. Originally built in 1901 as an opera house, the Farris was modeled after the Folly. The Farris Theatre has been fully restored for use as a performance theater, movie house, and community center by a not-for-profit group called Friends of the Farris. The Saturday morning cartoon series is a lot of fun for kids.

Ray County Museum. 901 W. Royal St.; (816) 776-2305. This odd-looking Y-shaped building, constructed in 1910, was designed so that all 54 rooms would have lots of sunshine. Today it is home to a number of artifacts that tell the story of this region, including Native American, Civil War, and Mormon history. It is open year-round, Wed through Sat 10 a.m. to 5 p.m., and closed on holidays. Free.

United Methodist Church. 212 Main St.; (816) 776-2122. This lovely limestone church is remarkable for its 15 stained-glass windows of various sizes. But unique to a church in 1918 was the inclusion of an in-ground swimming pool and library, both open to the public. Although neither exists today, the public is welcome to visit anytime to see the windows and lovely woodwork rarely found in construction projects today.

where to eat

Jeffery Kyle's Restaurant. 908 E. Main St.; (816) 776-5308. A massive buffet here offers great comfort food, such as real mashed potatoes and gravy and homemade pies, or you can order from the menu and be served by some of the most pleasant staff in the hospitality business. Open 7 days a week. $.

day trip 03

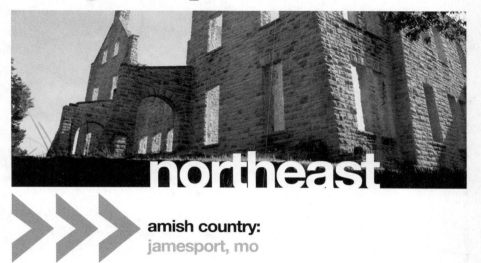

northeast

>>> **amish country:**
jamesport, mo

jamesport, mo

In Jamesport, the Amish community offers a glimpse of a bygone era. These people are part of the Old Order Amish, who are direct descendants of the Mennonite Anabaptists, a group that developed during the Reformation in Germany and Switzerland. Today there are Amish settlements in at least 21 states and Canada. In the early 1950s the Amish immigrated to Jamesport, now the largest settlement in the state. Currently about 2,200 Amish reside on the rich farmland of the area.

They shun the use of modern conveniences and travel by means of horse-drawn vehicles. Their peaceful lifestyle revolves around a close-knit family, their faith, and farming. They use no electricity, no cars, no televisions or radios. Their education ends at the eighth grade. Many of the Amish farmhouses now have indoor plumbing, and most Amish families use oil furnaces, kerosene- or wood-burning stoves, and kerosene lamps.

Amish men are expert farmers who still use plows pulled by horses to till their fields. They dress modestly in black broad-brimmed hats, white shirts, and black trousers.

The women excel in the home arts. They wear plain, long cotton dresses held together with pins (they consider buttons worldly). On their heads they wear white prayer caps at all times. Their conversation often lapses into something called "Ferhoodled English," a combination of German, Dutch, and English.

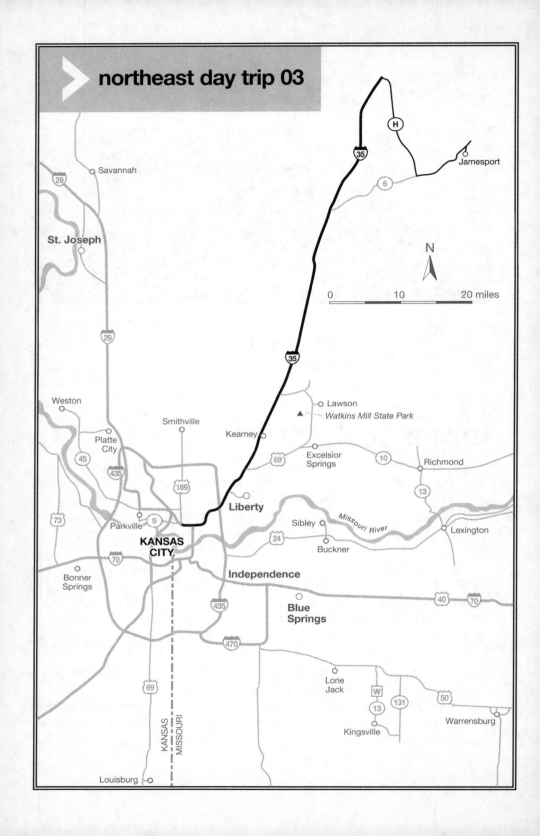

Jamesport has prospered as a tourist attraction because of the Amish, and they, in their practical way, have taken advantage of public curiosity. The Amish typically do not want their pictures taken, since it violates their religious beliefs. As a courtesy, ask permission before you shoot.

If you're looking for authentic Amish foods, goods, and services, be aware that "Amish style" does not necessarily mean that something is Amish-made.

A visit to Jamesport can be fun if you tour it with the idea that there are two separate reasons for coming here. The first is to visit the Amish-owned stores, where you will find authentic Amish foods, quilts, and other items. The second reason is to enjoy the antiques, craft, and specialty shops; restaurants; and bed-and-breakfasts, most of which are not Amish-owned.

If you want to determine whether an establishment is Amish or Mennonite, check the days it is open; Amish shops close on Thursday and Sunday. If you like to can or preserve your own fruits and vegetables, plan your visit to Jamesport to coincide with the **Produce Auction.** The days of the week vary, depending on the growing season. Anyone can attend, but all produce is sold in larger quantities. Call for details at (660) 684-6844.

Many farm stores and related businesses are found along gravel country roads, and street addresses are ineffective for those locations. Therefore, pick up a free map of the area at any of the local businesses.

For more information, contact the Jamesport Community Association, PO Box 215, Jamesport, MO 64648; (660) 684-6146; www.jamesportmissouri.org.

getting there

From downtown, take I-35 north about 75 miles to exit 84, which is Highway H. Turn right, heading east about 8 miles. There will be lots of signs for Jamesport. Be alert to horse-drawn buggies.

where to shop

Broadway Pavilion Mall. 204 S. Broadway; (660) 684-6655. The mall has a large assortment of antiques, collectibles, furniture, glassware, pottery, records, old books, and more. Open daily.

DeVaul Art Gallery. 107 S. Broadway; (660) 684-6010. This gallery features the work of western artist Lee Teeter, along with pottery and other handcrafted items by Missouri artists. Closed Sun and Mon.

The Farmhouse Collection. 113 S. Broadway; (660) 684-6704; www.jamesport-farmhouse.com. Actually 5 buildings connected, this store has almost 9,000 square feet of home decor and handmade furniture. Come early in the day and you might catch the owners in the process of pouring hand-dipped candles, something they do every morning. You'll also find nice collections of handmade soaps and lotions here.

Firehouse Antiques. 101 S. Broadway; (660) 684-6789; www.aowboyandcabindecor .com. Located in the former firehouse that served Jamesport from the 1930s to the 1970s, this store carries a mix of old and new, including antique furniture but new western and lodge decor. Closed Sun.

Homestead Creamery. East on County Road F, then south on County Road U; (660) 684-6970. This family dairy farm is picturesque in its own right, but come on Tuesday to witness the cheese-making process, directly from the milk from the Jersey cows in the adjacent pastures. Otherwise, bring a cooler to fill up from the gift shop. Closed Thurs and Sun.

Kramer-Yoder Country Store. Located 2 miles west on County Road NN. You may need a map to find this place, but it's so worth it to get out on the country roads and see the Amish homes and farms. And don't call for directions. There is no telephone. This Amish-owned store carries natural farm-raised meats, homemade goodies, and crafts. Open Mon, Wed, and Fri.

Pastime & Carlyle's. 100 Auberry Grove; (660) 684-6222; www.pastimefurniture.com. Early country furniture and decorative items, plus original painted furniture, are sold here along with old-fashioned candy and collectibles. You can also order custom-made furniture for your home. Closed Sun.

This 'N That. 102 S. Broadway; (660) 684-6594. A little bit of everything, including furniture, jewelry, and glassware, is sold here. Closed Sun.

Wholly Cow Custard and Fudge. 107 S. Broadway; (660) 605-0575. Make this your first stop for an introduction to Amish life. The 30-minute documentary *Old Order Amish* is played on a continuous loop in the shop's DVD player. Learn more about the community while you enjoy some fresh-made fudge or custard.

where to eat

Anna's Bake Shop. 1005 Old Hwy. 6; (660) 684-6810.This Amish shop is worth the drive to Jamesport just for the mouthwatering fresh-baked doughnuts, pies, breads, and cinnamon and dinner rolls. Closed Christmas through Feb 1 and the rest of the time when the day's goods are sold out. According to the owner, the phone works only "when the weather is above 20 degrees." $ (no cards).

Countryside Bakery. Located 0.5 mile south of Jamesport on MO 190. Leave room in your tummy and your car for some delicious, authentic Amish homemade baked goods. Or if you are inspired to bake yourself, you can choose from a number of cookie mixes already packaged for you. Closed Thurs and Sun. No phone. $ (no cards).

Gingerich Dutch Pantry. 107 Auberry Grove; (660) 684-6212; www.gingerichdutch pantry.com. Located at the four-way stop in downtown Jamesport, this Mennonite-owned restaurant specializes in Mennonite cooking using Old Dutch recipes. Homemade pies, breads, cinnamon rolls, and other baked goods are featured. A buffet and a complete menu are available for individuals or large groups. Closed Sun. $.

where to stay

Country Colonial Bed & Breakfast. 106 E. Main St.; (660) 684-6711. Sleep tight in an original pre–Civil War rope bed, the kind that instigated the term "sleep tight," in this 3-bedroom inn that is filled with antiques throughout. But don't snuggle in too tightly before enjoying a moonlight, horse-drawn carriage ride through the Amish countryside. And don't sleep too late or you'll miss Nina den Hartog's fabulous cinnamon raisin French toast. $$.

Marigolds Inn and Gift Shoppe. 305 W. Auberry Grove; (660) 684-6122. Located 3 blocks west of downtown Jamesport. If you like handmade quilts, you'll enjoy a stay in one of the 12 individually decorated rooms at Marigolds. Several have a garden theme; others have a western or bunkhouse look to them—all based on the bed coverings. And if you appreciate the craftsmanship of Amish carpenters, take a close look at the quality in this building constructed by local Amish. Breakfast is on your own, but with so many wonderful bakeries nearby, you won't go hungry. $.

east

day trip 01

east

history, a president's residence & red delicious:
independence, mo; sibley, mo; lexington, mo; waverly, mo

independence, mo

Founded in 1827, Independence became known as the Queen City of the Trails, heading three dominant routes west—the Santa Fe, California, and Oregon Trails. (The Santa-Cali-Gon Festival, held annually on Labor Day weekend, commemorates the opening of these prairie pathways.)

Fortunes were made here during the westward expansion and Victorian periods, and many of the charming homes built during these times have been designated with historic markers. Today Independence is best known as the home of the 33rd president, Harry S. Truman. Places related to his life here include his home, courtroom, and office, as well as the Harry S. Truman Museum and Library.

Just a few blocks from the Harry S. Truman National Historic Site (Truman home) is Independence Square, filled with restaurants and shops housing arts, crafts, antiques, and memorabilia. It's fun to go exploring around a historic area that has a great past. Smack in the middle of the square is the Jackson County Courthouse. Built in 1836, it was renovated in 1933 during the administration of Jackson County Judge Harry S. Truman.

On the east side of the courthouse is a full-size statue of Harry himself. *The Man from Independence*, a multimedia show highlighting Truman's life before his presidency, is shown on the hour inside the courthouse.

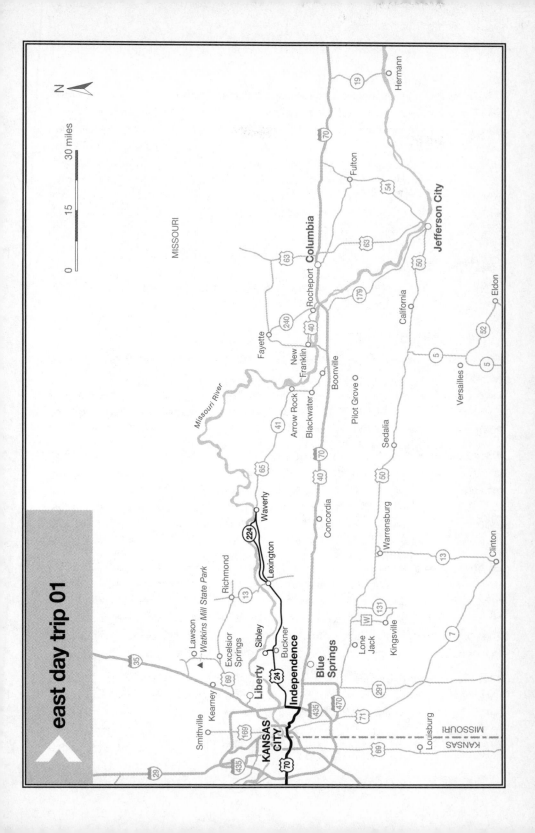

Three walking trails are available in Independence for historically minded leisure walkers. The Swales Walking Trail at the Bingham-Waggoner Estate winds along a 0.25-mile paved surface through the grounds, and 9 interpretive signs focus on wagon ruts that follow the Santa Fe trade route west. The second trail begins in front of the Harry S. Truman National Historic Site Visitors Center. This 2.7-mile trail features 43 brass plaques embedded in the sidewalks throughout the Truman neighborhood. Finally, the Missouri Mormon Walking Trail begins on the corner of Walnut and River and explores the religious history of the Mormons, illustrated by 14 brass sidewalk markers at locations of significance in the early days of the church.

getting there

From downtown, take I-70 East to I-435 North and the Truman Road exit; then take Truman Road east to Independence.

where to go

City of Independence Tourism Department. 111 E. Maple St.; (816) 325-7111; www .visitindependence.com. Pick up brochures for the walking tours here, as well as the latest news in town. Another option is to take a ride on the Truman Trolley between May and Sept. For just $1, the trolley will take you to 6 of the major sites in Independence, returning every 20 minutes to take you to the next site. Call (816) 512-5555.

The Auditorium. 1001 W. Walnut St.; (816) 833-1000, ext. 3030; www.cofchrist.org. This is part of the world headquarters for the Community of Christ. The 6,000-seat chamber features a world-famous 111-rank, 6,334-pipe Aeolian-Skinner organ, one of the largest church organs in the nation. Thousands of people use the building yearly for religious, cultural, and community-centered activities. Free organ recitals are offered daily from June through Aug and on Sun the remainder of the year. Guided tours are available daily.

Bingham-Waggoner Estate. 313 W. Pacific Ave.; (816) 461-3491 or (816) 325-7111; www.bwestate.org. Built in 1855, this private home eventually became the residence of Missouri artist George Caleb Bingham, who lived here with his wife, Eliza, until 1870. In 1879 the home was purchased by Peter and William Waggoner, who remodeled the original structure. The house served as the Waggoner family home until 1976. The 26-room residence is open to tour from Apr 1 to Oct 31 and throughout the month of Dec. Admission fee.

1827 Log Courthouse. 107 W. Kansas Ave.; (816) 325-7111. The first courthouse in Jackson County, this is the oldest historic site open to the public in Independence. Originally a county courthouse, it was used as a private residence in 1832. During the 1920s and 1930s, the structure housed the headquarters of the Community Welfare League, with Bess Truman (Harry's wife) as honorary vice-chairperson. In 1932 Jackson County Judge

Harry S. Truman held court there while the main courthouse was being remodeled. Open year-round. Admission fee.

1859 Jail, Marshal's Home, and Museum. 217 N. Main St.; (816) 252-1892. Four buildings constitute this museum operated by the Jackson County Historical Society. These include the jail that held the outlaw Frank James, the marshal's restored home, a one-room schoolhouse, and a county museum. Open daily Apr 1 to Oct 31 and in the month of Dec. The complex is closed in Nov and Jan through Mar. Admission fee.

George Owens Nature Park. 1601 S. Speck Rd.; (816) 325-7115. This 85-acre gem of the Jackson County Parks system has 2 fishing lakes stocked with bass, channel cat, bluegill, and bullheads. A fishing license is required for people ages 15 through 64. There are 4 miles of nature trails for hiking, one of them wheelchair accessible, as well as a nature center whose outdoor habitat is filled with live deer, bats, geese, and snakes. Films are offered on Sat once a month. Group reservations must be made at least 2 weeks in advance. Open year-round. Closed Mon. Free.

Harry S. Truman Courtroom and Office. Independence Square Courthouse, Rm. 109, Main at Maple Street; (816) 252-7454. This is where the 33rd president of the United States began the political career that led him to the White House. You'll see Judge Truman's restored quarters and an audiovisual presentation about his life and courtship with Bess. Open Mon through Fri, 10 a.m. to 3:30 p.m. Admission fee.

Harry S. Truman Presidential Museum and Library. US 24 and Delaware Street; (816) 268-8200; www.trumanlibrary.org. One of 15 presidential libraries administered by the National Archives and Records Administration, this library houses exhibits and memorabilia of the Truman years, as well as a research facility. An extraordinary Thomas Hart Benton mural greets you as you walk through the door. Permanent museum exhibits on President _____ plica of the Oval Office and a glimpse into his dramatic 1948 _____ Dewey. Interactive exhibits allow visitors to participate in some _____ an made, including dropping the atomic bomb. Temporary _____ mented with special programs. The graves of President and _____ library's courtyard. Open daily. Admission fee.

_____ storic Site. 219 N. Delaware St.; (816) 254-2720; www.nps _____ S. Truman National Landmark District, this was the home of _____ , Bess Wallace Truman, until their deaths. Informative tours _____ at the ticket center and a 15-minute tour of the residence. _____ kets in person on a first-come, first-served basis on the day _____ Ticket and Information Center, 223 N. Main St., adjacent _____ daily Memorial Day through Labor Day. Closed Mon from _____ . Admission fee.

Leila's Hair Museum. 1333 S. Noland Rd.; (816) 833-2955; www.hairwork.com/leila. In 55 years as a hairdresser, Leila Cohoon has developed a fascination with hair and a fascinating collection. She has hundreds of pieces of hair art and jewelry, some dating to the 1680s. She is considered a leading expert on hair and has been consulted in criminal cases by the FBI. Her museum is the national headquarters for the Victorian Hairwork Society. Open Tues through Sat. Admission fee.

Missouri Pacific Railroad Station. Grand Street and Pacific Avenue; (816) 421-3622. This depot, which figured in Truman's 1948 "Whistle Stop" campaign, is listed on the National Register of Historic Places. There's daily Amtrak service into Kansas City. Round-trip group rates are available. Free (fee for Amtrak).

Mormon Visitors' Center. 937 W. Walnut St.; (816) 836-3466. Operated by the Church of Jesus Christ of Latter-day Saints (Mormons). The high-tech exhibits document the doctrines of the church. Visitors enter through a covered wagon and see the daily life of the Saints portrayed in a log cabin. Open daily. Free.

National Frontier Trails Museum. 318 W. Pacific Ave.; (816) 325-7575; www.frontier trailsmuseum.org. This acclaimed museum, library, and archival center is located at the principal jumping-off point of the Santa Fe, Oregon, and California Trails. It is the only interpretive center in the nation devoted to all three trails. The gripping story of the exploration and settlement of the American West is shown in an award-winning introductory film that prepares visitors for their interesting trip through the museum's many exhibits, which feature memorabilia and relics from the prairie pathways. The 2-story Chicago and Alton Depot, restored from the 1890s, is located on the grounds. Only two such 2-story depots remain in Missouri. Open daily. Admission fee.

Pioneer Spring Cabin. Southeast corner of Noland and Truman Roads; (816) 325-7111. The austere 2-room cabin was originally constructed in an Irish community known as Brady Town and moved to its present location in 1971. A spring outside the cabin has been re-created to represent the kind of welcome oasis that traders and emigrants may have found on their way west. Open daily Apr 1 to Oct 31. Free.

The Temple. 201 S. River St.; (816) 833-1000, ext. 3030. This unusual architectural structure is part of the Community of Christ World Headquarters complex. It includes 2 visitor theaters, a lecture hall, and classrooms, plus a museum, a bookstore, a library, and a chapel with an adjacent meditation garden, along with administrative offices. Highlighting the building is a 1,600-seat sanctuary and a 102-rank, 5,686-pipe organ built by Casavant Frères Limitée of Quebec, Canada. Fashioned after the nautilus seashell, the 150-foot spire rises from the sanctuary and can be seen from many areas of the city. The public is invited to attend the programs dedicated to peace and reconciliation, along with a daily prayer for peace, offered in the Temple sanctuary at 12:30 p.m. Public organ recitals are offered at 3 p.m. daily June through Aug and on Sun only the remainder of the year. Free.

Vaile Mansion–DeWitt Museum. 1500 N. Liberty St.; (816) 325-7111. One of the best examples of Victorian architecture in the United States, this 1882 mansion has a second-floor smoking room where woodwork is painted with dozens of little faces and animals. The home also has 9 beautiful fireplaces and an indoor water tower. Open daily Apr 1 to Oct 31, when it closes for a month to decorate for the Christmas holidays. The home is open throughout Dec. Admission fee.

where to shop

Lily Wolfgang. 206 N. Liberty; (816) 836-3822; www.lilywolfgang.com. Do you ever find yourself admiring home decor displays and thinking, "Why can't I make my house look like that?" Well, you can, because owner Lisa Holiman hosts workshops and special events in this fun boutique on taking the look to your own home. Here you can find new and repurposed furniture, along with fun home decor items. There's a boutique of new clothing as well as a resale clothing consignment area. They also carry a line of locally made children's accessories that includes fun things like tutus and butterfly wings, barrettes, hair bows, and more.

Primary Colors Gallery. 109 W. Lexington Ave.; (816) 254-2106; www.primarycolorsgallery .com. Not only can you find some locally crafted pottery, jewelry, and home decor in this shop, you can also take a class in raku and other art forms. Children's classes are offered on weekends. Or if you need art supplies, you'll find a nice little selection here. Open Tues through Sat.

Scandinavia Place. 209 N. Main St.; (816) 461-6633. Nina Anders' shop on the Independence Square is about as close as you can get to visiting Iceland without a passport. A native of Iceland, Nina has a mission, albeit a small one, to help others better understand and appreciate Scandinavian countries. In her little shop, you can buy rosette and almond cookies, dala horses, lingonberry jam, and other goodies that speak to those northern countries. Find flags, story books, and holiday ornaments unique to Scandinavian cultures. Nina's shop is one of the few places in the Midwest that carry these specialty items. Open daily.

Wild About Harry. 104 W. Maple St.; (816) 252-0100; www.wildaboutharryind.com. Before dabbling in politics, Harry Truman operated a haberdashery in downtown Kansas City. Haberdashery is a word that's fallen out of favor in the English language, but it's basically a men's clothing and accessory store, and that's what Wild About Harry is, with a modern twist. Yes, you can find men's ties, but they are the line Ties That Don't Suck. There are some cool hats and backpacks made from recycled canvas tarps. You can find manly hand lotions, drink decanters, and all sorts of offbeat gift items for men and women. Closed Sun.

where to eat

Courthouse Exchange Restaurant and Lounge. 113 W. Lexington Ave.; (816) 252-0344. Located right across the street from the old courthouse, this restaurant has been serving up good Midwestern fare since 1899. Open for lunch and dinner, the Courthouse Exchange offers everything from prime rib to homemade cinnamon rolls. The tenderloin sandwiches here are famous. The private banquet room can be reserved for groups. $–$$.

Ophelia's. 201 N. Main St.; (816) 461-4525; www.opheliasind.com. Located on Historic Independence Square, this trendy restaurant offers American cuisine, with the highest-quality seafood, steaks, chops, and pastas available for lunch, dinner, and Sunday brunch. $–$$.

where to stay

The Inn at Ophelia's. 201 N. Main St.; (816) 461-4525; www.opheliasind.com. Seven rooms and one suite afford the business or leisure traveler gracious accommodations, complete with private baths, voice messaging, modem capability, hotel amenities, and down comforters and pillows to make you feel at home. $$–$$$.

Serendipity Bed and Breakfast. 116 S. Pleasant St.; (816) 833-4719; www.serendipity bedandbreakfast.com. Housed in an 1887 home, this bed-and-breakfast features antique furnishings along with Victorian children's books and toys, china figurines, glassware, and books for guests to peruse. The backyard garden provides a hammock and swing for peaceful relaxation. Accommodations include the carriage house, with king and twin beds, a kitchen, and a sitting room on the ground level, as well as 2-room suites, one with a kitchenette. All 6 rooms have private baths. A full breakfast is served in the main dining room. The home also offers a Tour and Tea and antique car rides, weather permitting, for a fee. $–$$.

Woodson Guest House. 1604 W. Lexington Ave.; (816) 254-0551; www.woodsonguest house.com. This elegant 19th-century home features overnight accommodations complete with a full breakfast and evening hors d'oeuvres, plus a large 2-room suite and 2 lovely guest rooms with private baths. The home sits on an acre of ground and is tucked away in an all-natural setting filled with trees, gardens, shrubs, and herbs. $$.

Woodstock Inn Bed and Breakfast. 1212 W. Lexington Ave.; (816) 833-2233. Located near Independence's historic sites, this inn offers 10 rooms with private baths and 2 elegant suites. You can choose from king-, queen-, and double-bed accommodations that also include fireplaces and Jacuzzis. Breakfast is whatever you like it to be, and many choose to enjoy it at tables outside in the flower garden. Lunch and dinner are available by request. $$–$$$.

sibley, mo

Snuggled in on the banks of the Missouri River, Sibley is a great destination for fresh fruit and produce. The rolling hills and open farmland of eastern Jackson County are filled with orchards and gardens that provide everything from strawberries, peaches, and apples to asparagus, tomatoes, and green beans.

getting there

As you leave Independence, ignore I-70 and follow US 24 east, about an 18-mile drive that will take you about 30 minutes.

where to go

Fort Osage National Historic Landmark. 105 Osage St.; (816) 650-3278; www.fort osagenhs.com. When the Lewis and Clark expedition passed this bluff on the Missouri River in June 1804, William Clark noted in his journal that it would be a prime location for a military outpost. In 1808 he returned to supervise the building of this, the second outpost in the Louisiana Purchase. It operated as Fort Clark for several months but then became Fort Osage until it ceased operation in 1827. The fort is also a stop on the Santa Fe Trail. An impressive 15,000-square-foot visitor center explores the geology, flora, and fauna of the Missouri River basin, as well as the prehistoric Hopewell Indians and the namesake Osage Indians. A wide veranda filled with rocking chairs and benches provides wonderful views of the Missouri River and a place to contemplate this spot's role in American history. Open Tues through Sun year-round. Admission fee. The visitor center is wheelchair accessible, but many of the buildings—to retain their authenticity—are not.

Sibley Orchards. 3717 Buckner-Tarnsey Rd.; (816) 650-5535; www.sibleyorchards.com. Located 3 blocks from historic Fort Osage, the orchard offers blackberries and peaches in summer, along with sweet corn, tomatoes, and other seasonal vegetables. Peaches and apples are sold here in July. In fall apples, apple cider, and pumpkins are available. For barbecue enthusiasts, you can buy apple wood chips here to enhance the smoking flavor. Evening hayrides that take visitors through the orchard and weekend bluegrass concerts are another reason to visit. Open daily.

lexington, mo

Lexington was once one of the great river ports of this state. River trade made it a fine commercial center and an outfitting point for those heading west. A US land office was established in 1823, followed by a courthouse, a bank, churches, colleges, and more than 120 lovely antebellum and Victorian homes and buildings. Lexington has four historic districts on the National Register of Historic Places, and more than 120 antebellum and Victorian homes and buildings are listed on the register. The Vintage Homes Tour, held in September of odd-numbered years, allows the public a glimpse of the interiors of these elegant historic structures.

The cannonball embedded in one of the courthouse columns is a relic of the Confederate victory in the 1861 Battle of Lexington. The Anderson House, built in 1853 and located on the battlefield, was used as a field hospital and has been restored to its original elegance. For information: Lexington Tourism Bureau, 927 Main St.; (660) 259-4711; www .visitlexingtonmo.com.

getting there

The historic town of Lexington can be reached by meandering along MO 224, which is a designated Missouri Scenic Byway. The 38-mile route follows the curves of the Missouri River, and could take you an hour or more, depending on farm traffic at the time. Note: If the Missouri River has been out of its banks, the road will be closed or at least not very pretty as a result of the high water. A faster route is along US 24. It will take you about 30 minutes to drive the 24 miles.

where to go

Battle of Lexington State Historic Site. Northwest edge of town on Thirteenth Street; (660) 259-4654; www.mostateparks.com/lexington. Between September 18 and 20, 1861, Union forces suffered a major defeat when the pro-Southern Missouri State Guard, commanded by former Missouri governor Major General Sterling Price, led 12,000 men against the Union outpost at Lexington. The siege ended when the Union troops ran out of food, water, and ammunition. This is one of the few Civil War battlefields that has never been cultivated. Outlines of the trenches are still visible on the self-guided walking tour.

Also on the grounds is the Anderson House, which was used a field hospital during the Civil War. It was originally built in 1853 as a private home for Colonel Oliver Anderson. Battle damage is still visible inside and outside the home. There is a fee for guided tours of the home, but otherwise the state historic site is free. The visitor center is open daily and has a 15-minute film that explains why this has become known as the Battle of the Hemp Bales.

Farhmeier Family Vineyards. 9364 Mitchell Trail; (816) 934-2472; www.ffvineyards.com. The vines have been here since 1947, but in recent years, the Farhmeier family has begun bottling wine and opened their barn as a tasting room. It's a lovely afternoon to sip a glass of Missouri's famous Norton while enjoying the gardens on the property. Other wines offered here include Clark, Vidal, Catawba, Lewis, Chambourcin, Oren, Apple, and Port. Closed Mon.

Lexington Historical Museum. 112 S. Thirteenth St.; (660) 259-4711; www.visitlexington mo.com. Built originally as the Cumberland Presbyterian Church in 1846, the museum contains an extensive exhibit on the Pony Express, along with Civil War artifacts from the Battle

> ## the williamsburg of the west
>
> *Lexington at times has been called "the Williamsburg of the West" because of its numerous historic homes and the dedicated efforts of the community to preserve the city's historic and cultural integrity. Early settlers built a performing arts school and three women's colleges to cultivate the finer elements of life.*
>
> *A modern-era concert series known as "Live! in Lexington" brings renowned performers such as the Kansas City Symphony and the St. Louis Philharmonic to this small river town an hour east of downtown Kansas City.*
>
> *Despite its early emphasis on culture, Main Street Lexington was once known as Block 42 because of the number of saloons that thrived here. It has been said that proper women and children never were seen on the sidewalks of Block 42, which is now home to lovely shops and restaurants that do indeed reflect the finer elements of life.*

of Lexington, a coal-mining display, and a fine collection of early Lexington photographs. Open daily during summer; other times by appointment only. Admission fee.

Madonna of the Trail. At the corner of Highland Avenue and Cliff Drive. This monument is one of 12 placed in every state crossed by the national Old Trails Road, the route of early settlers from Maryland to California. It honors the pioneer women who helped settle the west.

***Saluda* Memorial at Heritage Park.** (660) 259-4711. In 1852 the *Saluda* steamboat's boilers exploded while it was docked at Lexington, killing approximately 100 people. The people of Lexington responded, providing medical care, housing, and, in some cases, adopting the children of those adults killed in the accident. The memorial was dedicated in April 2002 on the 150th anniversary of the accident.

where to shop

Main Street Lexington is peppered with more than a dozen interesting boutiques, specialty shops, and quality antiques stores. Come with plenty of cash in your pocket or an extended limit on your credit card because it's almost impossible to go away with your vehicle empty. A couple choice suggestions:

Missouri River Antique Co. 912 Main St.; (660) 259-3097. Straight from many old homes, barns, and businesses in rural Missouri, you'll find lots of primitives, architectural salvage items, and odds and ends. Open 7 days a week.

The Velvet Pumpkin/Gigi's. 920 Main St.; (660) 259-4545; www.thevelvetpumpkin.com. Georgia Brown operates two great stores accessed through one doorway. The first is the Velvet Pumpkin, where you'll find a refined selection of antiques and lots of fun decorative accents. Check out the creative line of greeting cards. Then cross the threshold into Gigi's for a high-caliber line of women's clothing. One-of-a-kind pieces of jewelry are perfectly matched to finish the look. Open 7 days a week.

where to eat

Maid-Rite. 1401 Main St.; (660) 259-444. While *Day Trips* is about taking people to places off the beaten path, this little Maid-Rite drive-in is worthy of inclusion simply for its longevity. Since 1946, the people of Lexington have been enjoying Maid-Rite's famous loose meat sandwiches and classic malts and milk shakes. It's quite possible that the sign or the building's exterior has not been refreshed since then, making it an antique, although not quite antebellum. Business continues to hum along, right in the shadow of a more modern set of golden arches. Closed Sun. $.

Riley's Irish Pub and Grill. 913 Main St.; (660) 259-4771; www.rileyspub.net. This downtown gathering spot is located in a restored 1890s building complete with original tile floors, stained-glass window, pressed-tin ceiling, and back bar. Irish specialties such as mulligan stew are offered, along with sandwiches and Southern specialties such as sweet potato fries. Closed Sun; no cards. $.

Victorian Peddler Tea Room. 900 Main St.; (660) 259-4533. Don't let the words "tea room" scare off the manly men with you. This spacious restaurant offers plenty of hearty, country-style food along with a healthy selection of soups, salads, and sandwiches for lunch and dinner. Try the warm bread pudding or fruit cobblers in season. Closed Mon. $.

where to stay

Inn on Main Street. 920½ Main St.; (660) 259-3600; www.innonmainst.com. Located in the downtown historic district, this 1840s building offers 4 king-size suites with private baths. There's no innkeeper living on site, so you could have the place all to yourself. Breakfast is not included. $.

The Parsonage. 1603 South St.; (660) 259-2344. This large, Queen Anne–style home was built in 1894 and served as the Methodist Church parsonage for many years. It features 2 nicely appointed guest rooms, a full breakfast, and a cafe area where cappuccino, tea, and wine are served. No cards. $$.

waverly, mo

US 24 has recently been declared a Missouri Scenic Byway, and you'll understand why when you drive this road between Lexington and Marshall. The shades of gold from fields of soybeans readying for harvest, punctuated by the hearty reds and greens of apple orchards loaded for the season, are enough to make Monet's garden at Giverny tip its hat in appreciation.

Along this roadway, you'll find nearly two dozen farms and orchards that sell everything from blackberries and asparagus to bedding and vegetable plants to Christmas trees. Many of these are U-pick, so bring a buck.

Situated right in the middle of this cornucopia is Waverly, where more than half of Missouri's apple crop is harvested each year. The Apple Jubilee each September features apple judging and apple eating, as well as entertainment, contests, and lots of family fun. Call the Waverly City Hall for details: (660) 493-2551.

getting there

A pleasant 20 miles away along US 24 is Waverly. It should take about 30 minutes to make the drive, unless you get behind a famer moving equipment from one field to another. Be patient and enjoy.

where to go

Baltimore Bend Winery. 27150 US 24; (660) 493-0258; www.baltimorebend.com. Harvesting more than 3 tons of grapes in a season, this little vineyard is quickly making a name for itself with Chardonel, Cynthiana, and Cabernet grapes. (The Cynthiana, by the way, is the state grape of Missouri.) The tasting room is open 7 days a week.

Five Oaks Christmas Tree Farm. Higginsville; (660) 584-8515; www.fiveoaksfarm.net. The easiest way to find this cut-your-own Christmas tree farm is to travel east on I-70 to the 49-mile marker and turn north on MO 13. Follow the signs. Open on weekends from Thanksgiving through Christmas. However, you can come early in November and tag your "Griswold Family Tree" to be cut later. The majority of the trees are Scotch and white pine with a few blue spruce. The Raucher family also has beehives on the farm and this is one place you can buy raw honey on the comb, or look for it in area grocery stores under the label Five Oaks Farm.

Peters Market. Located 1.5 miles east of Waverly on US 65; (660) 493-2368; www .petersmarket.com. Homegrown yellow and white peaches, as well as nectarines, abound here in season, along with delicious fruit butters and locally grown farm produce. Fall brings crops of Red and Golden Delicious apples, together with the popular Braeburn, Fuji, Granny Smith, and Staymen Winesap varieties. Peters holds a flea market in October that offers utility-grade apples at ridiculously low prices. During fall harvest season, free tours of the market and orchard are offered to organized groups by appointment only.

Schreiman Orchards. Located 2 miles west of Waverly on US 24; (660) 493-2477; www .schreimanorchards.com. This roadside market sells peaches in summer and apples in fall, along with homemade apple butter, raw honey, jams, jellies, apple-wood chips, cookbooks, and Amish-made foods. The Schreiman family has been in business here for more than 80 years. Open daily from mid-June through mid-Nov.

day trip 02

east

the katy trail corridor & boonslick country:
blackwater, mo; arrow rock, mo; boonville, mo; new franklin, mo; fayette, mo; rocheport, mo; columbia, mo; jefferson city, mo; california, mo; sedalia, mo

It's flat, free, and fun, and it snakes across Missouri for more than 235 miles from Clinton to 12 miles east of St. Charles. It's Missouri's Katy Trail, the longest rails-to-trails project in the United States. If you've never traveled the Katy Trail, you're missing some of the prettiest country in the Midwest. The Katy Trail can be traveled on foot, on horseback, or on two wheels. All along the way you can see glimpses of dense forests, wetlands, valleys, and rolling farm fields, and always the Missouri River is not far away. In spring there are flowering dogwood and redbud trees. Fall brings crimson colors of maple and sumac, along with an abundance of wildlife that includes woodpeckers, red-tailed hawks, waterfowl, deer, and other creatures.

The section of trail between Boonville and St. Charles has been designated an official segment of the Lewis and Clark National Historic Trail. The entire trail is part of the American Discovery Trail and a Millennium Legacy Trail.

The Katy Trail is a common denominator that has revitalized many small towns that once flourished along the railroad. The Missouri-Kansas-Texas (MKT) Railroad, known as the Katy, ceased operation in 1986 and donated its right-of-way for the Katy Trail State Park. The Department of Natural Resources acquired the Katy Trail through the National

35

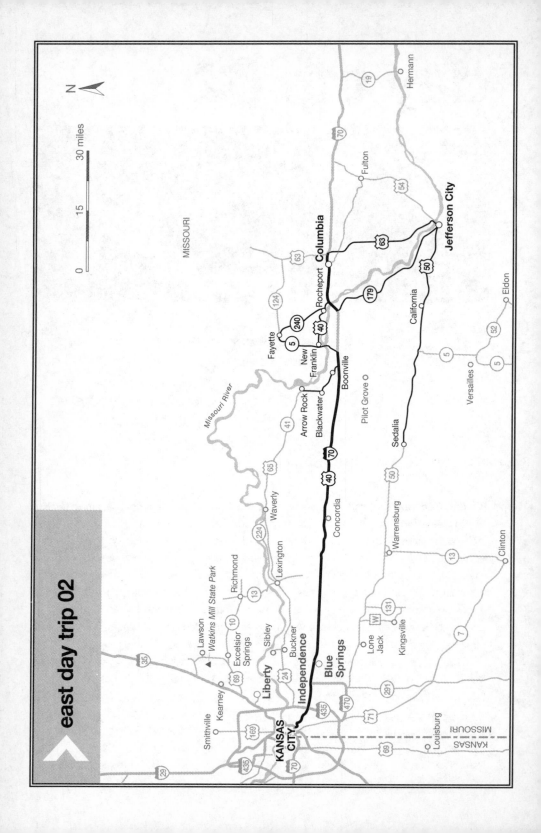

east day trip 02

Trails System Act—the "Rails-to-Trails" program that has helped turn inactive railroad corridors into recreational opportunities. Bed-and-breakfasts, restaurants, shops, and other services have prospered as a result.

Almost all the Katy Trail towns have bike-rental shops, and most offer a selection of mountain bikes, tandems, and toddler trailers for a modest hourly cost.

Although the trail is mostly flat, with a grade that seldom reaches more than 5 percent, it is very possible to overextend yourself, especially on a hot day. For in-depth information on the Katy Trail State Park, get a copy of *The Katy Trail Guidebook* by Pebble Publishing (573-698-3903; www.pebblepublishing.com). Otherwise, contact the Department of Natural Resources, (573) 449-7402; www.mostateparks/katytrail.

As long as you're traveling the Katy Trail, you might as well visit the **Boonslick region,** which takes its name from a salt lick in southwestern Howard County that was worked, about 1805, by Nathan and Daniel Morgan Boone, sons of the famed pioneer and scout Daniel Boone. (The actual location of the salt springs is now part of Boone's Lick State Historic Site, located 8 miles northwest of New Franklin near Boonesboro.)

The magic of the Boone name, plus the salt licks and fertile soil, drew early settlers to the area. There has been much speculation since that time as to why the e was left out of Boonslick. It may have been because then, as now, many people placed little importance on accurate spelling.

Boonslick Country is chock-full of history, for many of its towns brought politicians, land speculators, and entrepreneurs who later gained fame, such as painter George Caleb Bingham and frontier scout Kit Carson. Many of the gorgeous old homes in this area are listed on the National Register of Historic Places.

For those interested in Lewis and Clark history in this area, James M. Denny of the Missouri Department of Natural Resources, in conjunction with the Boonslick Historical Society, has written the booklet *Lewis and Clark in the Boonslick.* It is for sale through the Missouri River Communities Network in Columbia, (573) 256-2602; www.moriver.org.

blackwater, mo

This little town tucked along the tracks of the Missouri Pacific railroad almost disappeared off the map until brothers Mark and Bobby Danner, who grew up in Blackwater, returned in adulthood and harnessed the energy that had been hovering just beneath the surface of dozens of the little town's residents.

In its heyday as a railroad town at the turn of the 20th century, the population was just 600, but it dropped dangerously low in the 1980s as the rural agriculture economy took its toll on small towns. Today, the little green highway sign on Highway K lists the population as 199, but the energy along Main Street today makes it feel more like 200 or more. An extraordinary number of flowers bloom in this little town where an April weekend is dedicated to flower and plant sales.

Just about the entire town is the 2 blocks of Main Street, where you'll find a couple of good quality antiques and gift shops. For sale in almost any setting in Blackwater is Chef Leron's Strawberry Salad Dressing (www.chefleron.com), created by a native of Blackwater and sold in stores throughout the Midwest.

getting there

From downtown, take I-70 east almost 100 miles to exit 89 for Arrow Rock and Blackwater. Follow Highway K about 3 miles and turn right into town.

where to go

Blackwater City Hall. 125 Main St.; (660) 846-4411; www.blackwater-mo.com. Much of Blackwater is self-explanatory, but if you have any questions or just want to chit-chat for a while, check in with Mary Lee at City Hall. She'll have brochures about things to do in the community and the latest developments in town.

Bucksnort Trading Company. 111 Main St.; (660) 846-2224. Part museum with its quality Native American relics and collection of art, Bucksnort is a great place for re-enactors needing supplies or costumes. Owners Gerald and Connie Cunningham are re-enactors themselves, which is how they came across some of their unusual collection. If Gerald doesn't offer, be sure to ask about his bear skin, rawhide box, or Cherokee turban made of feathers. But he'll probably offer to show you. He's pretty excited about them, and no, they are not for sale.

Connie and Gerald also operate the Bucksnort Saloon next door. It's open daily, just like the Trading Company, but things really get to hopping on weekends when a ragtime piano player starts cranking out the tunes. Order a sarsaparilla and other non-alcoholic drinks from the bar. But don't drink too much because, just like the old west days, the outhouse is real and out back.

West End Theatre. 301 Doddridge St. (no phone). This is where the creative talents of Blackwater area residents are often on display with music, theater, poetry readings, and you name it. Visitors may appreciate the original stained-glass windows a bit more than the comfort of the original pews in this theater, located in a former church that dates to 1905. For a schedule of activities, check the city website or call City Hall at (660) 846-4411.

where to stay

Iron Horse Hotel. 101 Main St.; (660) 846-2011; www.ironhorsehotel.com. The original hotel that housed railroad workers from the 1880s, the Iron Horse is a focal point of the revitalization of the community. From the Katy Trail to the Marakesh Express, each of the 10 rooms is named for a prominent railroad or rail route. Some rooms have fireplaces and televisions, but all have claw-foot bathtubs and a sense of authenticity to the period and community. The lunch and dinner menu is reflective of much larger communities and the culinary experiences the owners received while living in New Orleans. Open daily from May through Sept, then on weekends or when something is happening in town. $–$$.

arrow rock, mo

As the state's first historic site, the Missouri River town of Arrow Rock is the western gateway to Boonslick Country. Founded in 1829, it was an important Santa Fe Trail rendezvous point and home of several distinguished Missourians, including three Missouri governors, painter George Caleb Bingham, and Dr. John Sappington, who pioneered the use of quinine for treating malaria.

On their epic expedition upriver in 1804, Lewis and Clark made note of the area, and later William Clark termed it a "handsome spot for a town." Just 25 years later, in 1829, a town was founded here. Indeed, Arrow Rock was then, as it is now, a beautiful place, and it has somehow retained its peaceful country character and managed to keep the look and feel of 19th-century America.

Once a bustling frontier village with a population of 1,000, it has only 55 year-round residents today. Each October during the annual Arrow Rock Craft Festival, that number increases as visitors come to enjoy historically authentic crafts interpreted in a period setting. The town hosts a variety of other events, including the Traditional Folk Music Festival in September and an antiques show in May.

For information about narrated tram tours of the village, call (660) 837-3231; www .friendsofarrowrock.org.

getting there

From Blackwater, go back to Highway K and follow it 5 more miles to MO 41, which will lead you right into Arrow Rock.

where to go

Arrow Rock State Historic Site Interpretive Center. 39521 Visitor Center Dr.; (660) 837-3330; www.mostateparks.com. This center is expansive not only in physical size but in the periods of history covered. Starting with the Osage and Missouri Indians through the Lewis and Clark expedition to the Civil War and finishing with issues of the 20th century, this facility provides a fascinating and in-depth interpretation of the region. From here, you can also sign up for guided tours of the village of Arrow Rock that take in the George Caleb Bingham Home (1837), the Saline County Courthouse (1839), the Sites Home (1875) and Gun Shop (1844), and the Print Shop (1868). Tours are conducted daily Memorial Day through Labor Day and weekends in spring and fall. Admission fee. The state site includes several picnic places and a camping area on the limestone bluffs overlooking the Missouri River.

Arrow Rock Lyceum Theatre. 114 High St.; (660) 837-3311; www.lyceumtheatre.org. The Lyceum is Missouri's oldest professional regional theater and the only professional theater serving rural Missouri. Popular, professional summer theater is presented here in rotating repertory from May through Aug and into parts of Oct. Buy your tickets early because these shows do indeed sell out quickly. Admission fee.

where to shop

Many Arrow Rock merchants and businesses operate seasonally with hours that are frequently subject to change. It's always best to call ahead to the Arrow Rock Area Merchants Association, (660) 837-3352; www.arrowrock.org.

Arrow Rock Antiques. Main Street; (660) 837-3333. This shop features period furniture and needlepoint. Open weekends or by appointment.

Arrow Rock Craft Shop. Main Street (in the Masonic Lodge Building); (660) 784-2441. Wood and fabric artwork, clothing, quilts, china, jewelry, and toys are offered here, plus breads, plants, confections, and seasonal produce. Open daily May through Oct and weekends only Dec and Apr.

Lot 2 On the Town Square. (660) 837-3167. As the name suggests, this antique and vintage clothing store is located in the second lot on the Town Square of Arrow Rock. You can't miss it. Closed Mon and Tues.

The House of Mary B. Main Street; (660) 837-3305. Find quality reproduction antiques and other gift items at this longtime establishment on Main Street.

where to eat

Catalpa. 500 High St.; (660) 837-3324. Liz Huff has a history of creating a gourmet dining experience in other area restaurants and she does it again here with steaks, seafood, and fowl. Catalpa is open only on weekends and nights the Lyceum performs, so call ahead. $$.

The Old Arrow Rock Tavern. Main Street; (660) 837-3200. Built in 1834, the tavern continues to serve the public as it served those who drove their wagons over the Santa Fe Trail. The fare includes catfish, country ham, and fried chicken. Private parties and groups are accommodated. Call for reservations. $$.

where to stay

Borgman's Bed & Breakfast. 706 Van Buren; (660) 837-3350. This 1850s-era home offers 4 rooms and 3 shared baths. A family-style breakfast is served in the kitchen and features the owner's home-baked items. You'll love the cinnamon rolls. Open year-round; no cards. $.

Bunny's Bed and Breakfast. 300 N. Seventh St.; (660) 837-3352. Bunny Thompson's home is just steps from all of the activities in Arrow Rock and includes a lovely patio on which you may enjoy a glass of wine upon check-in. With 5 guest rooms, each with a private bath, your accommodations here may be even more comfortable than you have at home. $.

DownOver Bed & Breakfast Inn. Main Street; (660) 837-3268. This unusual establishment features 6 distinctively decorated guest rooms with private baths and a fully equipped guest cottage. A full breakfast is served daily. There are lounge areas for games and a front porch for relaxing. A bicycle built for two is available. $–$$.

Switzler House Guest Cottage. 117 Sixth St.; (660) 837-3148; www.switzlerhouse.com. If you've ever wondered about living in one of the lovely homes in Arrow Rock, this is your chance to try it out. Guests at the Switzler House have the entire house to themselves. You'll be surrounded by the state park on 3 sides, but you're not entirely secluded, being just a block from the hub of activity. Guests are provided with a basket of freshly baked muffins along with a selection of juices, cereals, and milk so that breakfast is whenever you like. The kitchen is fully equipped if you would like to cook for yourselves. $$.

boonville, mo

Settled in 1810, Boonville is the oldest surviving town on the Missouri River. The town still exhibits the cultural mix of original Southern settlers along with the influx of German immigrants who settled here in the mid-19th century. Boonville's many restored historic buildings, restaurants, and bed-and-breakfasts make this a place worth visiting.

Boonville is also the county seat of Cooper County and the site of the first Civil War battle fought in Missouri (June 1861). South of Boonville are three interesting old plantation homes, including Ravenswood, Crestmead, and Pleasant Green Plantation House, that are open for tours.

Boonville was a town that made the transition from being a major river port to a booming railroad town. Many remnants of this era can still be seen, including the restored MKT depot.

Named for Daniel Boone (as was the Boonslick region), Boonville prospered during the late 1820s. German immigrants arrived 10 years later, and the river trade and Santa Fe Trail activity were the economic forces that sustained the town. The advent of railroads and the resulting confusion from the Civil War engagements fought in and around Boonville slowed the city's growth. Boonville today remains an important local center for transportation, tourism, and agribusiness.

Boonville contains 7 National Register Districts and 19 individual listed sites.

getting there

Boonville is a few miles farther east on I-70 from Arrow Rock.

where to go

Boonville Area Chamber of Commerce. Katy Depot, 320 First St.; (660) 882-2721; www .boonvillemochamberofcommerce.com. The restored 1912 depot houses the Katy Trail offices and the Boonville Chamber of Commerce. Katy Trail gift items are sold here.

Friends of Historic Boonville. 614 E. Morgan; (660) 882-7977; www.friendsofhistoric boonville.org. Pick up brochures for self-guided tours of the area and other information about the Boonslick region.

Cooper County Jail Museum, Jailers Residence, and Hanging Barn. Friends of His-toric Boonville, 614 E. Morgan; (660) 882-7977. Built in 1848, this venerable structure was the oldest continuously used county jail in Missouri until its closing in 1978. The last public hanging took place here in 1930, when a man named Lawrence Mabry was executed for a robbery and murder in Pettis County. This hanging was a factor in the elimination of capital punishment in Cooper County. The most famous prisoner held here was Frank James, brother of Jesse James. He was brought here on April 24, 1884, to answer a warrant for his arrest for a train robbery (what else?) that took place in 1876. Sympathetic citizens of Boonville raised his bond in a matter of hours, and the case was later dismissed for lack of evidence. Open daily. Admission fee.

Crestmead. 7400 Highway A, Pilot Grove; (660) 834-4140. Located 6 miles south of Pilot Grove, the Italianate mansion was built in 1859 by John Taylor. The 3-story home has a wide central hall that runs the length of the structure and features a massive octagonal newel post and 16 rooms with 8-foot windows and period furnishings. Although the home, which is on the National Register of Historic Places, was partially damaged by fire in 2008, it has been slowly and meticulously restored. Outbuildings include an ice and carriage house, restored slave quarters, and an old barn. The home has been owned since 1903 by the Betteridge family, who renamed it Crestmead, meaning "high meadow." The home is open to tour by appointment. Admission fee.

Katy Trail State Park. Cooper County trailheads in Boonville, Clifton City, and Pilot Grove; (800) 334-6946; www.mostateparks.com. As the trail heads east from Boonville, travelers experience some of the prettiest country in Missouri and are on an official part of the Lewis and Clark National Historic Trail because of its close proximity to the Missouri River. Heading west from these trailheads, the trail begins to move through open prairie away from the river.

Pleasant Green. 7045 MO 135, Pilot Grove; (660) 834-3945. Located 9 miles south of Pilot Grove, this Federal-style brick mansion is built of handmade bricks and native stone. It was begun as a one-room house, with additions added from the 1830s through the 1870s, and was once a plantation of 2,500 acres. Settled by Winston and Polly Walker of Virginia in 1818, it survived Civil War raids and years of neglect. Many original furnishings are part of the home, and the facade has been returned to its 1877 appearance. The home is listed on the National Register of Historic Places and includes outbuildings that feature an old hexagonal barn, a curing shed, and restored slave quarters. The 1870 Pleasant Green Post Office building was moved here to serve as a mini-gallery for local artists. The home is open to tour by appointment. Guides in antebellum dress serve coffee or tea in the dining room by advance request. Admission fee.

Ravenswood Farm. Located 12 miles south of Boonville on MO 5, Bunceton; (660) 882-7143. This impressive private home was built in 1880 by Captain Charles E. Leonard and his wife, Nadine. Five generations later it is still owned by Leonard descendants. Few changes have been made in the house: The furnishings and decorations are much the same as when it was built. Group and individual tours of the home are offered by appointment from Mar through Nov. Admission fee.

Roslyn Heights. 821 Main St.; (660) 882-5320. This 1894 Queen Anne home features Romanesque Revival structures, towers, turrets, gable dormers, and a porte-cochere with Moorish decorative elements. Paneled front doors open from the front porch into a reception hall, and the entrance hall's original tile floor is intact. The house is graced by a geometrically designed stairway with motifs that illustrate the use of machinery during the Industrial Revolution. The parlor features a hand-painted ceiling and mahogany fireplace mantel. The other rooms in the home also have ornate designs and elegant antique furnishings. Tours are by appointment only. The home is open to the public for meetings, luncheons, receptions, and special events. Admission fee.

Thespian Hall. Main and Vine Streets; (660) 882-7977; www.friendsofhistoricboonville .org. This restored Greek Revival opera house, built in 1857, is owned and managed by the Friends of Historic Boonville. It is the oldest theater still in use west of the Alleghenies and is on the National Register of Historic Places. If you can, time your visit to coincide with one of the music festivals held here. The Missouri River Festival of the Arts in August brings in fine performers, ranging from symphony orchestras and ballet companies to jazz, pop, and theater groups. The Big Muddy Folk Festival in April plays host to local and national musicians. Tours are available by appointment.

Warm Springs Ranch. 25270 MO 98; (888) 972-5933; www.warmspringsranch.com. This is a second home and breeding facility for the famous Anheuser Busch Clydesdales. About 100 horses enjoy the spacious pastures and rural living between Boonville and Rocheport. Tours are offered daily Apr through Oct except Wed and include the stables, pastures, fancy-schmancy trailers, and an up-close-and-personal photo op with those massive horses. Reservations are required. Admission fee.

where to eat

Glenn's Cafe. 501 High St., inside the Hotel Frederick; (660) 882-9191. Guests are often surprised, even blown away, that such a quality dining experience is available in rural mid-Missouri. Even the local favorites like Fried Missouri-Raised Catfish have a little some-thing extra to the flavor. However, for more adventurous palates, try the unusual offerings of items like Chicken Tchoupitoulas, a grilled free-range chicken breast served on a bed of griddled potatoes and topped with Hollandaise sauce. For dessert, the bread pudding and Hummingbird Cake are fabulous. Closed Mon. $–$$.

Riverside Diner. 203 Main St.; (660) 882-6333. Richard and Janice Held found themselves eating at this local diner so often that they finally bought the place for themselves. The diner is now famous for Fried Chicken Fridays, which delight the nose of anyone within 3 blocks of the downtown restaurant. Richard's big contribution to the menu is a breakfast sandwich his wife named "Richard's Full of Bologna." It's an egg, cheese, and fried bologna sandwich served on Texas toast. Open 7 days a week. $.

The Settlers Inn. I-70 and MO 135 (Arrow Rock and Pilot Grove exit); (660) 882-3125. For something very different, come and dine in this simple log home, where made-from-scratch food is cooked up in a small but mighty kitchen. The excellent family-style meals include main dishes such as beef and buffalo T-bone steaks, pheasant, country ham, game hen, buffalo brisket, smoked pork chops, and more. All dinners include salad, potato, veg-etables, home-baked desserts, bread, and beverage.

Because the restaurant is small, you will need reservations. Call well in advance, espe-cially if you have a large party. To expedite mealtime, the restaurant requests that you order your meat selection when you make your reservation. Seatings are at 5:30 and 7:30 p.m. on Fri and Sat evenings. Special group bookings are available during the week. Closed Sun. $$.

where to stay

Hotel Frederick. 501 High St.; (660) 882-2828; www.hotelfrederick.com. With a fabulous perch above the Missouri River, the Hotel Frederick has been welcoming guests since 1905. But after some less than glorious days, the hotel was renovated and reopened in glorious style in July 2007. The 24 guest rooms today are decorated as they would have been 100 years ago, but with modern and comfortable amenities such as towel warmers, freshly pressed bed linens, and complimentary wireless Internet. The designer soaps are by Indigo Wild in Kansas City, and the classic bathroom dividers are by Kansas City glass artists Bill Drummond and Peregrine Honig. Many of the lobby antiques are original to the hotel. Ask the front desk about the bicycles on loan to explore the Katy Trail, or schedule an in-room massage. A continental breakfast is included, but enjoy lunch or an evening meal at Glenn's Cafe. $$–$$$.

new franklin, mo

Like many communities that developed on the banks of a major waterway, New Franklin has flooded and moved to higher ground over the years as the mighty Missouri has changed its course. Although many people today consider Independence the beginning of the Santa Fe Trail, it was first New Franklin, before the town underwent many of its floods and relocations.

Today a sleepy little town on the north banks of the Missouri River, New Franklin has made some great contributions to state history and beyond. For example, the composer of "The Missouri Waltz," the state's official song, Edgar Settles, was born in and is now buried in New Franklin. Of more modern interest, country music singer Sara Evans, nominated for 2012 Female Vocalist of the Year by the Country Music Association, also calls New Franklin home.

getting there

New Franklin is 3 miles north of Boonville on MO 5.

where to go

New Franklin City Hall. 130 E. Broadway; (660) 848-2288; www.newfranklin.missouri .org. Here you'll find brochures about the community and people proud of their small town girl who made it big, Sara Evans, who was nominated for CMA's Female Vocalist of the Year in 2012.

Boone's Lick State Historic Site. Located 8 miles northwest of New Franklin, near Boonesboro; (660) 837-3330; www.mostateparks.com. Take MO 87 west from the northern approach to the Missouri River Bridge on MO 5 to MO 187, about 1 mile north of Boonesboro. Continue 2 miles west to the site of the salt springs, worked by the sons of Daniel Boone beginning around 1805. The year before, Captains Meriwether Lewis and William Clark noted this area and its potential for development in their journals. The state of Missouri has a kiosk here with information about the Boonslick region and the salt springs. A trail with informational signs winds through the woods by the remnants of the saltworks, and there's a shelter house with picnic tables, as well as public restrooms. Free. Artifacts from the industry are displayed at the Arrow Rock State Historic Site.

where to stay

Katy Roundhouse. 1893 Katy Dr. (Katy Trail Mile Marker 189); (660) 848-2232; www .katyroundhouse.com. Located on the grounds of a century-old restored train depot, the Katy Roundhouse stands on the site of the former MKT Railroad switching yard. The area offers a full-service campground with spacious, secluded campsites for tent camping, including picnic tables, fire rings, and bike racks. In addition, there are full RV hookups, modern shower facilities, public restrooms, a mini grocery, and tents for rent. Home-cooked dinners are served on Fri and Sat evenings by reservation only. The steaks are fresh cut and broiled outdoors over an open grill. There are also beer and wine gardens and occasional live music for a small cover charge. $–$$.

Rivercene Bed and Breakfast. 127 Country Rd. 463; (800) 531-0862; www.rivercene .com. Listed on the National Register of Historic Places, this 15-room mansion was built by Captain Joseph Kinney. The riverboat baron began construction in 1864 on the floodplain, leading locals to call the structure Kinney's Folly. Kinney was undaunted. Finding the highest flood point, he built the house 1 foot higher. Of course, he hadn't counted on the Great Flood of 1993. Jody and Ron Lenz purchased the home in 1992, only to be confronted by 4 feet of water in their living room during the flood, when Rivercene could be reached only by boat.

The couple has fully restored the mansion, incorporating the splendor of Kinney's original architectural masterpiece. The home has Italian marble for the 9 fireplaces, black walnut for the front doors, and a hand-carved mahogany staircase. (A few years after Kinney completed Rivercene, the architectural plan was duplicated for the present Governor's Mansion in Jefferson City.)

Rivercene offers tours of the home, as well as overnight stays with queen-size beds and private baths, or you can take your choice of a 2-room suite or a room with a whirlpool. A delicious breakfast is served in the large dining room. Group and individual tours are offered by appointment (admission fee). $$–$$$.

fayette, mo

Fayette is the seat of Howard County, thus the town is centered around the lovely 1900s-era courthouse. The delightful tradition of a town crier "crying" the results on election night still occurs on these courthouse stairs. The Fayette Cornet Band plays on the grounds most Thursday nights in the summer.

getting there

From New Franklin, travel 11 miles north on MO 5 to Fayette, the home of Central Methodist University.

where to go

The Ashby-Hodge Gallery of American Art. On the campus of Central Methodist University, 411 Central Methodist Sq.; (660) 246-6324; www.centralmethodist.edu. Opened in 1993, the Ashby-Hodge Gallery holds a special collection of oil paintings, lithographs, watercolors, bronzes, graphite drawings, and acrylics representing the work of American regional artists. The gallery holds rare pieces by Swedish-born artist Birger Sandzén, lithographs by Jackson Lee Nesbitt, an ink and wash by Thomas Hart Benton, a rare egg tempera on panel by Charles Banks Wilson, and many other interesting pieces. This little gem of a place also features special exhibits throughout the year, often bringing in the artists themselves to greet guests at gallery openings. Open Sun through Thurs afternoons. Free.

Morrison Observatory. Located on Park Road across from Fayette City Park; (660) 248-6371; www.centralmethodist.edu. Dating to 1875, this observatory still has its original lens and is the oldest observatory west of the Mississippi. Although it is now owned and operated by Central Methodist University, it was first built in nearby Glasgow for Pritchard College. The observatory is not open for regular hours, but opens to the public a few evenings each spring and fall, or when some interesting astronomical occurrence is expected. Free.

where to eat

Emmet's Kitchen and Tap. 111 Main St.; (660) 248-3363; www.emmetskitchen.com. People in these parts know that authentic Cajun food and a good time can be found at this hot spot on the square in Fayette. The shrimp po' boy and bourbon pecan pie are direct from Louisiana, but the Kansas City strip steak and double-smoked pork chop remind you that good food comes from the Midwest as well. The wine list is impressive. $$.

rocheport, mo

The town is a perfect romantic getaway close to home, yet it also offers Katy Trail access for family outings. Antiques shops, an art gallery, cafes, a winery and bistro with a panoramic river-bluff view, and superior bed-and-breakfasts are part of its charm. Each summer the town's population swells from 225 persons to as many as 30,000 visitors, many of whom are Katy Trail travelers.

Located on the Missouri River, Rocheport was founded in 1825 and grew rapidly as steamboat transportation brought business to town. In 1849 57 steamboats made 500 landings at Rocheport. Nine years earlier the Whig Party held its convention in Rocheport and thousands of delegates arrived by carriage, wagon, steamboat, and horseback to support William Henry Harrison's presidential campaign.

Rocheport has survived disasters, including the Civil War and the Great Flood of 1993, when the 243-foot-long MKT Railroad tunnel, built in 1893, was filled with 4 feet of water. Rocheport also affords one of the most beautiful views along the Katy Trail, parts of which wind along the river under the spectacular Moniteau Bluffs.

Rocheport is on the National Register of Historic Places and many of its residents live and work in restored 19th-century homes and buildings.

For more information on Rocheport, visit www.rocheport.com.

getting there

From Fayette, drop south on MO 240 just 12 miles into Rocheport. From New Franklin you can head east on US 40 to Route BB or head east from Boonville on I-70 to the Rocheport exit.

where to go

Mighty Mo Canoe Rentals. 101 Lewis St.; (573) 698-3903; www.mighty-mo.com. Guided tours of the Missouri River are offered each Saturday afternoon in warm weather months and when the river is not above flood stage. Reservations required. Admission fee.

Rocheport General Store. 202 Central St.; (573) 698-2282; www.rocheportgeneralstore .com. More of a cafe and coffee shop than a true country store, this is the scene of a number of special events in Rocheport. From live music on weekends to a street bowling competition on St. Patrick's Day, the good times originate at the Rocheport General Store. But yes, you can buy sundries here along with souvenirs and a nice sandwich, ice cream, or coffee.

Trailside Cafe and Bike Rental. 700 First St.; (573) 698-2702; www.trailsidecafebike .com. From Katy Trail Mile Marker 179, you can literally pedal into the parking lot of the Trailside Cafe. This nice little operation began as a small sandwich shop and eventually expanded into a dining room with an adjacent bike shop. The cafe is noted for its excellent pork tenderloin sandwiches that will feed two, plus fresh homemade baked goods. Fresh fruit and grilled portobello mushroom sandwiches are on the healthy side of the menu. Open for breakfast, lunch, and dinner, the Trailside Cafe has a wonderful patio where many choose to enjoy ice cream or just a big bottle of water and trail mix. You can buy or rent bikes here, or if yours has a problem, get it repaired. Child carts, tandems, and mountain bikes can be rented by the hour or by the day.

where to shop

Flavors of the Heartland/Rocheport Gallery. 204 Second St.; (573) 698-2063. This unique store sells a variety of Missouri-made specialty and gourmet food products. You can choose from herb and fruit-infused vinegars, delicious apple and pumpkin butters, mustards, barbecue sauces, salsas, Boone County hams, and much more. The store features custom gift baskets filled with goodies like Caramel Satin and Chocolate Satin Dessert Sauces (ooooh!) and Lemon Satin Dessert Sauce (yum yum!). The free samples are tempting. When you're through slurping and shopping, you can visit the adjoining gallery and ogle the original art.

White Horse Antiques. 505 Third St.; (573) 698-2088. This longtime favorite in Rocheport is located in the historic 1840 Waddell House, where the 19th-century antique country fur-niture, quilts, and primitives for sale come to life in their natural setting. You can also find a great selection of modern decorating accessories or sign up for a rug hooking class. Open Wed through Sun.

where to eat

Abigail's. 206 Central St.; (573) 698-3000; www.abigails-restaurant.com. This restaurant offers wholesome fare in a restored downtown building. The menu changes daily, but count on delights such as butternut squash ravioli, frittata with goat cheese, or duck breast with rhubarb sauce Open for lunch Wed through Sun; dinner by reservation. $–$$.

Les Bourgeois Vineyards, Winery, and Bistro. 14020 W. Hwy. BB (1 mile north of I-70 on Route BB); (573) 698-2300; www.missouriwine.com. This unique restaurant and winery makes a great place to unwind and enjoy a spectacular sunset from atop a river bluff. The land here offers rich soil and a microclimate that is ideal for grape production. Les Bourgeois produces red, white, and blush table wines from French hybrid grapes and native cultivars. The restaurant offers an outdoor wine garden and indoor dining featuring a variety of nicely prepared fish, chicken, and steak dinners, plus great desserts. $$–$$$.

where to stay

Katy Trail Bed and Bikefest. 101 Lewis St.; (573) 698-2453; www.katytrailbb.com. This modest Victorian home was built in 1880 and is on the National Register of Historic Places. The Katy offers 4 rooms, including a converted railroad boxcar in the backyard that sleeps up to 5 and has a private bath, refrigerator, and cable television. The upstairs of the main house offers a family suite with a private bath, queen-size bed, and futon. There is a smaller bedroom downstairs with 1 double bed. Above the garage is a large rustic room with 2 beds and a sleeper sofa, which serves as a bunkhouse for cost-conscious travelers. $.

Schoolhouse Bed and Breakfast. Third and Clark Streets; (573) 698-2022; www.school-housebandb.com. Touted as one of the country's top 10 romantic inns, the Schoolhouse has been the subject of greeting cards and magazine articles. Large framed prints of the famous Dick and Jane primer grace the walls of this former schoolhouse. Elegantly refurbished, it now offers 10 bedrooms with private baths, 2 of which have a "sweetheart" Jacuzzi. Each of the nicely appointed guest rooms is decorated in beautiful antiques. An upstairs dining room offers a full breakfast of coffee, fresh fruit compote, baked bread or muffins, and egg strata. $$–$$$.

The Yates House. 305 Second St.; (573) 698-2129; www.yateshouse.com. Completed in 1991, the Yates House is a pretty reproduction of an 1850 roadside inn. Guests have a choice of 2 bedrooms and a suite, all with private baths. A back porch, a courtyard patio, and flower and herb gardens are yours to enjoy. The garden house next door has 2 bedrooms with private baths and a suite with a fireplace and jetted tub. $$–$$$.

columbia, mo

You don't have to be a college student to enjoy yourself in Columbia, though it is home to the University of Missouri, Stephens College, and Columbia College. On any given summer night, you can listen to live jazz and blues outdoors or catch a concert by noted artists such as Wilco, Ray LaMontagne, or Hot Tuna at the Blue Note, one of the best live-entertainment venues in the state.

If you're looking for one-of-a-kind finds, visit downtown Columbia's shops, which sell everything from handmade Brazilian tables, regional art, and rare books to items that reflect social, political, and environmental issues. Despite a thriving mall on the west side of the town, Columbia's downtown is vibrant and energetic at all hours.

Nation's Restaurant News has touted Columbia as the best up-and-coming place to open a dining establishment. Several youthful restaurateurs have taken it upon themselves to impart fresh and vigorous menus that have boosted the city's image as a restaurant town. Columbia now has a wide variety of choices that range from low-priced cafes to upscale eateries. Competition has spurred the upgrading of menus and ambience to keep pace with demand.

The city was the recipient of a $22 million non-motorized transportation grant in 2005 that has transformed Columbia into a very bike-friendly town with nearly 200 miles of bike paths, marked bike lanes, and abundant bike parking.

getting there

From Rocheport, return to I-70 and travel just 10 miles east to Columbia.

where to go

Columbia Convention and Visitors Bureau. 300 S. Providence Rd.; (573) 875-1231 or (800) 652-0987; www.visitcolumbiamo.com. The office is located just across the street from Flat Branch Park and the MKT Trailhead, so as you pick up your brochures and get your questions answered, you may study your options in a beautiful outdoor setting.

The Blue Note. 17 N. Ninth St.; (573) 874-1944; www.thebluenote.com. For more than a quarter-century, one of central Missouri's best live-entertainment venues has been located in this restored vaudeville theater that features renowned blues, reggae, rock, and folk artists. Two full cocktail bars are located on the premises. The popular College Trivia Challenge, a fundraiser for Special Olympics each October, is an opportunity for parents to see what their kids are (not!) learning at school.

Columbia College. 1001 Rogers St.; (800) 231-2391; www.ccis.edu. This was the first institution of higher education for women chartered by a state legislature west of the Mississippi River. Founded in 1851, the coeducational school is located on 26 acres in the midst of the city. Day trippers may enjoy checking out the student and local work featured in the Sid Larson Gallery. Or if you love volleyball, the women's team at Columbia is one of the best in the US. Check out their schedule on the college website.

MKT Trail. Fourth and Cherry Streets (downtown) to Scott Boulevard (Route TT); (573) 874-7460. Walk, jog, or bike on this 8.9-mile wheelchair-accessible trail, which varies from an urban walkway to ___sely wooded passageway. Parking is available at Stadium, Forum, and Scott B___. The MKT is Columbia's spur connection to the Katy Trail. The Martin L___ ___hitheater is located at the Stadium access.

Rock Bridge M___ ___(573) 449-7402; www.mostate parks.com. Thi___ where a stream flows beneath a na___ ___usic areas, and a wilderness d___ ___e park is best known for ___ ___h more than 6 miles of p___ ___ch fall, the Devil's Icebox V___

Y___ ___ssages that can be rathe___ ___ony of gray bats. Call the ___ Open daily.

S'___ ___erinsurance.com. Here's ___5-acre garden in the heart ___ well as 15,000 annuals and ___tural landscaping that fills the ___ns is a place of repose within a ___oy a quiet walk through the tree- ___unday evenings in June and July. ___se relocated from Brunswick, Mis- ___varieties of grandifloras, floribundas, ___. In addition, there are a shaded pool ___e is enough to calm you down after a

Stephens College ___) 876-7207; www.stephens.edu. Founded in 1833, Stephens College ___dest women's college in the nation. It offers programs in the arts, business, pro___al studies, and liberal arts and sciences. The performing arts department is well respected for its productions and summer stock throughout the Midwest. The Firestone Baars Chapel features a unique 4-foyer design created by Eero Saarinen, who also designed the St. Louis Gateway Arch. Also on campus in Lena Raney Wood Hall (6 N. College St.; 573-876-7220) is the Historic Costume Museum, a collection

---

(Overlaid rotated document — Return Policy):

eBooks, digital downloads, and used books are not returnable or exchangeable. Defective NOOKs may be exchanged at the store in accordance with the applicable warranty.

Returns or exchanges will not be permitted (i) after 14 days or without receipt or (ii) for product not carried by Barnes & Noble or Barnes & Noble.com.

Policy on receipt may appear in two sections.

Return Policy

With a sales receipt or Barnes & Noble.com packing slip, a full refund in the original form of payment will be issued from any Barnes & Noble Booksellers store for returns of undamaged NOOKs, new and unread books, and unopened and undamaged music CDs, DVDs, vinyl records, toys/games and audio books made within 14 days of purchase from a Barnes & Noble Booksellers store or Barnes & Noble.com with the below exceptions:

A store credit for the purchase price will be issued (i) for purchases made by check less than 7 days prior to the date of return, (ii) when a gift receipt is presented within 60 days of purchase, (iii) for textbooks, (iv) when the original tender is PayPal, or (v) for products purchased at Barnes & Noble College bookstores that are listed for sale in the Barnes & Noble Booksellers inventory management system.

Opened music CDs, DVDs, vinyl records, audio books may not be returned, and can be exchanged only for the same title and only if defective. Magazines, newspapers, purchased from other retailers or sellers are returnable only to the retailer or seller from which they are purchased, pursuant to such retailer's or seller's return policy. Defective NOOKs are not returnable or exchangeable. eBooks, digital downloads, and used books are not be exchanged at the store in accordance with the rough___ of more than 13,000 pieces of clothing by designers from around the world. Each semester, students create new exhibits that interpret how the clothes we wear reflect our culture.

Twin Lakes Recreation Area. 2500 Chapel Hill Rd.; (573) 874-7460. This family-oriented facility offers swimming, boating, fishing, hiking, and nature study. The 6-acre swimming lake has a deck, a diving platform, water slides, and a large sand beach. There's a water playground separate from the lake for small children and paddleboats available for rent. Bring your best friend to the dog park.

University of Missouri-Columbia. Eighth and Elm Streets; (573) 882-2121; www.mizzou.edu. The first public university west of the Mississippi River, "Mizzou" was founded in 1839. The 1,340-acre campus has an enrollment of nearly 28,000 students. UMC is one of the few institutions in the country that houses journalism, law, medicine, agriculture, engineering, and veterinary medicine on a single campus. The Mizzou journalism school was the first such school in the world and remains the respected leader in training professional journalists.

The center of the campus is the historic Francis Quadrangle, at the entrance of Eighth and Elm Streets. Its 18 surrounding buildings are on the National Register of Historic Places. The row of 6 Ionic columns that adorn the center of the Francis Quadrangle once supported the portico of Academic Hall, the first building erected on campus. The open area around the columns is the center of the cluster of redbrick buildings known as the Red Campus. It is modeled after Thomas Jefferson's design for the University of Virginia. Walking through those columns into the quad is a freshman class orientation rite, and passing through the columns, back into the world, is a treasured memory at graduation.

UMC houses the first monument erected for the grave of Thomas Jefferson. When Virginia decided to erect a new monument for Jefferson's grave and give the original away, UMC was first in line to grab the valuable castoff. Since President Jefferson was instrumental in acquiring UMC as the first state university in the Louisiana Purchase Territory, Mizzou was the logical choice to house the prized stone slab. (Virginia has since regretted its decision to give up the original grave marker, but UMC has no intention of returning it.) The entire campus is considered a botanic garden with 9 individual gardens identified on campus. Thomas Jefferson would have liked that.

If you are not interested in the academics and just want a tour of campus, call (800) 856-2181.

Mizzou Arena. 600 Stadium Blvd.; (573) 884-PAWS. The Mizzou Arena, officially opened in 2004, seats 13,000 people for basketball, volleyball, and concerts.

Museum of Anthropology. 100 Swallow Hall; (573) 882-3764. The Museum of Anthropology is one of those tucked-away-and-taken-for-granted places that doesn't get much fanfare. As early as 1885 UMC began accepting gifts of ethnographic materials, finally organizing them into a cohesive collection in 1902. The only anthropology museum in the state and one of the few in the Midwest, its archaeological collection is the largest holding of prehistoric Missouri artifacts in the world, including those dating from 9000 BC to modern times.

The Grayson Archery Collection housed here is one of the largest and most comprehensive collections of its kind in the world. Unusual thumb rings of carved jade used by Chinese archers represent only a fraction of the materials that are showcased in the museum's exhibit hall.

There are a number of Native American exhibits, dating from 11,000 years ago to the present. Works by Hopi artist Iris Nampeyo, plus Santa Clara pottery and authentic Hopi kachinas, are showcased. There is also a prehistoric section of Native American work that features Hohokam and Anasazi pottery. Both the museum exhibit hall and the exhibits in the Museum Support Center are open to the public. Tours are available by appointment. Open Mon through Fri. Free.

The Museum of Art and Archaeology. Pickard Hall; (573) 882-3591. One of the best-kept secrets in the Midwest, this gem of a museum is worth the drive to Columbia. It houses 13,000 pieces of art and artifacts from 6 continents and is the third-largest collection of its kind in Missouri. The Saul and Gladys Weinberg Gallery of Ancient Art is one of the most comprehensive in the state and features exhibits from ancient Egypt, Palestine, the Near East, Greece, Italy, and the Roman world. Particularly noteworthy is the oldest piece in the museum, a 250,000-year-old ax handle, as well as a 4,000-year-old cuneiform tablet and case that afford a glimpse into an early form of human communication before computers and texting. A Cypro-Archaic vessel, thrown before 600 BC, is a reminder that the venerable craft of pottery is blessed with longevity, while coins and gaming pieces from Egypt, Alexandria, and Rome tell the story of leisure-time spending sprees long before riverboat casinos. Closed Mon, open late on Thurs. Free.

The Walters–Boone County Historical Museum and Maplewood Home. 3801 Ponderosa St.; (573) 443-8936. Located 3 miles south of the junction of MO 63 and I-70, the visitor center is housed in a traditional family farmhouse. The museum contains the history of the area from prehistoric to present day in its 16,000 square feet of exhibition space. The Montminy Art Gallery located on-site showcases the talents of mid-Missouri artists as well as the outstanding collection of half a million photographic images that are part of the Boone County Historical Society Photo Archives, which date from the late 1800s to the mid-20th century. The museum also can be used for banquets, meetings, workshops, weddings, and receptions.

Just north of the museum is the Maplewood Home, a historic Victorian residence built in 1877 that is listed on the National Register of Historic Places. Boone Junction Village, a historic town, consists of an 1820s-era log cabin, a Victorian home, and a 1920s-era general store, one-room schoolhouse and other buildings. Open Wed through Sun afternoons. The museum is free, but a charge is necessary for guided tours of the historic village.

where to shop

Central Columbia Association Special Business District. 11 S. Tenth St.; (573) 442-6816; www.discoverthedistrict.com. Columbia's downtown district is filled with fine restaurants, shops, galleries, bookstores, museums, and one-of-a-kind specialty stores that cover 45 square blocks surrounding Broadway. Some of the downtown establishments interconnect, making them easily accessible during inclement weather. Below are just a few noteworthy places:

Bluestem Missouri Crafts. 13 S. Ninth St.; (573) 442-0211; www.bluestemcrafts.com. This unusual store is actually a partnership of craftspeople who feature their own ceramic jewelry, weaving, pottery, and batik work. In addition, Bluestem is a showcase for an extensive collection of handmade functional and decorative work by other artists. Pottery, glass, wood, metal, and fiber art are represented here. Baskets, wooden boxes, toys, cards, and clothing made in Missouri are part of the colorful displays. The "Neighboring States Gallery" features the work of equally talented artisans from the states that border Missouri and includes a large selection of pieces by Decorah, Iowa, artist Brian Andreas. Open daily.

Calhoun's. 911 E. Broadway; (573) 443-3614. This pleasant gift shop reminds those who forget it that Columbia is home to more than college students. It's a fun place to browse, where you may find some unusual jewelry, a fresh scent for candles, a raucous birthday gift for an adult friend, or maybe something for newborn babies. Gift wrapping is free and creative.

The Candy Factory. 701 E. Cherry St.; (573) 443-8222; http://thecandyfactory.biz. This bright and cheery candy store is renowned for its delicious handmade chocolates, including chocolate-covered strawberries and scrumptious truffles. For real chocoholics, there's always the Ultimate Pizza, a gourmet treat featuring 1.5 pounds of deep-dish chocolate topped with fresh pecans, cashews, walnuts, cherries, and marshmallows, and drizzled with white chocolate. Closed Sun.

Columbia Art League Gallery. 207 S. Ninth St.; (573) 443-8838; www.columbiaartleague.org. Art lovers will find an eclectic collection of paintings, ceramics, jewelry, photography, and works in wood, metal and fiber at this bright and contemporary gallery, which has been showing work by local and regional artists for more than 50 years. A changing schedule of exhibits in the main gallery is testament to the myriad forms of creativity in this mid-Missouri art colony. Closed Sun and Mon.

Columbia Books. 1907 Gordon St.; (573) 449-7417; www.columbiabooksonline.com. An independently owned bookstore is such a rarity nowadays, and this place is really a classic laid-back place to browse and buy. It offers a mix of 60,000 new and used books that includes everything from rare publications dating back four centuries to the latest best-sellers. The store has a wealth of children's illustrated books, gardening tomes, and first editions. Open Mon through Sat.

Cool Stuff. 808 E. Broadway; (573) 875-5225. Globe-trotting owner Arnie Fagan has a great sense of humor and an eye for the unusual. By his own definition, he seeks all things "cool, unusual, practical, and fun"—much of it from Africa, Asia, Central and South America, and parts of Europe and the Middle East. The place offers an eclectic mix of ethnic items that range from Southwestern sage smudges to Israeli dreidels. There are more than 4,000 varieties of beads and thousands of candles, plus toys, jewelry, accessories, and clothing. Unless he sells it prior to this book's publication, there's a one-of-a-kind Indonesian ricksha for sale with an asking price (don't ask) of $5,000. Open daily.

Poppy. 920 E. Broadway; (573) 442-3223; www.poppyarts.com. Easily one of the best places in the country to find authentic American crafts, this store has been a fixture in down-town Columbia for more than 30 years. Poppy offers an excellent collection of contemporary artwork in clay, fiber, metal, wood, glass, and jewelry, as well as 2-dimensional art. This is one of the few stores in Missouri that carries the Sticks furniture line from Des Moines. If you're looking for something different, this is the place to come. Open daily.

Orchids and Art. 10 W. Nifong Blvd.; (573) 875-5989. Displays by local and regional artists are surrounded by flowering orchids, which are also for sale. The gallery collection rotates often and includes prints, mixed media, paintings, drawings, and photography. Closed Sun.

where to eat

Boone Tavern. 811 E. Walnut St.; (573) 442-5123; www.boonetavern.com. Prime rib, fresh seafood, steak, pasta, sandwiches, and salads are served at this popular establishment, which also offers outdoor dining. Located next to downtown's Boone County Courthouse, the restaurant features large banquet rooms and has driver and escort service available for groups of 40 persons or more. Open daily for lunch and dinner. $$.

Broadway Diner. 22 S. Fourth St.; (573) 875-1173. This working-class establishment opened in 1949 and is the only remaining diner of its style in Missouri. It features breakfast anytime and daily lunch specials for under $5. Come here for real hash browns and freshly mashed potatoes. Open daily for breakfast, lunch, and dinner. $.

Buckingham Smokehouse Bar-B-Q. 3804 Buttonwood Dr.; (573) 449-1490. You smell this no-frills spot, named for rock guitarist Lindsey Buckingham, long before you arrive at it. Owner Mark Brown spent several years on the road with rock bands, including Fleetwood Mac. Today Brown specializes in hickory-smoked beef brisket, pork loin ham, and turkey. The horseradish coleslaw is guaranteed to burn on the way down. You can sample at least a dozen famous barbecue sauces here, or simply go with the house favorite. And then enjoy a big fat cupcake for dessert. $.

Buck's Ice Cream Place. Eckles Hall, East Rollins and College Streets (on the UMC Campus); (573) 882-0591. Under the supervision of UMC's Department of Food Science and College of Agriculture, Buck's is a student-run research, teaching, and service operation. It's also a gathering spot for aficionados of good ice cream. Mizzou's "Truman the Tiger" mascot is the inspiration for Buck's Tiger Stripe ice cream, a mixture of vanilla and chocolate, with some orange coloring thrown in to account for the tigerlike hue. All ice cream is freshly made, is available in dipped and packaged forms, and weighs about 30 percent more per serving than most commercial products. Closed Sun. $ (no cards).

C.C.'s City Broiler. 1401 Forum Blvd.; (573) 445-7772; www.ccscitybroiler.com. This excellent steakhouse is renowned for its corn-fed Black Angus beef, hand-cut daily on the premises and cooked exactly as you like it. The signature item is a bone-in filet mignon, accented with a special seasoning that makes the flavor sing. If you want something even bigger, try the gorgeous 23-ounce porterhouse. All steaks come with the restaurant's famous jalapeño twice-baked potato, burgundy mushrooms, salad or soup, and fresh, hot sourdough bread. On the lighter side, the char-grilled seafood is always fresh, and you can mix and match a meal of steak and shrimp, steak and oysters, or steak and lobster tail. The prime rib, served only on Fri and Sat, sells out fast. There's a wall-to-wall wait on weekends, so come early. Dinner is served 7 nights a week. $$–$$$.

Columbia Star Dinner Train. 6501 Brown Station Rd.; (573) 474-2223; www.dinnertrain .com. For something a little different, make reservations for a Friday or Saturday evening ride and dinner, or Sunday morning brunch, in 1 of the 4 dining cars on this 1950s-era locomotive. The rails run north out of Columbia on a 2.5-hour ride. The dinner train runs year-round. $$.

Ernie's. 1005 Walnut St.; (573) 874-7804. This venerable art deco storefront establishment has been in business since 1934 and was recently upgraded from a greasy spoon to a not-so-greasy spoon that even features a short wine list. It still serves up good food at great prices. Hearty breakfasts, classic sandwiches, and luncheon specials are offered here, as are espresso, cappuccino, and lattes. One of the best things about Ernie's is the ambience. The eclectic assortment of patrons ranges from babies to bearded octogenarians. Blue-collar workers elbow in side by side at the counters with college students and faculty. Open daily until 3 p.m. $.

Lakota Coffee Company. 24 S. Ninth St.; (573) 874-2852.This popular coffee roastery, located in the heart of downtown, is the only Columbia coffee shop to roast its own beans daily. The owner named the place for the Lakota Sioux, who loved the taste and smell of hot, strong coffee and who would, in their caffeine quest, raid wagon trains and steal the beans for their own coffee klatches. The establishment's lattes and cappuccinos are served in enormous *Alice in Wonderland*–size cups. You have your choice of scones, croissants, biscotti, lox and bagels, and other edibles for dipping and sipping. The Lakota also sells coffee to take home and is especially proud of its hard-to-find varieties. Open daily. $.

The Main Squeeze. 28 S. Ninth St.; (573) 817-5616; www.main-squeeze.com. Start your morning with a 16-ounce Elvis Parsley—a mixture made with beets, spinach, parsley, celery, carrots, and garlic—which provides the equivalent of 5 servings of vegetables. Have a smoothie or go for the homemade soups, hearty sandwiches, salads, or fresh baked goods. There are no preservatives or artificial colors or flavors in anything you'll eat here. Breakfast can be free-range organic eggs, whole-grain pancakes, organic roasted potatoes, scrambled tofu, breakfast burritos, or biscuits with soy sausage gravy. There are also wheat-free nondairy entrees for vegans. Open daily 7 a.m. to 4 p.m. $.

63 Diner. 5801 SR 763; (573) 443-2331. This 1950s-style diner features neon lights, jukebox music, and the art and architecture of the era. Specialties include open-face roast beef and mashed potatoes, homemade ham and beans with grilled corn cakes, country-fried pork fillets, and country-fried chicken or pork cutlets with home-style gravy, mashed potatoes, and green beans. There's also a broccoli walnut casserole for those who swoon at the thought of ingesting too many calories. Sandwiches include almost any variety of burger known this side of Mars. Save room for homemade breads, rolls, pies, cobblers, and a hot fudge brownie sundae, complete with whipped cream and a cherry. Closed Sun and Mon. $.

Sophia's. 3915 S. Providence Rd.; (573) 874-8009. This popular restaurant has a laid-back, cosmopolitan ambience that goes well with its southern European fare that includes tapas, pastas, fresh seafood, steaks, and more. For after-dinner sport, there's always the bocce-ball court located next to the outdoor patio. There is usually a 30- to 40-minute wait to get in, but early birds could luck out. For late-night owls, Sophia's stays open until 11 p.m. during the week and until midnight on weekends for the restaurant; until 1 a.m. for the bar. $$–$$$.

Sycamore. 800 E. Broadway; (573) 874-8090; www.sycamorerestaurant.com. Focusing on local suppliers and seasonal ingredients, Sycamore is an excellent choice for a lunch with soups and salads or dinner with large plates of steak, duck, and trout. Unexpected offerings like a swordfish club or carrot cashew soup on this ever-changing menu keep local foodies returning regularly. With more than 50 beers and as many wines on the menu, Sycamore has become known as a diverse dining destination. $$.

Uprise Bakery. 10 Hitt St.; (573) 256-2265. Located in the former Coca-Cola distribution center in Columbia, the bakery is a part of the Rag Tag independent film building. Come here for coffee and scones on Sunday morning before first time screenings next door. Everything is made on site, including the alcohol, the corned beef, the bread, and the butter, and most ingredients are supplied locally. The cookies and cupcakes are worth the drive all the way from Kansas City. $.

The Wine Cellar & Bistro. 505 Cherry St.; (573) 442-7281. Connoisseurs of fine wine and good food will enjoy a meal at this quiet, intimate bistro that features an ever-changing menu of eclectic and cross-cultural cuisine. You can choose from an interesting array of appetizers, entrees, and desserts, sample wines by the glass, or select from a number of superior bottled labels from around the world. Depending on the day and the disposition of the chef, dinner can be a gravlax appetizer of cured salmon with pressed crackers, onions soaked in cranberry juice, capers, and a mustard dill sauce. Entrees like roast pork with honey bourbon glaze served with orange mashed potatoes and a corn cobette with sun-dried tomato butter, or bouillabaisse—a fresh seafood stew of shellfish, fish, onions, tomatoes, wine, olive oil, garlic, saffron, and herbs—are not to be missed. Reservations recommended. Closed Sun. $$–$$$.

where to stay

The Gathering Place. 606 S. College Ave.; (573) 443-4301; www.gatheringplacebedand breakfast.com. Operated by Mizzou students pursuing a degree in hotel and restaurant management, this bed and breakfast inn receives an A+ in decor, service, and comfort. With 5 unique guest rooms offering complimentary wireless Internet access, it's a unique option for business and leisure travelers to Columbia. The 3-story Colonial-style home dates to 1906 and includes hardwood floors, stained glass windows, and fresh flower arrangements provided daily from the university garden. $$.

jefferson city, mo

Like two sides of a coin, Columbia and Jefferson City are separated by fewer than 30 miles, yet there's a world of difference between them. Located south of Columbia on US 63, Jefferson City is exactly the opposite of Columbia with regard to atmosphere and ambience. Columbia is a liberal and laid-back college town with a high degree of tolerance for unconventional appearances and beliefs. Jefferson City is an old, conservative city that thrives on influence, politics, and power lunches, most likely taken at acceptable restaurants with acquaintances grouped according to social behavior and dress code. In Jefferson City moderate nonconformists fit in as long as no boats are seriously rocked.

Jefferson City is full of lovely residences and old refurbished homes, and a genteel, rather Southern influence permeates the town, which touts itself as a great place to raise a family. While Columbia places its emphasis on fun, food, and shopping, Jefferson City views history, architecture, and tradition as its most important assets. Travelers on the Lewis and Clark Trail will find several points of interest here.

Jefferson City's unique art and architecture are not to be found elsewhere. As the state capital, it holds the magnificent State Capitol Building, where the Missouri legislature convenes. The Governor's Mansion and Governor's Garden, Jefferson Landing State Historic Site, Cole County Museum, and other historic points of interest are also worth visiting.

Visitors can come to town along the Katy Trail. Binder Park campgrounds are the closest camping spot to the trailhead on US 54 and State Road West. However, it still is a 10-mile ride by bike through traffic to the heart of the city.

If you decide to spend the night, you'll find a number of accommodations that cater to business and leisure travelers alike, as well as a smattering of good restaurants. Leave time for a visit to the Runge Nature Center and Missouri's most delicious secret, the Central Dairy.

getting there

From Columbia you have a couple of ways to reach Jefferson City. Heading back west on I-70 to MO 179, the road takes you through some pretty countryside that passes the Runge Nature Center on the way to Jefferson City. US 63 South is faster and connects with US 54, the mid-Missouri gateway to the Lake of the Ozarks region.

where to go

Jefferson City Convention and Visitors Bureau. 100 E. High St.; (800) 769-4183 or (573) 632-2820; www.visitjeffersoncity.com. Visit this downtown office for answers to lots of questions, but also to pick up your MP3 player for a walking tour of the downtown business district.

Clark's Hill/Norton State Historic Site. Osage Hickory Street, Osage City; (573) 449-7402; www.mostateparks.com. This unit of the Missouri State Park System is near Osage City just east of Jefferson City. This 13-acre property, donated to the state by William and Carol Norton of Jefferson City, is believed to be where William Clark camped on June 1, 1804, at the mouth of the Osage River. The area also includes Native American archaeology that will be preserved in an interpretive center.

Cole County Historical Museum. 109 Madison St.; (573) 635-1850. Located across from the Governor's Mansion, the museum is housed in an 1871 building that features a collection of inaugural ball gowns of the former First Ladies of the state, along with other vintage clothing and Victorian furnishings. One floor of the 4-story building is devoted to the Civil War in Missouri. Open Tues through Sat, or by appointment. Admission fee.

Governor's Mansion. 100 Madison St.; (573) 751-7929. Built in 1871, the official residence of Missouri's First Family has an interior that is authentically restored to the Renaissance Revival period and includes a winding stairway, marble fireplaces, elaborate ceiling stenciling, and period furnishings. Portraits of Missouri's First Ladies are showcased on the walls. Docents in period costumes conduct tours of the first floor Tues through Thurs except during Aug and Dec. The grounds also hold the Carnahan Memorial Garden, dedicated to Governor Carnahan, his son, and an aide who were killed in a plane crash. It is filled with flowers, pools, and walkways and can be reserved for special events. Christmas Candelight Tours are held at the mansion 2 evenings in Dec. Free.

Jefferson Landing State Historic Site (Lohman Building and Union Hotel). Jefferson and Water Streets; (573) 751-2854; www.mostateparks.com/jeffersonland.com. The 3-story Lohman Building, constructed of limestone in 1839, is thought to be the oldest structure in Jefferson City. It served steamboat passengers during the city's heyday as a busy river town. Charles Lohman, a native of Germany, operated an inn here at that time. A small museum on the premises depicts the history of the area. Adjacent to the Lohman Building is the Union Hotel. It was built in the 1850s, when the community was a busy center for rail and river traffic; it operated as a hotel following the Civil War and continued to do business until the decline of steamboating. The Elizabeth Rozier Gallery in the building is open for exhibits featuring Missouri's arts, artists, and cultures. An Amtrak station is located on the first floor of the Union Hotel. Both buildings are open Tues through Sat. Free.

Lincoln University. 820 Chestnut St.; (573) 681-5599; www.lincolnu.edu. Established in 1866, the university is situated on 52 rolling acres and is a source for cultural events, sports activities, and continuing education. The Soldiers Memorial at the center of campus is an impressive bronze sculpture that pays homage to the soldiers of the Civil War who eventually established Lincoln University. Free tours are available.

Missouri State Capitol Building. 201 W. Capitol Ave.; (573) 751-4127; www.visitjefferson city.com. Ranked number 2 among the nation's capitols for its art and architecture, the Missouri State Capitol sits on 3 acres of ground and rises 262 feet to the top of its dome. Completed in 1918, the Renaissance-style building is where Missouri's state senators and representatives meet from Jan through May to enact laws that govern the state. On Tues, Wed, or Thurs morning, you can watch the political process unfold from the visitors' gallery. The Missouri Museum, located on the first floor, features exhibits of outstanding historical significance, including portraits of Meriwether Lewis and William Clark. The large state seal in the center of the first-floor rotunda is wrought in bronze and can be viewed from a higher location during a tour of the building. The guided tours, conducted by docents, take in the legislators' chambers, architecture and design, and the Benton Mural. The Gallery of Famous Missourians is located on the third floor. Tours are given daily, except holidays. A Christmas concert is held annually the second Tues of Dec. Free.

The Benton Mural. House Lounge, on the third floor, west wing of the Missouri State Capitol. One of the most important and best reasons to visit the Missouri State Capitol is for the Thomas Hart Benton Mural, an expansive, stunning masterpiece that reflects the enormous genius behind it. Painted in 1936, the work covers 4 walls with a breadth and scope that reflect the legends, history, landmarks, industry, and people of Missouri. Entitled *A Social History of the State of Missouri*, the mural offended many people because of its "lack of refinement." Refined, Benton was not, since he wanted to portray "activities that did not require being polite." His mural, in addition to its niceties, also depicts racist actions, hangings, and other messy and corrupt things that human beings—even Missourians—did in their zeal to build a state.

So enraged were the legislators by Benton's masterpiece that they deliberately defaced the mural, dashing out lighted cigars on it. They were about to whitewash it altogether when Benton's famous temper erupted. He took his case to the media and to the Missouri people, who backed him. The politicians relented and the painting stayed. There is no charge to see the restored work. Benton would have liked that.

Missouri State Highway Patrol Museum. 1510 E. Elm St.; (573) 526-6149. Part education/safety center and part museum, this museum includes patrol cars, uniforms, weapons, and other equipment dating to the department's inception in 1931. Interactive exhibits test a driver's speed and reflexes as items appear on the screen. There's a train safety quiz for children 3 to 6 years old and an interactive train crossing exhibit in which kids can drive the train. Kids will also love Otto, the talking car. Open Mon through Fri, 8 a.m. to 5 p.m. Free.

Missouri State Penitentiary Tours. Tickets sold at 101 W. High St. (directions will be provided to the appropriate gate at the penitentiary, based on tour times); (866) 998-6998; www.missouripentours.com. This is certainly one of the most memorable tours you'll ever take, and no matter how creepy it sounds at first, you really should tour the old state pen. Built in 1836, the Missouri State Penitentiary operated until 2004—the longest operating penitentiary west of the Mississippi. At one point it held 5,200 inmates, making it the largest prison in the world. It accepted its first prisoner the week the Alamo was under siege. It was open and holding prisoners 100 years before Alcatraz became a prison. In the 1950s and 1960s, it was called the bloodiest 47 acres in America because of the violence inside.

It's one of only three state penitentiaries open for tours in the US: Alacatraz, Eastern Pennsylvania, and now Missouri. Sonny Liston learned to box here and a mural of him painted by another inmate can still be seen on the exercise field wall. James Earl Ray escaped here in November 1967 in a bread box with the intent of assassinating Martin Luther King. Blanche Barrow of the Bonnie and Clyde gang did time here, as did Pretty Boy Floyd and a number of minor gangsters of the period.

The 2-hour tours, often led by former prison guards, begin in dungeons in the oldest parts of the prison and end at the execution chamber. In between, you learn a surprising amount about the evolution of American culture and its philosophy of incarceration and punishment. The buildings have no lighting, no heating or air conditioning, and no working plumbing. If you have mobility issues, this may not be the tour for you because there are many stairs and uneven surfaces, and no place to sit and rest.

Two tips: Bring a flashlight to see better in some buildings. And don't be cute by pulling a cell door closed behind you. There are few remaining keys to most cells. You could stay for a long, long time. Admission fee.

Native Stone Vineyard and Bull Rock Brewery. 4301 Native Stone Rd.; (573) 584-8600; www.nativestonewinery.com. This 300-acre family farm and business on the river bluff northwest of Jefferson City includes a tasting room, microbrewery, gift shop, and antiques. The lovely old farmhouse dates to the 1800s and the owners have added a restaurant and large patio for dining and sipping wine. Take a hike along a wood-chip path to a scenic overlook on the Missouri River to see Bull Rock, noted by Lewis and Clark in their journals as they passed this way in 1804.

Runge Nature Center. MO 179; (573) 526-5544; www.mdc.mo.gov/areas/cnc/runge. This 3,000-square-foot facility west of downtown is the Department of Conservation's showpiece. Missouri's habitats are explored in a variety of exhibits and dioramas that feature the state's wetlands, agricultural lands, rivers and streams, ponds and lakes, prairies, glades, forests, and caves. Hiking trails, outdoor demonstrations, and naturalist-guided programs are offered over 112 acres 7 days a week. Indoors is a lovely bird and wildlife viewing area with lots of seating. Free.

where to eat

Arris Cafe and International Market. 409 W. Miller; (573) 634-8400, www.arriscafe.com. Part cafe, part coffee shop, part international market—the Arris family has brought authentic Mediterranean cuisine to the state capital. Sun-dried tomato mozzarella paninis with fresh ciabatta and an Aegean Sandwich, which is grilled eggplant, pepper, zucchini, and mozzarella cheese, are highlights of the menu. Or shop for Papagalos coffee, souvlaki, lupine beans, hibiscus nectar, or chocolate noisetta, among other goodies. $.

Central Dairy. 610 Madison St.; (573) 635-6148. In Jefferson City the milkman still makes deliveries to your door twice a week, courtesy of Central Dairy, a mid-Missouri operation that sells products made in its plant from locally produced milk. The owner keeps his prices low at the ice-cream store as a goodwill gesture to the community, so everybody can afford to come here. Cones still sell for around a dollar, including sales tax, and prices are minuscule for colossal blockbuster sundaes and splits so top-heavy with triple dips of ice cream, marshmallow, and hot fudge toppings and nuts that you'll need several napkins just to clean up. Hand-packed pints and quarts are so affordable that serious aficionados will want to bring a cooler and plenty of dry ice to take some back home. $ (no cards).

Das Stein Haus Restaurant and Lounge. 1436 Southridge Dr. (off US 54, next to the Ramada Inn); (573) 634-3869; www.dassteinhaus.com. This is an authentic German restaurant operated by Helmut Stein, a native of Berlin. He came to this country in 1968 and first cooked in New Orleans at Brennans. He moved to Jeff City in the 1970s. His chef, Dieter, is also from Berlin. German specialties here include beef rouladen, Wiener schnitzel, smoked pork chops with sauerkraut, sauerbraten, and bratwurst. Dinners also feature chateaubriand for two, veal medallions, frog legs, and Long Island Duckling Flambé, topped with orange sauce and served with spiced rice and red cabbage. The lounge features live music on Sun evening. $$.

Ecco Lounge. 703 Jefferson St.; (573) 636-8751. In 1838 the land on the corner of Jefferson and Dunklin was purchased for $32; in 1840 the back parking lot was bought for $26 more. The building was erected in 1858 and served as a "beer saloon." *Lounge* has replaced the word *saloon,* but beer is beer, and Ecco serves it up along with giant beer-battered onion rings and hefty burgers made from ground chuck and topped with blue cheese. Specialties are hot spiced shrimp, prime rib, and steak. The funky, working-class surroundings are fun. $.

Prison Brews. 305 Ash St.; (573) 635-0678; www.prisonbrews.com. Building on the popularity of the state penitentiary tours just a few blocks away, this dilapidated old building was saved in 2008 to become Jeff City's first microbrew. Actual cell doors from the old penitentiary separate booths and pictures from the prison's notorious past line the walls. The bar area itself is located in a cell and if you're looking for the restrooms, follow the signs to the gas chambers. A bocce ball court is located outside and league play is an exciting event in town. Wood-fired pizza, salads, and Reubens fill the menu, and they are all really good. $–$$.

where to stay

Briar Rose Inn Bed and Breakfast. 306 E. Dunklin St.; (573) 338-0284; www.briarrose innbnb.com. Two separate and complete apartments are great for an overnight or long-term stay. The small kitchen allows you to fix a morning coffee or late-night snack, but a full breakfast is provided in a separate dining area by your hosts Randy and Jeanette Wilkerson. $–$$.

Capitol Plaza Hotel and Convention Center. 415 W. McCarty St.; (800) 338-8088 or (573) 635-1234; www.capitolplazajeffersoncity.com. The 9-story atrium setting and 5-story waterfall set the scene for this pleasant hotel located in the heart of downtown. Nicely appointed rooms and suites open to the atrium. The hotel also offers a fully equipped exercise room, as well as restaurants featuring an array of items for breakfast, lunch, and dinner. $$–$$$.

Hotel DeVille. 319 W. Miller St.; (800) 392-3366 or (573) 636-5231; www.devillehotel.com. This small, moderately priced downtown hotel offers shuttle service to and from the Katy Trail. There are 98 guest rooms equipped with coffeemaker, refrigerator, high-speed wireless Internet, and other amenities. $$.

california, mo

For most people, California is just a zip-through spot on US 50, but if you take time to turn into the little village, you will find the heart of America. California is just one of those places with lots of hard-working middle-class citizens who take pride in maintaining their homes and their communities. And, oh yes, they love their barbecue here.

getting there

From Jefferson City, head west on US 50 about 20 miles to the hamlet of California.

where to go

Burgers' Smokehouse. 32819 MO 87 South; (800) 705-2323 (tours) or (800) 624-5426; www.smokehouse.com. The 18th-century art of meat preservation is still used by this family-owned operation to smoke and cure turkeys, chickens, and meats the old-fashioned way. You can pig out on pork in the form of country-cured bacon and naturally aged smoked ham. The visitor center contains some interesting displays about the history of smoking meat. There is a covered bridge, as well as dioramas with educational themes that point out the importance of the changing seasons as they relate to natural curing, drying, and aging of country-cured ham. Open Mon through Fri and on Sat from mid-Sept through Dec.

sedalia, mo

Sedalia's history dates back to 1857, when General George R. Smith decided to found a new town amid the prairie grasses. He envisioned a prosperous railroad city and named it Sedville, after his daughter's nickname. Friends eventually persuaded him to use the more mellifluous "Sedalia" to commemorate his progeny.

When the Civil War erupted, Sedalia was in the thick of the fighting. Missouri, though a slave state, did not secede from the Union as did other slave states. Sedalia was captured and held by the Confederates, and later was made the seat of Pettis County.

The railroad, as Smith foresaw, did indeed play an important role in the town's growth. Sedalia flourished and drew people with talent, such as Scott Joplin, who became known as the King of Ragtime. His sound spread across the country with compositions like the "Maple Leaf Rag," one of the finest pieces of ragtime music ever written. A historical monument was built at the Maple Leaf Club site in the 100 block of East Main Street, where Joplin lived and worked.

The Scott Joplin Ragtime Festival is held annually the first full weekend in June in Sedalia. The 4-day event is the only classical ragtime festival in the world and commemorates the noted composer's work, bringing musicians and visitors from around the globe to the birthplace of ragtime. Food, crafts, and free performances on the Maple Leaf Club grounds are part of the fun.

Aside from its musical past, beautiful architecture can also be found in Sedalia. The old homes that line Broadway (US 50), the buildings on the State Fairgrounds, and the downtown area are all of interest. A free walking tour brochure that highlights 57 historic buildings in Sedalia is available at the chamber.

getting there

From California head west 35 miles on US 50 to Sedalia.

where to go

Sedalia Chamber of Commerce. 600 E. Third St., Katy Depot Historic Site; (800) 827-5295; www.visitsedaliamo.com. The MKT Depot was built in 1896. In addition to housing the chamber offices, there's a remarkably interesting exhibit about the history of Sedalia and train travel. A children's area allows kids to dress up as an engineer and manually operate a wooden train along its tracks. Katy Trail souvenirs and Missouri gift items are for sale in a well-stocked gift shop. The Katy Trail passes directly in front of the depot. Here you can pick up all sorts of brochures about things to do in the city.

Art Impressions. 412 S. Ohio St.; (660) 826-4343; www.artimpressions.net. More than 30 local and regional artists are represented in the light and airy gallery in the historic district. Glass works, fiber art, and oil and acrylic paintings are for sale along with soaps, jewelry, and decorative note cards. On occasion an artist will demonstrate his or her technique, such as a glass-blowing demonstration on the street in front of the gallery. Matting and framing services are also available. Open Tues through Sat or by appointment.

Bothwell Lodge Historic Site. 19349 Bothwell Park Rd.; (660) 827-0510; www.mostate parks.com. Located 6 miles north of Sedalia on US 65, this 180-acre park offers visitors scenic bluffs and wooded trails, including 3 miles of mountain-biking trails. It features picnic areas and Bothwell Lodge, a century-old lodge built atop 2 caves open for tours year-round. Admission fee to enter the lodge.

Daum Contemporary Art Museum. 3201 W. Sixteenth St.; (660) 530-5888; www.daum museum.org. Located on the campus of State Fair Community College, these 9 galleries exhibit paintings, drawings, prints, photographs, and sculptures by Midwestern artists. A focal point is a chandelier in the atrium created by glass artist Dale Chihuly. The museum rotates exhibits 4 times a year. Guided tours are available. Free. Closed Mon.

Liberty Center Association for the Arts. 111 W. Fifth St.; (660) 827-3228. This renovated 1920s theater in downtown serves as the center for performing and cultural arts in the area. Visual artists display their work at Gallery 111, and the Sedalia Community Theatre's all-volunteer troupe stages 3 productions a year. Stop in for a cup of coffee at the

Bean Coffee Shop, located on the premises. A calendar of performances is listed at www .visitsedalia.com.

Missouri State Fair. State Fairgrounds, 2503 W. Sixteenth St.; (800) 422-FAIR or (660) 530-5600; www.mostatefair.com. The 397-acre showplace for agriculture and industry comes alive with color and excitement in late August for 10 days of shows, exhibits, and competitions, drawing nearly 400,000 people every year. Admission fee.

Nostalgia Vintage Apparel. 219 S. Ohio St.; (660) 829-0564. Carolyn Miller has built a home for her love of vintage fashion in the former C.W. Flower Department Store. Part museum, part lecture hall, and part resale shop, Carolyn provides a fascinating look at how fashion has shaped our culture, and vice versa. For groups of at least 20 or more, Carolyn will provide a lunch, dessert, or treats as the program dictates. By appointment only.

Paint Brush Prairie Conservation Area. Located 9 miles south of Sedalia, off US 65 (watch for signs); (660) 530-5500. This 300-plus-acre natural area captures the historic atmosphere at the time of homesteading. Unique plant species have been restored to the area, encouraging the return of native animals like prairie chickens, upland sandpipers, and Henslows' sparrows. Missouri Audubon has designated it an important bird area. Hiking trails wind throughout the area.

Scott Joplin Store. 103 E. Fourth St. (inside the Hotel Bothwell); (660) 816-2217; www .scottjoplin.org. This is the home of the Scott Joplin Foundation, which coordinates the annual festival each June. You can buy tickets here, but also find out just about anything you want to know about the musician who called Sedalia home. His music is for sale here along with lots of other memorabilia. Open Mon through Fri.

where to eat

Eddie's Drive-In. 115 Broadway; (660) 826-0155. If you own a classic car, on warm summer evenings you'll often find others of your kind gathered in the parking lot of this 1930s-era diner. But even if you drive a 21st-century vehicle, you'll enjoy the classic burgers, fries, and old-fashioned malts. $ (no cards).

Wheel Inn. 2101 S. Limit; (660) 826-5177. If you like peanuts, you'll love the Wheel Inn. In business for more than 50 years, the Wheel Inn touts its claim to fame on its menu as a "Guberburger." This is a hamburger topped with melted peanut butter and garnished with fresh lettuce, tomatoes, and your choice of mayo, ketchup, mustard, and onions. Some sage advice: Don't knock it before you try it. Why not be bold and surprise your taste buds with a Guberburger and a thick, rich peanut butter milk shake? Too much overstimulation? Not to worry: There are other popular items, such as fresh-squeezed limeades and lemonades, homemade chili, and the best foot-long chili dog in town. The Wheel Inn is the last of a dying breed—one of those rare and admirable restaurants that still have carhops, giving patrons the opportunity to dine inside or in the privacy of their cars. $ (no cards).

drive-through déjà vu

*Fans of Winstead's hamburgers in Kansas City may experience déjà vu as they dine at **Eddie's Drive-In** in Sedalia. Built in 1937, three years before Kathryn and Nelle Winstead set up shop at 1200 Main St. in Kansas City, Eddie's was also a Winstead family endeavor.*

Kathryn and Nelle began their restaurant experience with a root-beer stand in Springfield, Illinois. Their youngest sister, Fannie, married a gentleman named A.C. Garst and moved to Sedalia in 1937.

Fannie and her husband opened and operated Garst's Drive-In, the first drive-in restaurant in the state of Missouri. Business records show that monthly rent was paid to Kathryn and Nelle, who had since moved to Kansas City. You'll notice the art deco–style building of Eddie's is identical to Winstead's in Kansas City.

The business operated as Garst's Drive-In until 1970, when Fannie's brother-in-law Eddie purchased the business and changed the name. The current owner, George Geotz, purchased the property in 1983. Many old-timers in Sedalia still call the restaurant Garst's and have encouraged George to change the name back. Others, who knew Eddie, insist that he keep the name the same.

No matter what the name, Eddie's Drive-In serves the same style steakburger, onion rings, and malts that have drawn crowds to Winstead's in Kansas City for generations.

where to stay

Hotel Bothwell. 103 E. Fourth St.; (660) 826-5588; www.hotelbothwell.com. This National Historic Landmark hotel originally opened to the public in June 1927 and over the years hosted such names as Harry S. Truman, Bette Davis, and Clint Eastwood. The Hotel Bothwell preserves much of the original class and charm that drew thousands through its doors for more than 75 years. Original telephone booths in one corner of the lobby and a 6-story mail chute contribute to the feeling of yesteryear, as do original marble floors, walnut woodwork, and a lower-level "speakeasy." The hotel has 48 rooms, each unique in its furnishings and decor. Some of the rooms have been renovated into suites and long-term apartments, and 6 have been remodeled to their exact appearance in 1927. A coffee shop, restaurant, and gift shop add plenty of pizzazz to this familiar face in downtown Sedalia. $.

day trip 03

east

natural beauty:
blue springs, mo

blue springs, mo

This Kansas City suburb offers a high standard of living, good schools, and popular parks and wildlife areas that bring people from around the region to this part of town. It is those parks that make a drive to Blue Springs so enjoyable.

getting there

From downtown, head east on I-70 20 miles to exit 20.

where to go

Blue Springs Chamber of Commerce. 1000 SW Main St.; (816) 229-8558; www.blue springschamber.com. For ideas about festivals and other events taking place, be sure to give the chamber a call before heading east.

Burr Oak Woods Conservation Nature Center. 1401 Park Rd. (MO 7 North and Park Road); (816) 228-3766; www.mdc.mo.gov/areas/cnc/burroak. The center is nestled within 1,100 acres of mixed hardwood forest, prairies, glades, and limestone outcrops. Exhibits include hands-on displays of Missouri's fish, forest, and wildlife resources, including live animals. In addition, there are a 3,000-gallon aquarium stocked with native fish and reptiles, a 155-seat auditorium, and an indoor wildlife viewing area. Four outdoor hiking trails and

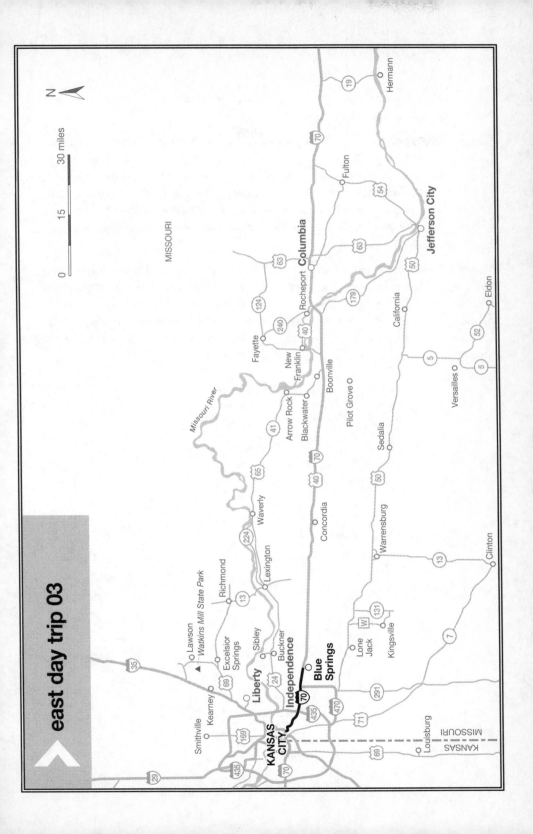

east day trip 03

wildlife food plots afford a glimpse of deer, turkeys, and raccoons. Two trails are wood-chipped, and two are paved. Picnic areas are available. Free.

Burrough's Audubon Center and Library. Fleming Park (off Woods Chapel Road, near Lake Jacomo Marina); (816) 795-8177. You can learn all about nature at the 5-acre center, which contains exhibits of birds' nests, insects, and butterflies and hiking trails through the wildflower gardens. Outdoor feeders bring in a variety of birds to watch. The natural history library on site allows visitors to check books and videos out for 4 weeks. A gift shop on the premises sells birdseed, feeders, bird guides, and related items. Closed Mon, Wed, and Sun. Free.

Missouri Town 1855. Fleming Park; (816) 503-4800. Head east on I-70, then south on MO 291; take a left at the Colbern Road exit to Cyclone School Road, then go left and follow the signs. This reconstructed 1850s farming community comprises more than 30 original structures that make up a charming village. Barnyard animals such as free-ranging chickens, sheep, and horses add an authentic touch. The volunteer staff, dressed in period attire, demonstrates chores done by frontier Americans. Admission fee. Closed Mon.

day trip 04

east

from garden getaway to higher learning:
lone jack, mo; kingsville, mo;
warrensburg, mo

lone jack, mo

A historic Civil War battlefield, one of the largest botanical gardens between Kansas City and Denver, a first-class bed-and-breakfast, and a dog that made national history back in 1870 are part of this unusual day trip that will acquaint you with this fascinating yet relatively undiscovered region.

getting there

From downtown, take US 71 (Bruce Watkins Parkway) south to US 50 East about 35 miles to reach Lone Jack.

where to go

Bynum Winery. 13520 S. Sam Moore Rd. (3 miles east of Lone Jack on US 50); (816) 566-2240. The Bynum family has been making alcoholic beverages in this part of the world for more than 125 years. Sweet and dry varieties of Seyval Blanc, Villard Blanc, and Chancellor Noir are made here, along with apple, cherry, and other fruit wines in season. Fresh fruits and vegetables are also for sale in season. Open daily.

Lone Jack Civil War Museum and Cemetery. 301 S. Bynum Rd. (1 block south of US 50); (816) 697-8833. This is the site of the August 16, 1862, Battle of Lone Jack, where 5

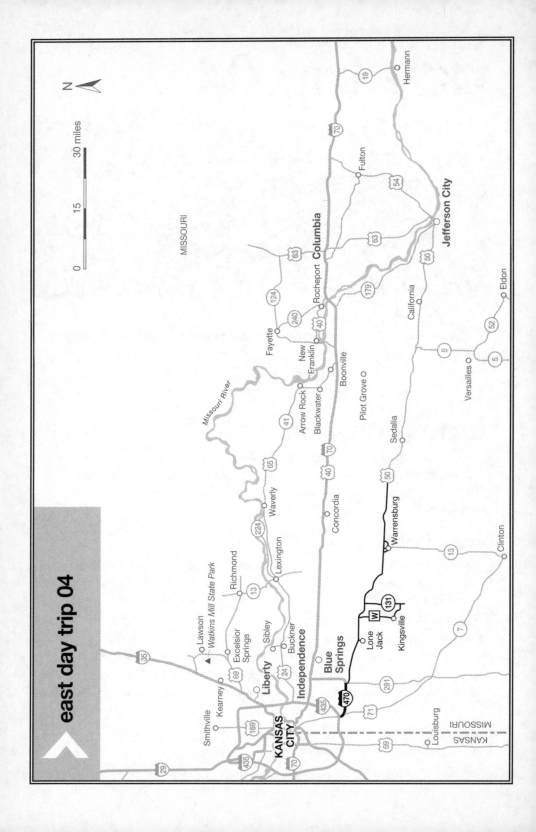

east day trip 04

N

0   15   30 miles

MISSOURI

Hermann
19
70
Fulton
54
Columbia
Rocheport
63
63
Jefferson City
179
50
California
5
5
Eldon
52
Fayette
124
240
New Franklin
40
Boonville
Pilot Grove
Arrow Rock
Blackwater
70
Sedalia
50
41
Versailles
Warrensburg
Missouri River
65
Waverly
40
Concordia
13
Clinton
224
Lexington
131
W
Richmond
Kingsville
13
7
Lawson
Watkins Mill State Park
Excelsior Springs
Sibley
Buckner
Lone Jack
69
Liberty
24
Independence
Blue Springs
291
Kearney
470
Smithville
169
71
Louisburg
KANSAS CITY
435
69
35
29
70
KANSAS
MISSOURI

hours of bloody, hand-to-hand fighting ensued. The event is depicted in dioramas, artifacts, and other displays that showcase what happened on this Civil War battleground. An annual commemoration is held the weekend closest to the original battle date. Open daily Apr through Oct; weekends Nov through Mar (donations suggested).

kingsville, mo

Kingsville is a rather low-key community where most activities center around the high-school sports teams and Little League baseball. Its residents, for the most part, live on a bit of acreage where they enjoy their horses and other outdoor pursuits. The village was put on the map when the state's largest botanical garden opened here in the 1980s.

getting there

Continue east on US 50 another 20 miles to reach Kingsville and Powell Gardens.

where to go

Powell Gardens. 1609 NW US 50; (816) 697-2600; www.powellgardens.org. Powell Gardens is a not-for-profit, 915-acre botanical garden dedicated to beautifying and preserving the natural environment. Established in 1984 through a generous gift from the Powell Family Foundation, Powell Gardens is an outdoor paradise for gardeners and nature lovers, offering a changing palette of colorful flowers and plants throughout the year.

Powell Gardens utilizes horticultural displays, education, and research to serve the Kansas City community and surrounding areas. Gardens of annuals, perennials, native plants, ornamental grasses, and other seasonal plantings make up this spectacular facility.

Visitors may enjoy strolling through the Perennial Garden, Rock and Waterfall Garden, the Island Garden, and the Terrace Gardens at the Visitor Education Center. Other highlights include the magnificent structures designed by architects Fay Jones and Maurice Jennings. These include the Marjorie Powell Allen Chapel, the Visitor Education Center, and the Wildflower Pavilion.

Powell Gardens offers year-round special events, educational classes, and environmental programs for children and adults, a lovely gift shop, and an excellent cafe where you can refresh and relax before or after your visit. Open daily. Admission fee.

warrensburg, mo

Warrensburg has plenty of antiques stores, specialty shops, restaurants, and cafes to visit. The town is the home of the University of Central Missouri, known for its outstanding technology and aviation programs. Amtrak has 2 stops daily from Kansas City in Warrensburg.

Consider taking the train for the day, or carrying on to Sedalia or Jefferson City for this day trip (see East Day Trip 02, p. 35.)

getting there

From Kingsville, continue east along US 50 for 35 miles to Warrensburg.

where to go

Warrensburg Chamber of Commerce. 100 S. Holden St.; (660) 747-3168; www.warrens burg.org. Here you can learn what treasures this community has tucked away from the spotlight's glare on the university. The chamber offices are located in the former Missouri Pacific Railroad Depot, which also serves as an Amtrak station.

Blind Boone Park. 402 W. Pine St.; (660) 747-3268; www.blindboonepark.org. Once representative of segregation in Warrensburg, this long-forgotten park has been restored and is now the pride of the city. The park is named for former Warrensburg resident Willie Boone, the son of an escaped slave, who lost his eyesight at 6 months but grew to be an accomplished concert pianist. Today's park includes a statue of Boone along with other sculptures, a gazebo, and a sensory garden, all designed around the needs of the visually impaired. There's also a shuffleboard court, horseshoe pits, and a great picnic area. The park is the location for a music festival each June.

Old Drum Monument. Market and Holden Streets (on the grounds of the Johnson County Courthouse); (660) 747-3168. In 1870 Senator George Graham Vest won a court battle and the hearts of dog lovers when he paid his famous tribute to the dog during the *Burden v. Hornsby* court case in 1870. That eulogy won the case for Charles Burden, whose favorite hound, Drum, was shot by Leonidas Hornsby, a neighbor. Burden sued for damages, and the trial became the focus of national attention, as each man became determined to win. After several appeals the case reached the Missouri supreme court. Vest's eulogy, which he made in his final appeal to the jury, became a classic speech that reached the hearts of dog lovers around the world. He said, "The one absolutely unselfish friend that a man can have in this selfish world, the one that never deserts him, the one that never proves ungrateful or treacherous, is his dog." Who could resist a speech like that? Burden was subsequently awarded $50 in damages for the loss of this favorite dog. Old Drum remains a prominent figure in many Warrensburg activities.

University of Central Missouri. Office of Admissions, Administration Building 104; (660) 543-4111; www.ucmo.edu. Founded in 1871, UCM, still commonly referred to as Central Missouri State University, despite legislative efforts otherwise, offers a wide range of academic programs in applied sciences and technology, arts and sciences, business and economics, and education and human services. The 1,050-acre campus offers opportunities to attend events and exhibitions of fine and performing arts, including those featuring celebrities in the entertainment

farther east on us 50

Extend your trip a bit farther on US 50 and enjoy the fruit of the vine at these two local vineyards and tasting rooms.

Bristle Ridge Vineyards. *Junction of US 50 and County Road P, Montserrat; (660) 422-5646; www.brvwine.com. Montserrat is just a dot in the road between Warrensburg and Sedalia, but one worth seeking out because of the outstanding sweet red wines produced here for more than 30 years. The tasting room is open every day except Mon, and when the weather turns yucky.*

Montserrat Vineyards. *104 NE 641 Hwy., Knob Noster; (660) 747-9463. Just about 5 miles from Bristle Ridge is the Montserrat Vineyards. The traditional Missouri Norton is one of the bronze medal winners here, but while you're tasting, take a sip of the chocolate wine. Yum.*

and musical fields. The James L. Highlander Theater offers 2 main-stage or dinner-theater productions each semester. The UCM Archives and Museum, located in the James C. Kirkpatrick Library, houses a diverse display of artifacts that changes themes monthly. The Gallery of Art and Design, located in the Art Building at 217 Clark St. (660-543-4498), has exhibits of student work and visiting artists. It's open Mon through Sat free of charge.

where to eat

Heroes Restaurant and Pub. 107 Pine St.; (660) 747-3162. Popular with college students and local businesspeople for lunch, this spacious pub in the downtown district is famous for its huge helpings of onion rings and cheese fries. Other than that, you might catch a Mules or Jennies sporting event on TV while enjoying your choice of salads, burgers, steaks, and pastas. The homemade desserts, such as carrot cake, are the best! $.

where to stay

Cottage on the Knoll at Cedarcroft Farm. 431 SE Y Hwy.; (660) 747-5728; www.cedar croft.com. Located on the 1867 John A. Adams Farmstead, now on the National Register of Historic Places, Cedarcroft has been beautifully renovated with modern comforts. The farm is surrounded by 80 acres of woods, creeks, and meadows. Wildlife—such as deer and wild turkey—abounds. The hosts provide guests with plenty of information about the area, including where to shop and how to find antiques and bargains galore. Guest quarters feature a guest cottage with wood-burning fireplace. There's also a parlor and gathering room. A large evening snack and a full country breakfast are included with your stay. $$$.

southeast

day trip 01

southeast

water, water everywhere:
clinton, mo; the lake of the ozarks, mo

clinton, mo

Located approximately halfway between Kansas City and Springfield at the intersection of MO 13 and US 7, Clinton is popular for boaters and anglers who enjoy the quiet pace of Truman Lake's 55,000 acres. Hunting is popular in the area as well. It is also the westernmost trailheld of the Katy Trail.

Day trippers will appreciate more than 100 shops, restaurants, and businesses thriving in the 4 blocks of Main Street, including 7 antique shops. Look for the unusual murals painted on downtown buildings, including the one with all the baby chicks. Clinton claims to have once been the Baby Chick Capital of the World. If you're looking for unusual collectibles from Missouri communities, a miniature village consisting of the courthouse, the Katy Trail Depot, and the other buildings is for sale at area businesses. The downtown square comes alive for Old Glory Days, a 4-day festival surrounding July 4.

getting there

From downtown Kansas City, Clinton is a straight shot on US 71 (Bruce Watkins Parkway). Rush-hour traffic will slow you considerably, but otherwise, plan on about an hour and 20 minutes to make the 75-mile drive. If you're traveling from Warrensburg, drive 28 miles south out of Warrensburg on MO 13 to the community of Clinton.

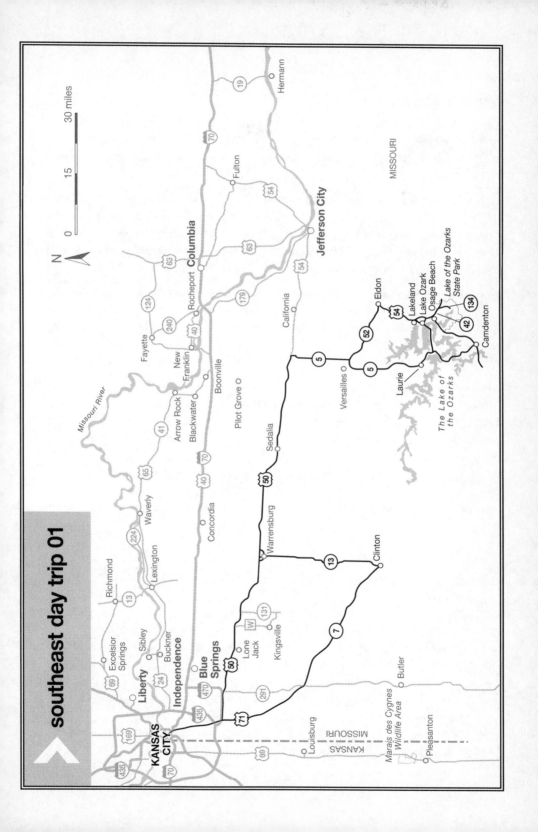

southeast day trip 01

where to go

Clinton Chamber of Commerce. 200 S. Main St.; (660) 885-8166; www.clintonmo.com. Located in a storefront building that dates to the 1880s, like much of downtown Clinton, the Chamber of Commerce will have information for all that there is to do and see in the little community.

Dorman House. 302 W. Franklin St.; (660) 885-2121. When this house was built in the 1850s, it was all the gossip for being the first 2-story brick house in Clinton. Owned by Jerubial Dorman and his wife Udolpha, the home was a hideout and resting place for both Union and Confederate soldiers during the Civil War. Many of the furnishings are original to the family. Tours by appointment.

Henry County Museum and Cultural Arts Center. 203 W. Franklin St.; (660) 885-8414; www.henrycountymomuseum.org.. A fully restored Anheuser-Busch distribution center (built in 1886) serves as the main building of the museum. The annex features building facades that would have been found here in the late 1800s. The museum includes the former Henry County Bank, built in 1887, which now serves as a performing arts center.

Kiddn' Around. 104 S. Main St.; (660) 885-6614. Whether you are into knitting and weaving or not, you should stop in this fun shop for a look at the antique spinning wheels. Owner Lois Schuck has 9 spinning wheels on display (more at her home) that date all the way to the 1600s. One is a rare trolley-wheel spinning wheel that dates to 1811. Also ask to see her antique hand spindles from around the world.

The building in which Lois sells yarn and weaving supplies dates to 1848 and was Simes Shoe store in Clinton for more than 100 years. Lois carries supplies for bobbin lace, teaches quilting classes, and takes custom orders for woven rugs. Some of the yarns she

clinton's checkered past

In 1923 Lawrence Brown opened a manufacturing company in Clinton that many credit with inventing the game of Chinese checkers. In reality, the game was invented in Germany in the 1830s, but Brown was the first to create the colored, star-patterned board that we associate with Chinese checkers. The boards were hand-made and painted by the thousands from the 1920s to the 1950s in Clinton. Today they are highly collectible and sell on eBay for up to $50 a board, living up to Lawrence Brown's trademark that it is "a game for all ages."

A collection of these boards and other inventions by Lawrence Brown are on display at the Henry County Museum.

sells are made from fibers from corn, soybeans, and bamboo, but most of her yarn comes from the 100 goats she raises on a farm outside of town (thus the name of her shop, Kiddn' Around). Open Tues through Sat, 10 a.m. to 5 p.m.

Wagoner Park. Sedalia Avenue and 52 Highway. Depending on how you look at it, Missouri's magnificent Katy Trail begins or ends in Clinton at this 19-acre park. There's plenty of parking if you want to hike or bike a few miles of the trail from here. Or stop by the baseball complex and check out some of the fine Little League action in town.

where to eat

Ben Franklin Coffee House. 106 Main St.; (660) 890-2021. Once a Ben Franklin Dime Store, this coffee shop rivals anything that Starbucks can brew up. In addition to whole bean or ground coffee that you can take home with you, and any whipped-up latte or mocha combination you could ask for, the fruit smoothies are wonderful on a hot summer day. Come in early for Belgian waffles with nuts and whipped cream ($3) or lunch sandwiches (starting at $4) named after Ben Franklin and his contemporaries. Enjoy your treats and free wireless Internet access at one of the many antique tables, which are for sale along with other primitive antiques. Closed Sun. $.

where to stay

Bucksaw Resort and Marina. 670 SE 803 Rd.; (660) 477-3900; www.bucksaw.com. This casual, family-friendly resort has a bit of everything to satisfy your weekend getaway needs. Guest rooms, although sparsely furnished, are clean and comfortable. The outdoor pool and deck are as inviting as a day on a pontoon boat, available for rent at the marina. Fishing boats are also available, along with all the trappings for a day on the lake. For campers and RVers, the campground is equally clean and comprehensive. $.

the lake of the ozarks, mo

Located 165 miles from Kansas City, the Lake of the Ozarks is one of the Midwest's premier playgrounds. The largest lake in Missouri, it offers 1,150 miles of shoreline (more than the Pacific Coast of California).

The lake covers 59,600 acres, surrounded by 100 marinas, dozens of waterfront restaurants and watering holes, and hundreds of shops, services, and businesses. Water activities abound from Apr through Oct. Off-season is a good time to go to the lake because it's less crowded. Even winter provides things to do, from holiday festivities to romantic cold-weather getaways at large resorts that stay open at this time of year.

There are plenty of places to camp, with more than 1,800 private campground sites, ranging from rugged, wooded locations at the water's edge to paved parks with full hookups.

In addition, the Lake of the Ozarks is a prime fishing and golf destination, hosting prestigious tournaments such as Bass Masters and the PGA Club Pro Championship.

When it was created back in 1931, the Lake of the Ozarks was considered the world's largest man-made body of water. The construction of Bagnell Dam by the Union Electric Company was hailed as the most skillful engineering feat of its day. The 2,543-foot-long dam's reservoir holds 650 billion gallons of water, covering parts of Miller, Camden, Morgan, and Benton Counties.

On the lake's eastern edge above the dam are the tiny towns of Lakeside and Lakeland. Below the dam, on the Osage River, is the village of Bagnell, for which the dam is named. The first mile south of the dam is known to tourists as the Strip, which houses shops, arcades, amusements, and restaurants, along with family resorts, motels, and hotels.

South of the Strip are US 54 and State Road HH. They lead to Horseshoe Bend's lush golf courses, resorts, restaurants, condominiums, and residential subdivisions. South of here is Lake Ozark, followed by Osage Beach, a popular 8-mile-long community of shopping malls, outlet stores, restaurants, country sampler shops, and many other attractions.

Following US 54 south leads you across the Grand Glaize Bridge to State Road KK, the pathway to Turkey Bend. Here you'll find more golf, luxury estates, homes, condominiums, resorts, restaurants, and marinas.

Past State Road KK is Linn Creek, a residential community that is home to the Camden County Museum and Big Surf Water Park. South on US 54 is Camdenton, the dividing point between the west and east sides of the lake. Here are the small towns of Sunrise Beach, Laurie, and Gravois Mills that provide a growing number of resorts, motels, campgrounds, and shopping and dining places.

North from here, at the crossroads of MO 5 and MO 52, is Versailles (pronounced versayles by residents). It holds the Morgan County Historical Museum, retail shops, and the Hilty Inn, a bed-and-breakfast establishment.

Eldon—east of Versailles on MO 52 as you drive southeast toward Osage Beach— boasts shops, antiques stores, and eateries.

Most of the lakeshore is privately owned, and there is little public access to boating, swimming, or fishing. There are 2 public beaches, campgrounds, and boat-rental facilities at Lake of the Ozarks State Park. Both Osage Beach and Lake Ozark provide entrance to the park, the largest in Missouri. Ha Ha Tonka State Park, west of Camdenton off US 54, includes unusual rock formations, castle ruins, and wheelchair-accessible trails.

Renowned as the Cave State, Missouri has more than 5,000 registered and mapped caves, with 300 "wild" caves and 3 show caves in the 3 counties surrounding the Lake of the Ozarks. There are 3 show caves located within 30 miles of one another.

getting there

The drive to the Lake of the Ozarks area from Clinton is going to be about 2 hours on winding, curvy two-lane roads. Choose your medicine: MO 7 or US 54, depending on what area of the lake region you plan to visit first.

where to go

Lake Area Chamber of Commerce/Willmore Lodge. Business US 54, Lake Ozark; (800) 386-5253; www.funlake.com or (573) 964-1008; www.willmorelodge.com. Just northeast of Bagnell Dam, Willmore Lodge was completed in 1930 for Union Electric during the construction of the dam. The Adirondack-style 6,500-square-foot lodge, built of white pine logs from Oregon, has been refurbished as a visitor center and museum operated by the Lake Area Chamber of Commerce. In addition to receiving brochures on lake area attractions, visitors can tour exhibits on the area's pre-lake history. The huge picture window provides a spectacular view of the Gravois Arm of the lake. Open daily; hours vary. Free.

boat rentals, marinas & scenic cruises

One way to enjoy the lake is on a boat. With more than 100 marinas, it's impossible to list all the facilities here.

Celebration. 5076 Davis Dr., Osage Beach, just west of the Grand Glaize Bridge; (573) 480-3212; www.cruiselake.com. If you prefer to have someone else take the stern, you might try a ride aboard the *Celebration*, the most elegant cruise ship on the lake. The 80-foot yacht features open-air decks and climate-controlled interior salons. Dinner excursions are available, as are special private charters for corporate functions, weddings, and groups.

Tropic Island Cruises. The Lodge of Four Seasons, State Road HH, Lake Ozark; (573) 348-0083; www.tropicislandcruises.com. This 75-foot luxury motor yacht offers daily scenic cruises. It can also be rented for special events, such as family reunions, weddings, business meetings, and parties. It holds 150 passengers, and catered food service is available for groups.

caves

Bridal Cave. Thunder Mountain Park, 526 Bridal Cave Rd., Camdenton; (573) 346-2676; www.bridalcave.com. Located north of Camdenton off MO 5 on Lake Road 5-88, this 46-million-year-old cave is the oldest in the area and one of the three most scenic in America. It is the site of a legendary Indian wedding ceremony held in the early 1800s. More than 2,000 couples have been married in the cave's breathtaking Bridal Chapel. The cave is accessible by car or boat. Open daily year-round; hours vary. Admission fee.

steering the titanic

I felt like the captain of the Titanic trying to avoid an iceberg, except that it was 85 degrees, under a perfect blue sky, and I was in the middle of the Lake of the Ozarks.

My friends and I had the pleasure of spending a few summer days on a houseboat at the lake. And not just any houseboat, mind you, but a 65-foot-long, 14-foot-wide VIP boat from Forever Resorts, one of the largest vessels to ply the waters of central Missouri. We had grown up on the waterways of the Midwest, my friends and I, and were comfortable with ski boats, Jet Skis, and watercraft that could turn on a dime—but we were perhaps not as adept as we thought with a larger vessel.

We had just gotten under way from the Lake of the Ozarks Marina when we had our first Titanic experience. The massive pillars of the Niangua Bridge loomed ahead like an iceberg, and no matter how hard I turned the wheel, nothing seemed to happen. Then ever so slowly, the nose of our freighter began to swing starboard, until we were safely away from danger. With my stomach clenched, I realized immediately that this would be no powerboat race. Instead, we were in for a slow-paced, 5-mile-an-hour tour of the shoreline.

The point of my story is two-fold: First, no matter how many times you visit the Lake of the Ozarks, there's always a new way to enjoy the beauty of the region.

Our lazy tour turned out to be refreshing and relaxing, allowing us to appreciate scenery that we had only zipped past before. Later, snuggled in a cove at Lake of the Ozarks State Park, we screamed down the boat's 2-story slide into the cool lake waters. And that night, we sipped wine under a starlit sky while enjoying the pleasures of our top-deck hot tub.

Second lesson: Look out for other boats and don't assume they are going to move out of your way. Whether you are the boat or the iceberg, the consequences of a crash are not much fun.

Jacob's Cave. 23114 Hwy. TT, Versailles; (573) 378-4374; www.jacobscave.com. This is the largest cave in the area and the only walk-through cave in Missouri that is wheelchair-accessible. The cave, known for its depth illusion, features the world's largest geode, reflective pools, musical stalactites, prehistoric mastodon bones, and unusual strawlike formations. The rock shop on the premises features a black-light rock display, along with native minerals, crystals, and geodes for sale. Open daily year-round. Admission fee.

Ozark Caverns. Lake of the Ozarks State Park, 823 Ozark Caverns Rd., Linn Creek; (573) 346-2500; www.mostateparks.com/lakeozark/cave.htm. This state-owned cave is located inside the park, off US 54 on Route A. Visitors receive handheld lanterns as guides take groups through the spectacular highlighted sights, which include Angel's Shower, a continual flow of water that falls from the rock ceiling into 2 massive stone basins below. Closed in winter. Hours vary. Admission fee.

music shows

Main Street Music Hall. 1048 Main St. (the Landing on Main Street); (573) 348-9500; www.lakemusichall.com. Toe-tapping country music and sentimental favorites from the 1950s and 1960s are performed here. Open May through Oct; hours vary. Also open in late Nov to the Sat before Christmas with a special Christmas show; hours vary. Reservations required.

golf courses

The Lake of the Ozarks offers excellent and affordable places to hit the links. In excess of 260 holes and 16 courses varying in length, degree of difficulty, elevation changes, water hazards, and strategic layouts make the courses appealing for all levels.

Major players, including Arnold Palmer, Lee Trevino, and Tom Watson, have lent their skills to numerous tournaments.

Most of the lake's courses are open daily year-round, weather permitting. Even if you don't golf, these courses include some of the best dining options at the lake. For a complete list and golf package information, contact the Lake of the Ozarks Golf Council at (800) 490-8474; www.golfingmissouri.com.

The Lodge of Four Seasons Championship Golf Resort & Spa. Lake Ozark; (800) THE-LAKE or (573) 365-3000; www.4seasonsresort.com. The Lodge's Witch's Cove Course is a classic Robert Trent Jones Sr. design that features rolling fairways, large greens, and spectacular par 3s. The design of this 18-hole, 6,567-yard, par-71 course utilizes land that juts out into the lake, creating challenging golf and some of the most beautiful scenery in the Midwest. Seasons Ridge Course is one of the top public courses in the state.

Old Kinderhook Golf and Marina Community. Lake Road 54–80, Camdenton; (573) 346-4444; www.oldkinderhook.com. This 638-acre recreational community includes a Tom Weiskopf championship golf course complete with undulating zoysia fairways, large bent-grass greens, 4 elevated tee boxes on each hole, and natural rock waterfalls. The 6,855-yard, 18-hole, par-71 design makes this one of the best crafted and most uniquely playable courses in the Midwest.

Osage National Golf Resort. Lake Ozark; (573) 365-1950; www.osagenational.com. Nestled between the lake and the lush Osage River Valley, the first Arnold Palmer–designed course in Missouri boasts a lovely course that incorporates wandering creeks, several lakes, and greens ranging from 29 to 47 yards in depth. The par-72, 27-hole, 7,150-yard layout is challenging for all skill levels and offers 3 possible 18-hole combinations.

Sycamore Creek Golf Club. Lake Road 54–56, 1270 Nichols Rd., Osage Beach; (573) 348-9593; www.sycamorecreekgolfclub.com. Fish-filled ponds serve as combination golf course water hazards and spawning pools for catfish! The 18-hole golf course and fishery are located on a wooded, 300-acre valley surrounded by gorgeous upscale homes. Amenities include a snack bar, a lounge, and rental clubs. There are zoysia tees, midiron Bermuda fairways, Crenshaw bent-grass greens, and, of course, catfish.

Tan-Tar-A Resort, Golf Club, Marina, and Indoor Waterpark. State Road KK, Osage Beach; (800) 826-8272 or (573) 348-3131; www.tan-tar-a.com. The Oaks Course, designed by Bruce Devlin and Robert Von Hagge, is a masterful 18-hole, par-71 layout, with 6,432 yards of demanding approaches, 9 water hazards, and breathtaking elevation changes along a tight terrain. In 1994 this was the host headquarters course for the PGA Club Pro Championship. Another course, Hidden Lakes, offers 9 holes, par 35, and fairways set amid stunning lake views and difficult sand traps.

museums

Morgan County Historical Museum. Old Martin Hotel, Versailles; (573) 378-5530 or (573) 378-5889. As the seat of Morgan County, Versailles has a history that dates to 1833. Much of the town's memorabilia has been preserved by members of the Morgan County Historical Society, who staff the museum inside the old Martin Hotel. Historical treasures found here include a library with bound volumes of Morgan County newspapers from 1877, a century-old square grand piano, and an old beauty shop with artifacts from yesteryear, plus a barbershop, a weaving room, a war relics room, and more. Closed Sun and Mon, and from Oct to May. Admission fee.

shrines

National Shrine of Mary, Mother of the Church. MO 5 between Versailles and Camdenton, on the grounds of St. Patrick's Church, Laurie; (573) 374-6279; www.mothersshrine .org. Dedicated to Mary, Mother of the Church, this remarkable shrine is housed in a natural grotto on the premises of St. Patrick's Church. The shrine is surrounded by a terraced amphitheater that seats several thousand worshippers and features the Mother's Wall of Life of polished black granite. The project was designed by Frank Grimaldi of Kansas City, and the epic statue that personifies Mary is by sculptor Don Wiegand. Available for viewing daily year-round. Free.

state parks

Ha Ha Tonka State Park. Camdenton; (573) 346-2986; www.mostateparks.com/haha tonka.htm. Accessible by water or land; located between mile markers 14 and 15 in the Big Niangua Arm. By car it's just west of Camdenton off US 54 on State Road D. By boat, be aware that the park's famous ruins are up a 300-step staircase from the docks below. The ruins are of an early 1900s castle and estate, conceived and developed by Robert McClure Snyder, a Kansas City businessman who acquired 2,500 acres of land and built his private retreat, importing Scottish stonemasons to ensure authentic construction techniques. In 1942 Ha Ha Tonka burned, the fire caused by a spark from one of its many fireplaces. The castle was gutted, and what remains today are the outside walls. The state of Missouri purchased the estate in 1978 and opened it to the public as a state park. The 3,527-acre grounds feature scenic trails, and there are natural bridges, caves, and other geologic wonders to be found here. Open for day use only, year-round, dawn to dusk.

Lake of the Ozarks State Park. US 54 to MO 42, east to MO 134, Kaiser; (573) 348-2694; www.mostateparks.com. Missouri's largest state park offers 17,000 acres and 85 miles of shoreline. The park provides rare public access to 2 beaches, plus boat-launching areas. There's even an on-site airport, with a 6,500-by-100-foot runway, plus terminal building, parallel taxiway, and fuel and tie-down service. Hiking trails, horseback riding, and 4 organized youth camps are offered. The free sand beaches provide swimming opportunities, and nearby picnicking and hiking areas are available. You can also reserve a picnic shelter here for large groups. Open daily, dawn to dusk, year-round.

Along the park's lakeshore is the Ozarks Aquatic Trail, designed for boaters, with stops marked by buoys. A free booklet keyed to the buoys is available at the park office. Naturalists present programs in an open-air amphitheater during the summer; the park also provides guided hikes and a variety of other programs.

where to shop

The Lake of the Ozarks has hundreds of shops, ranging from a factory outlet mall to strip malls, antiques and craft shops, and specialty stores. The places at which to browse and buy are too numerous to list here, but we've included a few unique shops that are worth a visit.

Casa de Loco Winery. 16952 N. MO 5, Sunrise Beach; (573) 374-8801; www.casa delocowinery.com. The unusual name for this winery comes from its stint in the 1950s and '60s as a home for mentally ill patients. A small museum at the winery—which was originally built as a private vacation getaway, not a mental institution—tells the story of the facility. Owner Larry Owens gets some flak about the political incorrectness of the names of his wine: Straightjacket Syrah, Schizo Bianco, Labottleme Zinfandel, and Group Therapy

Champagne. In reality, he's quite respectful about mental health care and uses these wines as a launching point into discussion of a time when we were ignorant about mental health issues.

The property offers one of the best views of the Ozarks that you'll find. It's a lovely spot to enjoy a glass of wine on the patio or a walk through the trails along the river bluff, and to pick up a few bottles of the more than 50 varieties offered here.

Ozark Bar-B-Que and Boutique. MO 5 to State Road F to State Road TT, Sunrise Beach; (573) 374-7769. Devour plates of excellent ribs, fries, and pies at the adjacent barbecue eatery and then go shopping at this unique store that sells a variety of clothing, sun gear, and souvenirs. There's everything from glitzy sequined caps to comical berets such as the "Carmen Miranda," complete with bananas and other assorted fruit. The upstairs and downstairs provide buyers with a wide array of beautiful handmade clothing, soft and gauzy dresses from Indonesia, and swimsuits to fit every figure. Open Apr through Oct.

Seven Springs Winery. 846 Winery Hills Estates, Linn Creek; (573) 317-0100; www.seven springswinery.com. A lovely dining spot and spectacular view of the Ozarks are among the reasons to find your way up the hill from US 54 to this relative newcomer to the Missouri wine scene. Known for their Vignoles, Seven Springs also has a small microbrewery. Open year-round.

Victoria Station. 5465 Osage Beach Pkwy. (1.5 miles west of the Grand Glaize Bridge), Osage Beach; (573) 348-2416. For more than 25 years, this bright shop has been a destination within the lake community. The selection here includes everything for your home and lots of gift items, such as cookbooks, note cards, and candles. If you like the nautical theme, you'll find a huge array of practical and whimsical items that bring the feel of the lake back home. The original flower arrangements are created by Misti Atkisson, the owners' daughter. Open year-round.

where to eat

More than 100 restaurants are located on the lake, and some have access by both water and land. The fare ranges from fast food to gourmet, from Italian and Mexican to French and American, along with Ozark-style delicacies such as catfish, trout, and barbecue. Sunday brunch is served at several restaurants, and many establishments offer hearty breakfasts and refreshing drinks.

Andre's. 1622 Horseshoe Bend Pkwy., Lake Ozark; (573) 365-2800; www.andreslakeoz .com. Upscale dining with a view is the specialty at this cozy restaurant. Andre's is the only restaurant on the lake to specialize in Mediterranean cuisine. Chef/owner Andre Torres and his wife bring expertise acquired in Japan, Kenya, Tunisia, Switzerland, and France. Open daily for dinner year-round. $$$.

Baxter's. 2124 Bagnell Dam Rd., Lake Ozark; (573) 365-2669; www.baxterslakesidegrill .com. For the best sunset at the lake, and a fabulous water view any time of day, this is the place to be. An excellent selection of salads and a swordfish caprese sandwich are memorable items on the menu. But who can remember anything after enjoying their signature drink, Baxter's Sunset, which is part mango margarita and part raspberry daiquiri? $$.

Larry's on the Lake. Pier 31 Road at mile marker 31, Camdenton; (573) 873-5227; www .larrysonthelake.com. Open for lunch and dinner, this floating restaurant is accessible by boat or car. The lunch and dinner menu features an assortment of nicely prepared sandwiches, salads, steaks, and fish. If you want your hamburger for free, try to finish the 5-pound Big Larry's Challenge in 30 minutes. Days and hours vary seasonally. $–$$.

On the Rise Bakery & Bistro. 5439 Osage Beach Pkwy., Osage Beach; (573) 348-4224; www.ontherisebakery.com. This classy European-style eatery is a momentary step away from the Ozarks. Try the European flatbread sandwiches that come on wood-fired, oven-roasted sourdough in 5 flavors, including Tuscan, Napa, Margherita, vegetable, and, of course, Ozark. For a refreshing treat on a hot afternoon, have a glass of Monkey Juice— bananas, strawberries, and orange juice served frozen with whipped cream. The home-made potato chips, served with Parmesan and peppercorn seasonings, are as memorable as the huge cinnamon rolls and other bakery items for carry-out. Open daily. $.

Traditionally Stewart's Restaurant. 1151 Bagnell Dam Blvd., (US Business 54), Lake Ozark; (573) 365-2400. If you're looking for a place that isn't upscale, trendy, or themed, this is the spot. For breakfast the "biscuits" are mammoth-size, mouthwatering, mini-loaves that weigh about a pound each. Equally monstrous are the cinnamon rolls, which are big enough for three. Return for lunch. Then you can choose from simple, tasty offerings such as salads, sandwiches, and entrees like fried catfish and Ozark sugar-cured ham. Open year-round for breakfast and lunch. $–$$.

Vista Grande. 4579 Osage Beach Pkwy., Osage Beach; (573) 348-1231. The Schell family has owned this California-style Mexican restaurant at the lake since 1984. For those who like a milder salsa, the original recipe is smooth and gentle on the stomach. Of the many fun items on the menu, which also includes chicken and spinach chimichangas, is an unusual dish called La Mot. One half of this large burrito is smothered in salsa verde, the other half in salsa roja. Although it sounds French, La Mot is simply named for its creator Tom Schell. Mot is Tom spelled backwards. Open year-round. $$.

where to stay

There are numerous places to stay at the Lake of the Ozarks—from no-frills fishing cottages and motel rooms to upscale family resorts, houseboats, and beautiful condominiums with a view. Many places are family owned and offer waterfront housekeeping units and play-grounds for the kids. The east side of the lake is the more frequented, with plenty of places to stay and resorts large enough to hold huge conferences. The west side is less crowded, with fewer places to stay but with more natural beauty to see. Here's a sampling of some accommodations you may find to your liking:

Country Club Hotel and Spa. State Road HH and Carol Road, Lake Ozark; (800) 964-6698 or (573) 964-2200; www.countryclubhotel.com. This world-class resort and racquet club offers luxurious amenities, unique services, and European decor that appeals to upscale tastes. Guests are treated to scenic views from their spacious rooms, suites, or villas. They can take advantage of amenities such as an excellent health club and fitness facility, indoor and outdoor swimming pools, indoor and outdoor tennis courts, racquetball courts, a restaurant and lounge with live New Orleans–style jazz, and more. $$$.

Forever Resorts. Lake of the Ozarks Marina, MO 5 North at the Niangua Bridge (north side of bridge and west side of MO 5), Camdenton; (800) 255-5561; www.foreverresorts.com. These floating homes range from 56 to 65 feet long and are equipped with everything you'll need, including 4 staterooms, a sofa bed, a dining area, a full kitchen with 2 refrigerators, a gas stove, microwave, and television. All houseboats come with full-size sundecks, built-in waterslide, and gas barbecue grill. Your kitchen equipment, towels, and linens are provided. There are 2 bathrooms in case you bring along the whole family. A houseboat costs a bit more than a hotel but can sleep up to 12 people, so you can split the cost. For the most peace and privacy, come during the week or in the off-season. $$$.

Hilty Inn Bed and Breakfast. 206 E. Jasper St., Versailles; (800) 667-8093 or (573) 378-2020; www.bbim.org/hilty. This elegant, historic Victorian home offers a change from resort condominiums and cabins. Accommodations include 4 guest rooms with private baths and a special bridal suite. A full breakfast is served. A tea room offers English high tea and gourmet dinners by reservation Mon through Fri. Open year-round. $$.

The Lodge of Four Seasons. Horseshoe Bend Parkway, Lake Ozark; (800) THE-LAKE or (573) 365-3000; www.4seasonsresort.com. Named one of *Condé Nast Traveler*'s 50 Best Golf Resorts and ranked as a Connoisseur's Choice Resort by *Resort and Great Hotels Magazine*, the lodge is one of only four resorts in the Midwest to be so designated. The lodge's elegant Spa Shiki, which means four seasons in Japanese, has been featured on the *Today* show and is recognized as a "Best Value" spa in the Midwest by *Spa Magazine*. The resort also has a full-service marina, 4 swimming pools, children's programs, and a cinema. There are a variety of shops and beautifully landscaped Japanese gardens to stroll through. Several restaurants on the premises feature wines, fresh specialties, and scenic views. Open year-round. $$$.

Lone Oak Point Resort. 25 Lone Oak Court, Sunrise Beach; (573) 374-7992; www.funlake.com. The nicest resort on the west side of the lake can be reached by taking MO 5 south from Versailles to Route F; then go left on State Road TT and follow the signs. Located on a wooded, 9-acre peninsula with a superb lake view, Lone Oak Point is owned by an environmentally aware couple who have maintained its architectural integrity by pre-serving the land around it and not overbuilding. The resort has an enclosed fitness spa with indoor pool, sauna, and exercise room. Other amenities are an outdoor pool, a wading pool, an enclosed fishing area, and covered boat stalls. Open Mar through Nov. $$–$$$.

Tan-Tar-A Resort, Golf Club, Marina, and Indoor Waterpark. State Road KK, Osage Beach; (800) 826-8272 or (573) 348-3131; www.tan-tar-a.com. Open for nearly 50 years, Tan-Tar-A is a 420-acre resort with more than 950 guest rooms, 185 suites, and meeting space totaling 93,000 square feet. Tan-Tar-A has 2 championship golf courses and a full-service marina that includes parasailing, a fishing guide service, and boat rentals. Relax at the Arrowhead Pool, an outdoor pool complex with a 125-foot waterslide, toddler splash pool, and whirlpool. Other amenities include an indoor pool area with a fitness center and tanning beds, the Windjammer Spa & Salon, Timber Falls indoor waterpark, bowling, horse-back riding, miniature golf, and tennis. The Black Bear Lodge offers a hunting lodge setting with hearty Ozark favorites. Enjoy fine dining and a beautiful sunset at the Windrose. Ameni-ties for children include in-room babysitting and a kid's camp. Open year-round. $$–$$$.

south

day trip 01

south

precious moments:
butler, mo; carthage, mo

butler, mo

Fans of nice courthouse squares will enjoy a walk around downtown Butler and the court-house. The streets still boast their original brick pavement, and the courthouse lawn, complete with gazebo, is a pleasant place to sit on a park bench and take it all in. Butler is quite proud of its history as the first community west of the Mississippi to have electricity—several months before lightbulbs burned in St. Louis or Kansas City.

getting there

Take US 71 south out of Kansas City 65 miles into Butler.

where to go

Bates County Museum. 802 Elks Dr.; (660) 679-0134. Once the county poor farm, today this historic building contains the riches of Bates County's past. The Bates County Historical Society has its offices and research materials here. The second floor of the museum is devoted to 8 theme rooms, including opportunities to learn more about the talents of former Butler residents Robert Heinlein, a renowned science fiction writer, and Charles Fisk, a big band leader. The former dormitory wing is a "time line" room that begins with the history of the Osage Indians and the Harmony Indian Mission, which opened in 1821. Two former

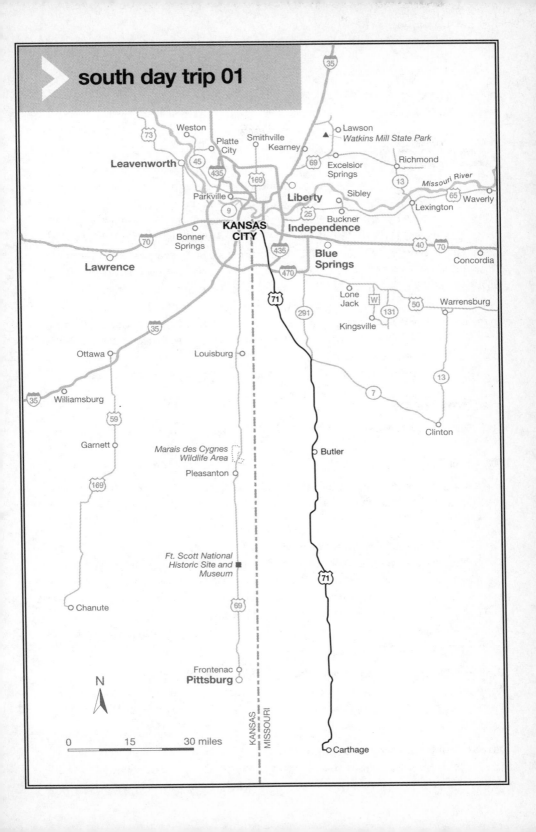

Weston

73

Platte
City

Smithville

Lawson
Watkins Mill State Park

Leavenworth

45

435

169

Kearney

69

Excelsior
Springs

Richmond

13

Missouri River

Parkville

9

Liberty

Sibley

65

Waverly

Lexington

KANSAS
CITY

25

Buckner

Independence

70

Bonner
Springs

435

40

70

Concordia

Lawrence

470

Blue
Springs

71

Lone
Jack

W

50

Warrensburg

35

291

131

Kingsville

Ottawa

Louisburg

7

13

35

Williamsburg

59

Garnett

Marais des Cygnes
Wildlife Area

Pleasanton

169

Butler

Clinton

71

Ft. Scott National
Historic Site and
Museum

Chanute

69

Frontenac
Pittsburg

N

KANSAS
MISSOURI

0   15   30 miles

Carthage

one-room schoolhouses from Bates County have also been moved to the site. Open Apr through Oct, Tues through Sat. Admission fee.

carthage, mo

Founded in 1842, Carthage was the site of the first major land battle of the Civil War after the US Congress formally declared war against the South on July 5, 1861. Events of the battle are highlighted at the Battle of Carthage State Historic Site. The town was destroyed by guerrilla warfare in 1864. After the Civil War, Carthage drew investors and entrepreneurs, and by the end of the 19th century, it is reported to have had more millionaires per capita than any other US city. Much of the wealth came from mining the region's rich deposits of lead, zinc, and a gray marble. Elaborate Victorian architecture still stands to mark the heyday when the town had unlimited prosperity. A driving tour of several of the Victorian homes in the area or a walking tour of the Courthouse Square Historic District is a lovely afternoon in this community. The streets are lined with hundreds of mature maple trees that make the autumn months here spectacular.

Today the Precious Moments Chapel brings thousands of visitors here annually.

getting there

From Butler, continue down US 71 for 70 miles straight into Carthage.

where to go

Carthage Convention and Visitors Bureau. 402 S. Garrison St.; (417) 359-8181; www.visit-carthage.com. Pick up brochures of area attractions and walking tours here, and find answers to many of your questions.

"Battle of Carthage" Civil War Museum. 205 N. Grant St.; (417) 237-7060 or (417) 682-2279; www.mostateparks.com/carthage.htm. The museum features authentic artifacts and information about the battle at Carthage, as well as other skirmishes around southwest Missouri. An elaborate, detailed mural of the event, painted by local artist Andy Thomas, and a diorama depicting the battle are showcased here. There's also an entertaining exhibit on Carthage native Belle Star, the notorious female outlaw who rode with the Jesse James gang. Open daily. Free.

Battle of Carthage State Historic Site. Near East Chestnut and River Streets, east of downtown Carthage. This small park, less than 8 acres, remains relatively untouched since the battle here in 1861. A simple walking tour takes you over the grounds where both Union and Confederate troops camped, fought, and died. Open daily. Free.

Jasper County Courthouse. Between Third and Fourth Streets, 2 blocks east of Garrison Street; (417) 358-0421 or (800) 404-0421; www.visit-carthage.com. Designed in 1894 by

Maximilian Orlopp of New Orleans, the Romanesque Revival structure was constructed of native stone quarried by the Carthage Stone Company. It was completed in 1895 at a cost of $100,000 and is on the National Register of Historic Places. Inside, visitors can see several displays of Civil War artifacts and a mural by local artist Lowell Davis entitled "Forged by Fire."

The Emporium. 311 S. Main St.; (417) 358-5620. Fans of bluegrass music should plan a trip here the first and third Friday nights each month for a live bluegrass concert. Inside the Emporium, you'll also find Helen Ryan's pottery studio, a jeweler, and some great antiques. Closed Sun.

Powers Museum. 1617 W. Oak; (417) 358-2667. Made possible through a gift from one of Carthage's most prominent citizens, this museum explores the history of southwest Missouri and hosts numerous touring exhibits. An adjacent library houses genealogical records and archives, and a gift shop offers a great selection of regional books and gift items. Maps for Route 66 and other tourism brochures are available. Open mid-Mar through Dec. Closed Mon. Free.

Precious Moments Chapel. 480 Chapel Rd.; (800) 543-7975; www.preciousmoments .com. This is Samuel J. Butcher's "gift of thanksgiving to the Lord." Murals covering 5,000 square feet depict scenes from the Old and New Testaments. The Precious Moments Art Gallery showcases the history behind Precious Moments, original pieces of art by local artists, and personal family memorabilia. The visitor center is patterned after a European village. Cottage- and castle-like structures within the village house several shops. Gospel and bluegrass music shows are presented several times daily. The Fountain of Angels show is a water display choreographed to music and light. The Precious Moments Collectors Christmas Weekend, held the first weekend in December, features a candlelight service, dinner, classes, and tours of the Butcher home. Open daily. Free to tour chapel.

where to stay

Grand Avenue Bed and Breakfast. 1615 Grand Ave.; (888) 380-6786 or (417) 358-7265; www.grand-avenue.com. This Queen Anne Victorian home features spacious and elegant rooms with amenities that range from rooms with queen-size beds and private baths to a room with king-size bed and large private bath with Jacuzzi. A full breakfast is served in the formal dining room. There's also a pool available for guests. Group discounts are available with the rental of 4 or more rooms. Special packages and murder mystery weekends are also offered. $$.

The Leggett House. 1106 Grand Ave.; (417) 358-0683; www.leggetthousebb.com. Completed in 1901, this Victorian Carthage stone house offers 5 large rooms, an elevator, private or shared bath, and full breakfast in the formal dining room. The decor features beveled and leaded curved windows, an open staircase, paneled entry hall, and mosaic-tiled solarium with marble fountain. $$.

The White Rose Bed & Breakfast. 13001 Journey Rd.; (417) 359-9253; www.white rosebed-breakfast.com. For those who love all things Irish or are looking for a special place to celebrate St. Patrick's Day, come visit Jim and Jan O'Hara, whose families comes from County Claire and County Sligo, respectively. Much of the decor of their 5,000-square-foot inn includes family heirlooms and Irish lace and linens. Breakfast is also very Irish, including soda bread and scones with sweet orange marmalade, fruit soup, potatoes O'Hara, bangers, bacon, and tomatoes. The inn is open for lunch as well. $$.

southwest

day trip 01

southwest

apple cider, wildlife & history:
louisburg, ks; pleasanton, ks;
fort scott, ks; pittsburg, ks

When sojourning in southeast Kansas, remember that people here like things simple, especially food. Fried chicken or chicken-fried is the featured cuisine in many places. If you simply surrender yourself to iceberg lettuce rather than radicchio and don't expect Chez Panisse cuisine, you'll be quite happy here.

Southeast Kansas is filled with stores that tout themselves as antiques shops but in actuality are crammed wall to wall with flea-market "junque." Just as long as you know what to expect, it's fun to browse and you might discover an occasional treasure, but don't expect a Sotheby-style find.

Southeast Kansas does have unexpected charm. In small towns, such as Chanute, tree-lined cobblestone streets, gorgeous old homes, and whole city blocks have been preserved. Southeast Kansans take pride in their historic heritage, and the area holds many architecturally significant structures—including one of singularly weighty importance called Big Brutus.

louisburg, ks

If you ask most Kansas Citians about Louisburg, there's a good chance they'll think of apples. That's because of the Louisburg Cider Mill, which is a huge reason many people journey to the little community. Many of the residents here are active in the equine business. A drive along the back roads reveals spacious homes and barns, with show horses of

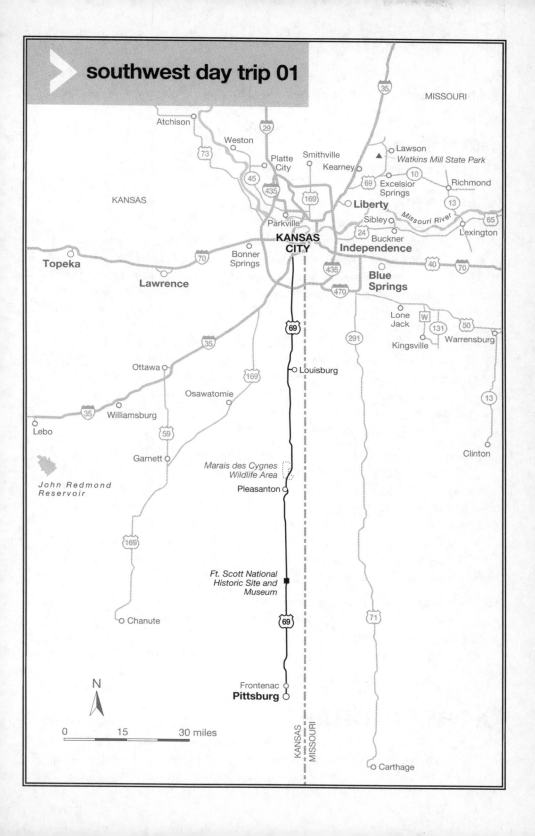

several breeds grazing in pastures outlined by white fences. If you ever want to take riding lessons, you'll find several farms in this area where they are offered.

getting there

Follow US 69 south out of downtown about 40 miles to the Louisburg exit.

where to go

Louisburg Cider Mill. 14730 KS 68; (800) 748-7765 or (913) 837-5202; www.louisburg cidermill.com. If the idea of cold apple cider, fresh-baked bread, and homemade cider doughnuts intrigues you, this is the place to go for a quick getaway. The store displays cider products and natural foods in old-time barrels and cases to give the feeling of a country emporium. While you're there, don't forget to sample the doughnuts. These cakelike goodies, made with cider, have a marvelous texture. You can watch the doughnuts being made and then take home the results.

The cider mill is also the home of the **Lost Trail Root Beer Company.** This special root-beer brew is refined in eastern Kansas from a family recipe passed down through generations to the present owners. Also try the Lost Trail Sarsaparilla, introduced for the bicentennial of the Lewis and Clark Expedition, which passed about 50 miles north of Louisburg.

Apples are pressed every day except Fri and Sun from Sept through Nov. The store is open 7 days a week except Thanksgiving and Christmas.

Powell Observatory. Just off 263rd Street and US 69 (3 miles northwest of Louisburg); (913) 438-3825; www.askconline.org. Run by the Astronomical Society of Kansas City, Powell Observatory houses a 30-inch computer-controlled telescope for public viewing of the night skies from May to Oct. Located in Lewis-Young Park, the facility has a heated classroom (with restrooms) attached to the 20-foot domed observatory, where star-observing parties are held twice a month. There is also a Junior Astronomers Group for kids 10 to 17. Children should be at least 36 inches tall to use the big scope and old enough to understand what they're seeing. Free.

Somerset Ridge Vineyard. 29725 Somerset Rd.; (913) 491-0038; www.somersetridge .com. Located 6 miles west of Louisburg, this boutique winery has about 10 labels produced from the 5,000 vines that the Reynolds family planted in 1998. They invite guests to their tasting room Wed through Sun all year round, but especially during Oktoberfest weekends.

pleasanton, ks

Despite its pleasant name, the entire region around Pleasanton experienced a great deal of bloodshed in Kansas's fight for statehood prior to the Civil War and is a part of the

Freedom's Frontier National Heritage Area. But today, it is a very pleasant place indeed, surrounded by protected areas for wildlife and migrating birds.

getting there

Continue south out of Louisburg on US 69 another 30 miles to reach Pleasanton.

where to go

Marais des Cygnes Wildlife Area. Managed by the Kansas Department of Wildlife and Parks, 16382 US 69, Pleasanton; (913) 352-8941. Those who have an eye for the unexpected can find wonder in the beauty of the Marais des Cygnes Wildlife Area. Located outside La Cygne in the picturesque floodplain of eastern Kansas, the refuge occupies more than 7,000 acres of man-made marshes rippling with natural lakes and laced with miles of rivers and creeks.

The area is a resting place for migratory waterfowl and other birds. Primitive camping is available, as well as hunting and fishing with the proper license.

The refuge takes its name from the Marais des Cygnes River, meaning "marsh of the swans," a title bestowed by the early French trappers who discovered it. Ironically, there is a good chance that what the trappers saw were not swans, but white pelicans that migrate through the area each spring. Flocks of these graceful, long-billed creatures can be seen floating in the water in early May, and their presence in the marsh pool, tinted a rosy amber by the setting sun, creates a surrealistic splendor.

Ducks, geese, herons, egrets, and birds of prey can also be spotted in the marshy
...nporary population of migrating ducks may
...ve been sighted at Marais des Cygnes, and
...nd green-winged teal, and Canada geese,

...rappies and catfish abound.
... the marsh banks for much of the day, hop-
...campers park alongside the water and sit in

...ge. (913) 352-8956; www.fws.gov/marais-
...llife Service, it's unique for its abundance of
...mmon species are pin and burr oak, pecan,
...warblers have been documented during the
... May in forested areas.

...13) 352-6441. This tiny spot played an impor-
...g in the 1850s. Here the pro- and antislavery
forces fought over whether the territory should enter the Union as a free or slave state. In 1858

a gang of pro-slavers massacred 11 free-state men near Trading Post. The men became martyrs to the abolitionist cause, and the site of their deaths is a registered National Historic Landmark called the Marais des Cygnes Massacre Memorial Park. Open Apr through Nov.

where to stay

Cedar Crest Lodge. 25939 E. 1000 Rd.; (913) 352-6533; www.cedarcrestlodge.com. If you can't get enough of the natural beauty of the great outdoors of this region, spend the night with Matt and Laura Cunningham at Cedar Crest Lodge. Their 7,000-square-foot home is situated on 113 acres of rolling hills, trees, and ponds. Their 11 guest rooms reflect their love of travel, and Laura is a great cook, preparing a breakfast you will remember for a long time. If you like to paint and decorate, ask them about their painting seminars. Or, if you need a massage or other spa treatment, they can make arrangements for that as well. Matt and Laura have children, and they will welcome your well-behaved children as well. $–$$.

fort scott, ks

All along the Overland Trails, US Cavalry forts, such as Fort Scott, sprang up to defend western settlement. Between 1838 and 1845 a military road was constructed through the Indian Territory to connect Fort Leavenworth in Kansas and Fort Gibson in Oklahoma. Throughout the years the road was traveled by soldiers, immigrants, Native Americans, outlaws, and traders.

Today the old military road no longer exists, but modern US 69 and other connecting pathways located near its original route have been designated the Frontier Military Scenic Byway. Fort Leavenworth and Fort Scott, two of the remaining historic Kansas forts that lie along that route, are open to tour today.

From Apr to Dec the restored military fort hosts a series of special events featuring activities that portray a vivid picture of life on a frontier post during the 19th century.

One of Fort Scott's most famous residents was internationally acclaimed photographer, filmmaker, and poet Gordon Parks, born here in 1912. Not until 2003 did the city of Fort Scott finally pay tribute to this accomplished African American, first with a permanent exhibit in the gallery space of Mercy Health Center and more recently with the Gordon Parks Center for Cultural Diversity at Fort Scott Community College. An annual celebration in October honors his contribution to the city of Fort Scott and the world.

And someday another celebration may take place for comedic genius Jason Sudeikis, a *Saturday Night Live* cast member and star of several movies. Sudeikis attended Fort Scott Community College on a basketball scholarship.

getting there

From Pleasanton, continue south on US 69 another 25 miles to Fort Scott.

where to go

Fort Scott Tourism Information Center. 231 E. Wall St.; (620) 223-3566; www.fortscott .com. Find a complimentary cup of lemonade or coffee waiting for you here, along with information about theme weekends, special living history programs, and seasonal celebrations. This is also where Dolly the Trolley tours start each day at 10 a.m., which take visitors through the historic city, including Fort Scott National Cemetery. The tours are completely narrated and leave hourly from the center.

Fort Scott National Historic Site. Old Fort Boulevard; (620) 223-0310; www.nps.gov/ fosc. The restored 1842 Frontier Military Fort was built to keep peace between the Indians and the settlers. The troops wound up policing the plains, supplying Union armies during the Civil War, and protecting railroad workers in the 1870s. A major tourist attraction that brings visitors from around the world, Fort Scott is the only completely restored frontier fort of the pre–Civil War period in the United States. Now designated a National Historic Site, the fort is located right in the center of the city, within walking distance of many shops and dining establishments.

Fort Scott's 18 structures, including a hospital, a guardhouse, a bakery, and barracks, tell the story of the mounted Dragoons, "bleeding Kansas," and the Civil War. Open for self-guided tours year-round; closed Thanksgiving, Christmas, and New Year's Day. Admission fee.

The Gordon Parks Center for Culture and Diversity. Fort Scott Community College, 2108 S. Horton; (800) 874-3722, ext. 515; www.gordonparkscenter.org. Honoring one of the city's most accomplished residents and one of the world's leading photographers, writers, and filmmakers, this facility on the campus of Fort Scott Community College is a resource for those who wish to explore social issues such as racism and poverty and understand how those issues influence the arts. Programs throughout the year delve into these subjects, and exhibits include the results of an annual photo contest and materials from Parks's private collection. Open Mon through Fri during the academic year. Free.

Gordon Parks Photo Exhibit. Mercy Health Center Foundation, 401 Woodland Hills Blvd.; (620) 223-7026. Famed photographer Gordon Parks donated 27 photographs and 5 poems to the Mercy Health Center Foundation upon the opening of a new wing in 2002. His work has appeared in *Life* and *Vogue* magazines, focusing on social injustice, poverty, and civil rights. A walking tour brochure of the Parks collection is available at the information desk. Free.

National Cemetery. 900 E. National Ave.; (620) 223-2840. The National Cemetery is older than Arlington and just as historically important. Indian scouts buried here include many with memorable names and histories. Soldiers interred on these grounds include black infantrymen from the country's first Colored Volunteer Infantry. Free.

Victorian Downtown. From Old Fort Boulevard to Sixth Street. The 6-block downtown area is on the National Register of Historic Places. Buildings from the period 1860 to 1919 have been restored and are the architectural showpiece of the city. Many homes feature ornate woodwork designs of gingerbread, stained and leaded glass, turrets, hitching posts, and stepping-stones for carriages. Walking-tour information is available from the Fort Scott Tourist Information Center.

where to eat

Sugarfoot and Peaches Barbecue. 1601 E. Wall St.; (620) 224-2888. If you're ready for some good Kansas City barbecue with a touch of Memphis thrown in there, check out John Embry's joint. Most everything is good, and smoked with a dry rub, but he has come up with a Dijon chipotle tenderloin that is worthy of your taste buds. Open Tues through Sat. $.

where to stay

Courtland Hotel and Spa. 121 E. First St.; (620) 223-0098; www.courtlandhotel.com. Originally built in 1906 to accommodate the railroad workers and travelers through Fort Scott, the Courtland and its 15 rooms have been renovated numerous times and continue to serve modern travelers. Frank and Cheryl Adamson are the owners who are on site every day to help your stay be comfortable. The Aveda Spa contributes to the relaxing getaway here. $.

The Lyons' Victorian Mansion and Spa. 742 and 750 S. National Ave.; (620) 223-3644; www.lyonstwinmansions.com. These two identical mansions were built by a wealthy banker for his two daughters in the 1880s. Today the homes become one with the gracious hospitality coordinated by Pat Lyons. Guest suites can accommodate couples, families, business travelers, and anyone looking for a home away from home. Seven guest rooms, some with claw-foot whirlpool tubs, are spacious. A full breakfast is served complete with country-fresh eggs, garden herbs, and produce. Other amenities include an in-room telephone with dataport, dedicated computer lines, a fax, a copier, and an answering service.

Behind the mansions, accessed via a lovely flower garden, is a guest house with 3 additional rooms as well as spa services. A hot tub may be reserved for special occasions.

The Lyons Twin Mansions specialize in event planning for business and social occasions, ranging from birthday parties and teas to sumptuous 9-course Victorian feasts for groups of up to 50. Business retreats, murder mystery weekends, an on-site spa, and educational tours are also offered. Breakfast and lunch are also open to the public here. $$–$$$.

pittsburg, ks

The "Fried Chicken Capital of Southeast Kansas," Pittsburg has several chicken emporiums from which to choose. It is also famous for being the jumping-off point for the attraction known as Big Brutus, a 16-story-high, one-of-a-kind mining shovel located just southwest of Pittsburg near West Mineral, Kansas.

At first glance you might not know that this town has a lot of Old World drama behind it. Pittsburg was actually an early-20th-century settlement of Europeans who came to work in the coal mines. Those who live here today are the descendants of people who traveled to this part of Crawford County from Sicily, Austria, and Bohemia.

Pittsburg, along with the tiny town of Frontenac, which borders it to the north, was a Crawford County mining community that appealed to those who wanted to escape poverty, oppression, and political injustice. Lured by the promise of work, the immigrants who toiled in the mines brought an unusual mix of cultural and ethnic backgrounds to southeast Kansas. Between 1880 and 1940 more than 31,000 people from 52 countries flocked here to begin deep-shaft mining, the most dangerous method of digging coal out of the earth.

Eventually the area became known as the Little Balkans region because of the number of Europeans who settled here.

Crawford County's colorful past is celebrated with a number of festivals. Little Balkans Days, held on Labor Day weekend, features bocce ball, a parade, polka music, arts-and-crafts booths, and ethnic foods. For more information: Crawford County Convention and Visitors Bureau, 117 W. Fourth St.; (620) 231-1212; www.visitcrawfordcounty.com.

getting there

From Fort Scott, continue south on US 69 another 30 miles to reach Pittsburg.

where to go

Crawford State Park. 1 Lake Rd., Farlington; (620) 362-3671. Located about halfway between Fort Scott and Pittsburg, this 500-acre state park is worthy of a bit of exploration. There's plenty of camping, a nice swimming beach, boat ramps, and other amenities, but also something that most other state parks don't have: Crawford Lake and the entire park were built by the Civilian Conservation Corps in the 1930s. They actually dug this lake by hand. An on-site memorial tells the entire history of the CCC, the Great Depression, how the men of the CCC learned to read and write, and how a camp in a community really helped lift that particular community out of the Depression ahead of other regions. On special holidays, the Avenue of Flags, featuring 50 state flags and 50 US flags, crosses the dam in honor of the men who built the lake and others who have donated to its upkeep.

Big Brutus. Located 6 miles west of the junction of KS 7 and KS 102, West Mineral; (620) 827-6177; www.bigbrutus.org. He's formally known as the Bucyrus Erie 1850 B, but his friends just call him Big Brutus. This 11-million-pound mining shovel is 16 stories high—something you see from a distance as you drive across the Kansas prairie. The Pittsburg & Midway Coal Mining Company purchased Big Brutus at a cost of $6.5 million—not to dig coal but to remove the dirt and rocks covering the coal seams. From 1962 to 1974, more than 9 million tons of coal was gouged out of the dirt, laying bare the land and leaving hundreds of "strip pits" behind. In 1974, when it was no longer cost-effective to operate Big Brutus, the steam shovel was shut down.

The legacy of Big Brutus could have been an environmental disaster; instead, it is a rare instance of a mined land reclamation success story. The Pittsburg & Midway Coal Mining Company donated the area surrounding Big Brutus to the Kansas Department of Wildlife and Parks, which, in turn, has reclaimed the 14,250 acres of land as a haven for hunting and fishing.

The Big Brutus Visitors Center tells the colorful history and heritage of the region. You can take a self-guided tour or climb up Big Brutus's boom, but you have to be at least 13 years old. There are primitive camping facilities and RV hookups on site, plus picnic tables and hot showers to meet the needs of campers and visitors. Open daily. Admission fee.

Crawford County Historical Museum. 651 S. US 69; (620) 231-1440. The colorful history of Crawford County is featured in interesting exhibits that include vintage clothing, coal-mining and farming artifacts, photographs, and horse-drawn vehicles. Miss America 1968 was from this area, and her handmade dress with 30 pounds of sequins is also on display. Outdoor displays include a one-room schoolhouse, an authentic neighborhood grocery store, and a coal-mining steam shovel. Open Thurs through Sun afternoons or by appointment. Free.

Hickory Creek Farms. 436 S. Thirtieth St., McCune; (620) 632-4294; www.hickorycreek farms.com. You're going to have to call for directions or make sure your GPS is fully functioning, but it's worth the effort to spend a lovely fall afternoon lost in the hay maze, picking out pumpkins, or taking a hay ride. Each year the Zimmerman family, who has lived here for five generations, adds new and different attractions. Admission fee.

Hotel Stilwell. 707 Broadway; (620) 235-1997. Built in 1880, the historic hotel has hosted guests who have included William Jennings Bryan, Eugene Debs, Susan B. Anthony, and Theodore Roosevelt. The building was restored in 1997 and is on the National Register of Historic Places. The architectural design features a grand stone entry flanked by brick columns on the first floor, wide bay windows, a circular leaded skylight, generous ornate plasterwork, and stained-glass windows. The upper floors have been converted to apartments for senior citizens, while the first-floor historic common areas are open to the public to tour. There are a few businesses operating inside, including Otto's Cafe, so it's certainly appropriate for you to come in and look around. You'll be impressed.

Mined Land Wildlife Area. Between Pittsburg and West Mineral; (620) 231-3173; www .kdwp.state.ks.us. Several hundred water-filled former strip pits dot the Mined Land Wildlife Area, a 14,000-acre region with about 1,500 acres of public waters near the communities of West Mineral and Pittsburg. More than 200 lakes in the area are managed for fishing. Sport fish are abundant here, with largemouth bass, spotted bass, channel catfish, walleye, and a specially stocked lake trout being favorites of anglers.

Native grasses have been reintroduced here, along with a variety of wildlife. Several marshes have been constructed to attract ducks and geese.

With its diversity of terrain and animal life, the Mined Land Wildlife Area is popular with photographers and wildlife observers, as well as hunters. Quail, white-tailed deer, and wild turkey are found in abundance, as are raccoons, muskrats, bobcats, coyotes, and a herd of rather photogenic buffalo. As the wildlife area covers parts of 3 counties, directions and addresses are impossible, but call the wildlife and parks office for input on the aspects in which you are most interested.

Pittsburg State University/Kansas Technology Center. 1701 S. Broadway; (620) 235-4122; www.pittstate.edu. This campus of 6,600 students on the south end of town has extensive landscaping, outdoor sculptures, a hike/bike trail, and other impressive features. The newest attraction on campus is the Veterans Memorial Amphitheatre, which features a number of patriotic bronzes, a half-scale replica of the Vietnam Veterans Memorial in Washington, D.C., and seating for 250. The university sponsors a Visiting Writers Series, a Performing Arts and Lecture Series, and a Solo and Chamber Music Series.

where to shop

Frontenac Bakery. 211 N. Crawford St., Frontenac; (620) 231-7908. Established in 1900, this bakery has had only four owners in more than 100 years. That list now includes Bryan and Jolynne Hite. Jolynne remembers coming here as a child for the Italian breads and bread sticks that are famous in this part of the state. The Hites welcome retail buyers Thurs through Sun mornings.

Pallucca & Son. 207 E. McKay St., Frontenac; (620) 231-7700. This off-the-beaten-path find is a fun place to stop and shop. Opened in 1912, Pallucca's is family-owned and -operated and specializes in imported Italian foods. The meat department carries everything you need for making a great Italian sandwich, from large imported Italian hams to handmade Italian sausage. Fine pasta, dessert items, candies, and sauces from Italy line the shelves, along with American-made products. Open daily.

where to eat

As the "Fried Chicken Capital of Southeast Kansas," Pittsburg is home to ethnic-influenced restaurants that serve fried chicken with German potato salad, coleslaw with garlic dressing, and peppers, tomatoes, and bread. This custom began in 1934, when Anne Pichler's husband was injured in the mines. Born near Budapest, the woman best known as Chicken Annie had a family to raise; therefore she started selling fried chicken out of her home to make a living. Eventually Chicken Annie opened her restaurant, which became so famous that it began to draw competitors. In 1943 Mary Zerngast opened her fried chicken restaurant across the road from Chicken Annie's. Chicken Mary and Chicken Annie went head to head as the famous southeast Kansas chicken wars heated up. Today, these and other family-owned restaurants still compete for business as the fowl play continues. The chicken places open at 4 p.m. for dinner only on weekdays; those open on Sun offer dinner from 11 a.m. to 8 p.m. They include the following:

Barto's Idle Hour. 201 S. Santa Fe, Frontenac; (620) 232-9834. Closed Sun and Mon. $$.

Chicken Annie's of Girard. KS 5 east of Girard. (620) 724-4090. Closed Mon and Tues. $$.

Chicken Annie's Original. 1143 E. 600th Ave., Pittsburg; (620) 231-9460. Closed Mon. $$.

Chicken Mary's. 1133 E. 600th Ave., Pittsburg; (620) 231-9510. Closed Mon. $$.

Gebhardt Chicken Dinners. 124 N. 260th St., Mulberry; (620) 764-3451. Open Fri through Mon. $$.

Pichler's Chicken Annie's®. 1271 S. 220th St., Pittsburg; (620) 232-9260. Closed Mon. $$.

other restaurants of interest

Jim's Steak House. 1912 N. Broadway; (620) 231-5770. Established in 1938, this third-generation family-owned and -operated restaurant has been in the same location for 70 years. Renowned in the area for its juicy steaks, the restaurant also offers chicken and seafood specialties. Jim's serves dinner only, starting at 4 p.m. Closed Sun. $$–$$$.

Otto's Cafe. 711 N. Broadway; (620) 231-6110. Built in 1945 as an annex to old Hotel Stilwell, this dining establishment is a throwback to the days when coffee shops were plentiful. Simple food, prepared well, is what you'll find here. Breakfast features everything from omelets and waffles to French toast and biscuits and gravy. If you're in the mood for Otto's excellent version of fried chicken, make plans for your lunch here. Leave room for homemade dessert. Open for breakfast and lunch. Closed Sun. $–$$ (no cards).

where to stay

Himmel House. 402 W. Euclid St.; (620) 232-9497; www.himmelhouse.com. Jeff and Sherri Stokes are now the owners of this beautiful home built in 1905. Of the 3 cozy rooms, the DeCuyper Room is perhaps the most romantic with its fireplace and balcony. Everyone enjoys the intimate, flower-lined patio and free wireless Internet access. $$.

day trip 02

southwest

civil war & safaris:
osawatomie, ks; garnett, ks;
chanute, ks

Don't head out on this trip expecting blockbuster attractions, but it's those unexpected little surprises that make this journey worthwhile. The towns listed here all have shady, tree-lined streets and historic old homes and buildings that have been lovingly preserved. It's a part of the world where people take pride in their homes and expect their neighbors to do the same, and where folks will greet you on the street and welcome you wholeheartedly into their communities. But with your first stop in Osawatomie, you'll find that has not always been the case.

osawatomie, ks

This pleasant community of less than 5,000 people is and always will be associated with the cause of freedom in the United States and around the world because of one resident who lived here for just about 9 months in 1855–56. His name was John Brown. He committed murder while living here, yet probably did more than any single individual to assure that Kansas became a free state and that slavery would eventually be abolished in the United States.

getting there

From downtown, head south on I-35 about 20 miles to exit 215, which is to US 169. Follow US 169 another 30 miles straight into Osawatomie.

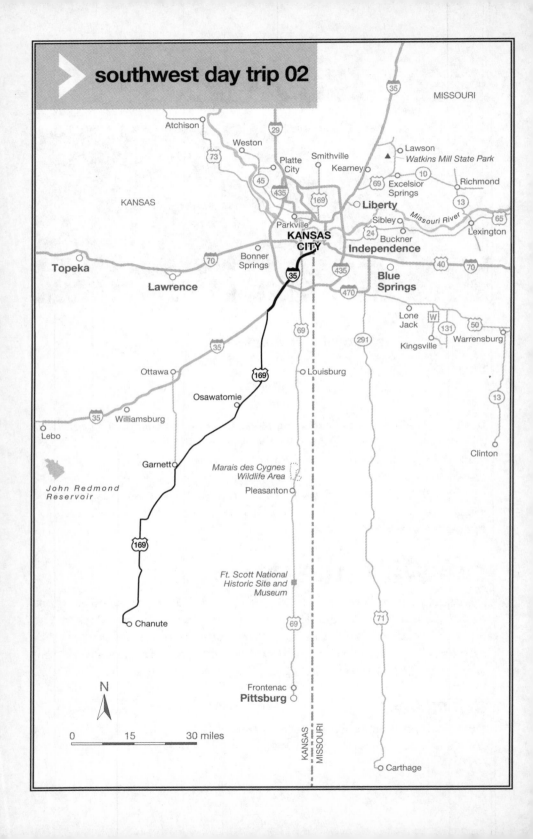

where to go

Osawatomie Chamber of Commerce. 628 Main St.; (913) 755-4114; www.osawatomie chamber.org. The chamber office is located inside a replica of the Union Pacific Railroad Depot that served this city for generations. When the railroad unceremoniously demolished the original depot, city leaders got together and recreated it in an empty lot on Main Street. The chamber offices are located here with all sorts of information about the community. A small museum and gift shop are also on the premises. Open daily.

John Brown State Historic Site. Tenth and Main Streets; (913) 755-4384. This little cabin in the John Brown Memorial Park actually belonged to the Reverend Samuel Adair and his wife Florella. It was a stop on the Underground Railroad and survived the Battle of Osawatomie in August of 1856. John Brown was a frequent visitor to this home and the story of his role in Kansas and US history makes the museum a valuable day trip. Open Tues through Sat.

garnett, ks

This small community features 3 lakes, more than 1,000 acres of parks, a hiking/biking trail, an unusual bed-and-breakfast, and a small but interesting museum that displays works of regional artists and more. For more information: Garnett Area Chamber of Commerce, 419 S. Oak St.; (785) 448-6767; www.garnettchamber.org; www.experiencegarnettks.com.

getting there

From Osawatomie head southwest on US 169 just another 30 miles to Garnett.

where to go

Anderson County Courthouse. Garnett Town Square; (785) 448-6767. Designed by prominent architect George P. Washburn, the courthouse was dedicated in 1902 and is listed on the National Register of Historic Places. A classic example of Romanesque architecture, it features a restored courtroom with stained-glass windows. Open weekdays. Free.

Cedar Valley Reservoir. Located 7.5 miles west of Garnett on Kentucky Road; (785) 448-5496. The beautiful scenery here provides the perfect getaway, with floating docks, boat loading ramps, picnic areas, and wilderness and RV camping facilities. Free. Boating, fishing, and camping permits required.

Lake Garnett. North Lake Road; (785) 448-5496. The 55-acre lake offers recreational facilities that include a golf course, campsites, sporting clay range, swimming pool, and much more. Free. Boating, fishing, and camping permits required.

Prairie Spirit Rail Trail. Kansas Department of Wildlife and Parks, 419 S. Oak St.; (785) 448-6767; www.prairiespirittrail.org. This 51-mile trail from Ottawa to Iola passes through Garnett on what was once the Santa Fe Railroad right-of-way. It provides a picturesque hiking and biking excursion in and around the city. Motorized wheelchairs are welcome. Trail permits are not required inside city limits but are needed for youngsters under 16 who venture outside town. Open daily during daylight hours. Free.

Santa Fe Depot. Main Street and Eighth Avenue. Built during the Depression years, this depot saw the passage of many trains until its closing in 1974. Beautifully restored in 1996, it now serves as a trailhead for users of the Prairie Spirit Rail Trail. The depot visitor center provides tourism information and has exhibits of railroad memorabilia on display, along with a wildflower garden. Free.

Valley View Elk Farm. 27640 NW Jewel Rd.; (785) 448-3085. Rodney and Rachelle Miller operate this elk farm and sell the very healthy meat at area farmers' markets or from their farm, where tours are offered. Tram rides to the pastures get you up close to the majestic animals, but completely protected by fencing. Products for sale include dropped elk antlers, velvet products, and a variety of meat products. Appointments are necessary, so call in advance. Fee.

Walker Art Gallery. 125 W. Fourth Ave.; (785) 448-3388. A rare collection of paintings, sculptures, prints, and drawings donated to Garnett by Maynard Walker features works by John Steuart Curry, Edouard Manet, and Jean Baptiste Corot. The conservators from Kansas City's Nelson-Atkins Museum of Art have restored many of the paintings. Docent tours are available by reservation. Free. Closed Sun.

where to eat

Maloan's Bar & Grille. 101 W. Fourth Ave.; (785) 448-2616. Housed in an 1883 building that was once a bank, the restaurant offers a fine-dining experience in a lovely setting that features high ceilings and oak furniture. Flavorful prime rib, steaks, and shrimp are favorites. Open Mon through Fri from 11 a.m. to 1 p.m. and Wed through Sat evenings from 5 to 9 p.m. Sunday brunch, served from 10 a.m. to 1 p.m., is worth the road trip to Garnett. $$.

chanute, ks

Close your eyes. Imagine, if you will, that you are in the middle of deepest Africa. All around you is the sound of jungle drums and pounding hooves of thousands of zebras and wildebeests. Well, open your eyes, get in your car, and head for Chanute, home of the Martin and Osa Johnson Safari Museum. Exhibits here showcase the life of two of the most extraordinary explorers, naturalists, and photographers of the 20th century.

getting there

Follow US 169 south out of Garnett for about 45 miles to Chanute.

where to go

Chanute Chamber of Commerce. 21 N. Lincoln St.; (877) 431-3350 or (620) 431-3350; www.chanutechamber.com. Here you can pick up brochures of driving tours past many of the community's fabulous Victorian homes. Another brochure highlights downtown businesses.

Chanute Art Gallery. 17 N. Lincoln St.; (620) 431-7807. The gallery provides a showcase for local area artists and Kansas Prairie Printmakers, such as Birger Sandzen and Charles Capps. Recent acquisitions include etchings by Luigi Kasimir. Unique for a small town, the gallery has more than 1,000 square feet of exhibit space and includes a gift shop featuring handcrafted items and original art. Special exhibits change monthly. Closed Sun.

Chanute Historical Society Museum. 101 S. Lincoln St.; (620) 431-1814. Sports fans will enjoy the exhibits on former KU and NBA star Ralph Miller and on Paul Lindblad, who played for the Texas Rangers, Oakland Athletics, and New York Yankees. Both are from Chanute. Other exhibits focus on the railroad history of the area. The museum is located in the historic Flat-Iron Building, constructed in 1907. The unique wedge-shaped building has been home to the Western Union Telegraph, a drugstore, a tavern, and a confectionery. Open weekends or by appointment.

The Martin and Osa Johnson Safari Museum. 111 N. Lincoln St.; (620) 431-2730; www .safarimuseum.com. The early work of Martin and Osa Johnson captured the first photographic records of remote and little-known regions of the world in the early decades of the 20th century. This museum offers a look at Africa in the early part of the 20th century, when it was still a mysterious, dark continent. At that time the American impression of Africa was confined to the machinations of movie moguls, who plied the public with yarns about Tarzan the Apeman and mega-monkeys like King Kong. At one time the cannibals of Borneo and game-choked savannas of Africa represented an overwhelming diversity of life on this planet. Yet deep in the heart of Kansas, in the little town of Chanute, there is the ultimate documentation of wilderness and cultures that have long since vanished from the earth.

The ultimate adventurers and explorers, this intrepid Kansas couple brought these secrets to life for more than 50 years in photography and field journals, which are now showcased in this museum.

The tangled forests of Borneo, the Congo, and the Solomons are displayed in a treasure trove of wildlife motion pictures, thousands of still photos, and an assortment of artifacts brought back from the primitive regions they described in their best-selling books and articles.

The Martin and Osa Johnson exhibit is located inside the restored Santa Fe Train Depot, where it shares space with a magnificent collection of masks and artifacts touted by *African Arts Magazine* as "the finest West African collection between Chicago and California."

Dioramas portray African art and artifacts from Mali, horned crocodile headdresses and wood carvings from Nigeria, carved masks from Guinea, 14-foot-high Sirige masks held in place by mouthpieces worn by warriors, and much more, plus a 10,000-volume natural history library and research facility that is open to the public to enjoy.

Educational programs on Africa, including special shows for groups of handicapped or visually impaired visitors, are also available. Do not miss the museum's extraordinary gift shop, which is filled with imported art and handcrafted items that you won't see elsewhere, unless you plan to travel to Africa sometime. Open daily. Fee.

Summit Hill Gardens. 2605 160th Rd.; (620) 212-3878; www.summithillgardens.com. Summit Hill was the location of the first school in Neosho County. That school has been restored, along with a historic home that has been moved to the site. However, many people come for the magnificent flower and herb gardens that surround the property. Pick your own blackberries in season, watch as soap is being made, and ask questions about gardening your favorite flowers. Open Sat only, or by appointment.

where to shop

Cardinal Drug Store. 103 E. Main St.; (620) 431-9150. This old-fashioned drugstore is owned by Jim Chappell, who bought it in 1972. At the time, the soda fountain had been torn out to make more sales space. Chappell spent a lot of time looking for soda-fountain furniture and found an impressive array of furnishings that included a 1914 solid oak back bar complete with stained glass and enormous mirror, plus a 1937 marble fountain and equipment. Four high-seated chairs with arms and a 1908 solid brass cash register complete the illusion that you've just entered another era. Coca-Cola is made the old-fashioned way, using syrup and carbonated water. You can also get everything from sodas and sundaes to limeades and phosphates. The soda fountain is flanked by cabinets displaying old patent medicines, such as Lydia Pinkham's Blood Medicine, still in the original box. Dr. Miles' Heart Tonic and Regulator and a bottle of Scarless Liniment dating back to 1910 are among the curiosities. Closed Sun.

where to eat & stay

Tioga Suites Hotel and Restaurants. 12 E. Main St.; (620) 431-3343; www.tiogasuites .com. This historic hotel that dates to 1926 has been lovingly restored by local businessman Todd Johnson. Suites are individually decorated, each named for a legendary Kansas figure—among them Wyatt Earp, Amelia Earhart, Dwight Eisenhower, and William Allen White. The decor of each suite is inspired by the figure for whom it is named. However, if you're traveling on a budget and really just need a bed and bathroom, you can skip the extras and sleep for about $40 a night. What a deal! But if you are looking to be pampered, the Heavenly Kneads Day Spa on site will make you feel like a celebrity.

The hotel includes 2 original eateries, open 7 days a week. Zarella's Pizza creates about 30 handmade specialty pies, plus lots of salads and other goodies. The Main Street Family Restaurant is a great place for breakfast. The French toast is really good, as are the homemade fries with lunch or dinner. But if you're just needing a treat any time of the day, the Wedge of Ice Cream covered with Oreos, caramel, and pecans should satisfy your sweet tooth. Restaurants: $–$$; hotel: $.

day trip 03

southwest

front porch to the flint hills:
ottawa, ks; williamsburg, ks;
lebo, ks; emporia, ks

This interesting day trip is one that hard-core foodies will like. It takes you to a truck stop, a barbecue joint, and an old-fashioned soda fountain where you can actually get a decent limeade.

Don't worry if you can't find the actual town of Lebo. You're basically looking for a big plateful of chicken-fried steak, and it can be found at a sprawling truckers' paradise called Beto Junction—which is designated as being in Lebo but is actually off US 75 at exit 155.

There's nothing much to do in Williamsburg but eat spicy pork ribs, play pool, and listen to the jukebox at Guy and Mae's Tavern. These are the simple things that make life so good.

ottawa, ks

Ottawa University, established in 1883, boasts architectural assets, as does the Franklin County Courthouse and the restored 200 block of the central business district, listed on the National Register of Historic Places.

Ottawa has plenty of shops that specialize in furniture, collectibles, primitives, and "junque." You may want to time your visit with Skunk Run Days, the second weekend in June.

But come election day, you may want to brag that you have visited this part of Franklin County for no other reason than to tell the story of the "Naked Voters."

This is a stop along the way on Franklin County Historical Society's Northeast Tour through Peoria, Wellsville, and other areas around Ottawa. This site commemorates 43

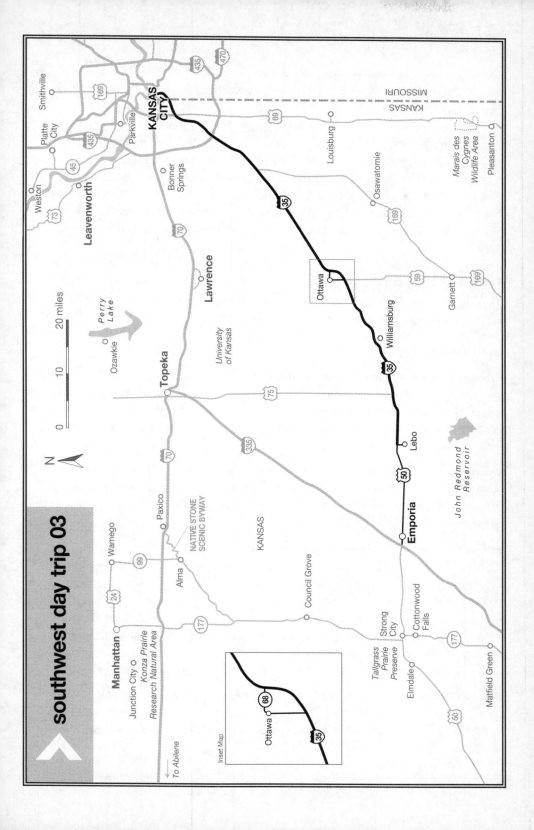

southwest day trip 03

free-state men who were so desperate to cast their ballots against slavery in 1858 that they skinny-dipped their way to the polls.

Granted, there's not much to see there now, but just imagine 43 zealous voters fording three turbulent creeks to vote. Ponder, if you will, whether Americans today would go to such lengths. Would they strip off all their clothing, drop it on the bank, and plunge into a creek—just to enact a new law? Would they show up naked at the polls, letting their birthday suits drip dry in the open air? Of course not: They'd be arrested. Yet in 1858 the free-staters who made it to the polls defeated the pro-slavery issue by a "bare" minimum. A kind neighbor, who did not require that they dress for dinner, fed them before they returned home.

getting there

From downtown Kansas City, take I-35 south for 53 miles to exit 187. Turn west on KS 68 and travel less than 2 miles into Ottawa.

where to go

Franklin County Convention and Tourism Bureau. 2011 E. Logan St.; (785) 242-1411; www.visitottawakansas.com. Located in what appears to be a Victorian home, the visitor center reflects the style of many homes in Franklin County. In addition to maps, brochures, and answers to your questions, you'll also find a nice gift shop of locally made products inside.

Dietrich Cabin. South of the Ottawa Library in Ottawa's City Park (Fifth and Main Streets); (785) 242-1232 or (785) 242-1411. The 1859 cabin is a memorial to a courageous couple who suffered hardships on the Kansas frontier. It has been moved from its original location to the park and is open to tour on weekends. Free.

Elizabeth "Grandma" Layton Exhibit. Wellsville City Library, 115 W. Sixth St., Wellsville; (785) 883-2870. Elizabeth Layton was a remarkable artist whose work gained recognition in her later years. Having been through years of therapy, shock treatment, and drugs to find relief from depression, she tried drawing self-portraits to lift her emotional spirits. So effective was the relief that "Grandma" Layton went on to become a painter. Her work has been represented in numerous galleries and museums around the country, including the Smithsonian's American Art Museum in Washington, D.C. Through her artwork Grandma Layton spoke out against racism, commercialism, and nuclear war. Free. Closed Sun.

Franklin County Courthouse. Third and Main Streets; (785) 242-1232. Built in 1893 by noted architect George P. Washburn, the courthouse features a complex, steep-pitched hip roof with intersecting gables and 4 square corner towers. It has a 4-sided clock, bell tower, and a statue of Justice that stands over the west gable. Tours are available from the Franklin County Historical Society. Free.

Midland Railway Excursion Train. 1515 W. High St., Baldwin City; (913) 371-3410 or (785) 594-6982; www.midland-ry.org. The Midland Railway is located just north of Ottawa on US 59. It operates an authentic re-creation of an American local passenger train and makes a 7-mile round-trip through scenic farmland and woods, using early-20th-century vintage coaches. Open mid-May through Nov. Call for hours and reservations. Admission fee.

Old Depot Museum. Located 1 block west of Main Street on Tecumseh Street; (785) 242-1250. Operated by the Franklin County Historical Society, the 2-story limestone building was constructed in 1888 as a depot for the Kansas City, Lawrence, and Southern Kansas Railway. Exhibits here include a model railroad and displays highlighting a number of Franklin County historical events. Admission fee. Open daily.

Ottawa Suzuki Strings. (785) 242-0242; www.ottawasuzukistrings.org. Students from throughout the area learn to play stringed instruments via this internationally renowned teaching method at the Carnegie Cultural Center in Ottawa and play at any number of community events. Nightly performances are held in June and July as professional musicians travel from across the country to work with these local students. Concerts are offered free or for a nominal fee, providing a phenomenal opportunity to experience world-class musical performances in a small town. Check the website for concert dates and locations.

where to shop

Ottawa Antique Mall. 202 Walnut; (785) 242-1078. Housed in a former soft-drink bottling plant, the mall features aisles of collectibles and furniture, plus lots of flea market–style merchandise. Closed Mon.

williamsburg, ks

South of Ottawa is the dot-on-the-map town of Williamsburg. Its sole claim to fame is Guy and Mae's Tavern, which is worth a trip if you like hearty ribs and tasty sandwiches of beef and ham.

getting there

Williamsburg is 16 miles south of Ottawa on 1-35.

where to eat

Guy and Mae's Tavern. 119 W. William St.; (785) 746-8830. It sits among some timeworn buildings on what appears to be the town's largest street. Inside you'll find thick sandwiches of lean beef and ham, plus hearty slabs of pork ribs served on butcher paper. The sweet and spicy sauce is served on the side; other side dishes include baked beans, coleslaw, and potato salad. Written up in regional and national magazines, the place offers an unusual ambience that features a jukebox, a pool table, and good food served at yesterday's prices. Closed Sun and Mon as well as the last week in July and first week of Aug. $–$$ (no cards).

lebo, ks

You've had ribs, beef, and ham in Williamsburg. Still hungry? Head to the truck stop in Lebo to fill up on some country-fried steak and other classic plates.

getting there

Continue another 23 miles down I-35 to exit 155 to reach Lebo.

where to go

Beto Junction. I-35 and US 75; (620) 256-6311. This sprawling truck stop takes its name from the first letters of four nearby cities: Burlington, Emporia, Topeka, and Ottawa. Food fans may want to make the trip just to chow down on trailblazer breakfasts that feature eggs with such meaty items as pork chops, chopped sirloin steak, ham, and Polish sausage. You might choose Beto Junction's fabulous chicken-fried steak with eggs, or order it for dinner.

Indeed, it is worth the drive just to savor the huge portions of this spectacular tenderized steak—dipped in a light, flaky batter and fried just right—nestled atop buttery, made-from-scratch mashed potatoes and crowned with country gravy. More than a meal, this is an all-you-can-eat experience. Catering to anybody on two wheels or more, the entire facility also includes a travel store that is great fun to browse through. If you're looking for a combination hair dryer/vacuum, you'll find it here, along with a wide range of Kansas gifts, greeting cards, and more. Open daily. $$.

emporia, ks

Emporia touts itself as the "Front Porch to the Flint Hills," an area that makes up the largest unbroken tract of tallgrass prairie in the county.

Founded in 1857, Emporia has made a name for itself by being the home of the National Teachers Hall of Fame and birthplace of Pulitzer Prize–winning journalist William Allen White. White died in 1944, having achieved success and fame. President Franklin Delano Roosevelt eulogized him, saying that he "ennobled the profession of journalism." White's birthplace in Emporia is now a state historic site.

getting there

Continue driving south on I-35 out of Lebo for 20 miles for the 3 exits to Emporia.

where to go

Emporia Convention and Visitors Bureau. 719 Commercial St.; (620) 342-1803; www
.emporiakschamber.org. Find out about the latest developments in the community and pick
up discount coupons here for some of the sites.

All Veterans Memorial Park. 933 S. Commercial St.; (620) 342-1803. In a continuing
effort to pay tribute to military veterans and Emporia's heritage of recognizing the service
of veterans, this park, dedicated in 1991, features a World War II–era Sherman tank and a
Vietnam-era Huey helicopter. The Kansas Purple Heart Monument is here, as is a monument to a local Medal of Honor recipient who gave his life for his country. The easily accessible park is located on the banks of the Cottonwood River, where lovely walking trails offer
an opportunity for reflection. Open daily, dawn to dusk.

David Traylor Zoo of Emporia. 75 Soden Rd.; (620) 342-6558; www.emporiazoo.org.
This is one of the five smallest accredited zoos in the country at just 8 acres. The mountain
lion and Nelson's elk are among the more popular exhibits. The zoo also has a nice assortment of birds, mammals, and reptiles housed in natural habitats. The zoo also features
exceptional botanical displays and spectacular holiday lights. Open daily, with extended
hours in the summer. Free.

Emporia State University. 1200 Commercial St.; (620) 341-5037; www.emporia.edu.
Founded in 1863, the university was the state's first school for training teachers. Located
on 200 acres, the campus offers special attractions of interest to tourists, such as the William Allen White Library. Manuscripts, correspondence, photographs, and other materials
about the life and times of William Allen White can be found here. The student union has a
Veteran's Wall of Honor that pays tribute to students and alumni who served in the armed
forces. The Johnston Geology Museum and the Peterson Planetarium are worthy of your
time. Free admission to all campus-related exhibits.

Flint Hills National Wildlife Refuge. Located 15 miles southeast of Emporia, near Hart-
ford; (620) 392-5553; www.flinthills.fws.gov. One of a system of 400 refuges administered
by the US Fish and Wildlife Service, the area is dedicated to the preservation and conservation of wildlife, primarily migratory waterfowl and bald eagles. Hiking, photography, boating,
picnicking, camping, fishing, wild-food gathering, and hunting are allowed. Open daily. Free.

Lyon County Historical Museum. 118 E. Sixth Ave.; (620) 340-6310; www.lyoncounty
historicalsociety.org. Located in the 1904 Carnegie Library Building, this is one of many sites
in Emporia listed on the National Register of Historic Places. The building still contains its
original leaded-glass windows, an ornate water fountain, beautiful oak woodwork, and other
unique features. It houses artifacts and exhibits on a rotating schedule that help illustrate
and interpret various phases of Kansas's Lyon County history and heritage. A great gift gallery specializes in items made by Kansas artisans. Closed Sun and Mon. Free.

National Teachers Hall of Fame. 1320 Commercial Dr.; (620) 341-5660; www.nthf.org. One of the city's premier attractions, the hall of fame nationally recognizes five teachers annually who have demonstrated a commitment to educating children from prekindergarten through high school. The walls hold tributes to some of the best teachers in America, and there are galleries with cultural and artistic exhibits of general interest. Closed Sun. Free.

Prairie Passage. Lyon County Fairgrounds, West US 50 and Industrial Road; (620) 342-1803. Eight massive limestone sculptures celebrating Emporia's origins and history were designed by artist Richard Stauffer and produced by the 1992 Kansas Sculptors Association. The sculptures present a variety of images about the land, its forces, and its people. Open daily. Free.

William Allen White State Historic Site. 927 Exchange St.; (620) 342-2800; www.kshs .org/places/white. William Allen White, born in Emporia in 1868, is the man for whom

honoring our nation's veterans

For a generation of Americans, November 11 was first known as Armistice Day— the 11th day of the 11th month in which at 11 minutes after 11 a.m., tribute was paid to those who had fought and died in World War I.

It was to have been the war to end all wars, but as Americans lost their lives in World War II and then in Korea, Alvin King of Emporia realized that wars would keep coming and that there was an ongoing need to recognize the veterans who fought in them.

In 1953 King approached his Congressional representative, Ed Rees of Emporia, and suggested the day be changed to Veterans Day to honor veterans of all military conflicts. Rees took King's proposal to Washington and to President Dwight Eisenhower, another Kansan and veteran of World War II.

The first nationwide observance of Veterans Day was on November 11, 1954. And each year, Emporia continues its recognition of veterans with a weeklong tribute that includes reenactments, lectures, parades, and other opportunities to learn about the contributions of military veterans. An All Veterans Park, at the intersection of Commercial Street and Soden's Road, is a must-see while visiting Emporia.

Many other parks and memorials around the community honor the contributions of veterans, including an exhibit at Emporia Service Area on the Kansas Turnpike honoring veteran Ken Bradstreet, who coordinated the work of many memorials and programs to Emporian veterans.

the University of Kansas School of Journalism is named. A prolific journalist who shaped public discussion on political and social matters nationwide for more than half a century, White won a Pulitzer Prize for editorials in his paper, the *Emporia Gazette*, and came to be respected around the world. His home is one of many sites in Emporia that explore the wit and wisdom that is studied today by journalists and educators around the world. Open Wed through Sat, Mar through Nov; weekends only Dec through Feb. Admission fee.

where to stay

White Rose Inn. 901 Merchant St.; (620) 343-6336; www.whiteroseinnemporia.com. This elegant Victorian bed-and-breakfast features 4 private suites with sitting rooms, Jacuzzis, and kitchen privileges. Guests arrive for afternoon tea and sumptuous treats and wake up the next day to the aroma of fresh-baked biscuits, coffee cakes, and muffins—or breakfast in bed for a special romantic treat. $$.

worth more time: wichita, ks

The largest city in Kansas is slightly more than 3 hours southwest of Kansas City on I-35. With the completion of Kellogg Avenue in 2011 (finally!), Wichita is easy to navigate with lots of little surprises here and there, along with a few big surprises as well. It has history, art, some intriguing restaurants, and a great farmers' market. Wichita is more than a day trip. It's a nice couple of days, and one worth more of your time.

where to go

Wichita Convention and Visitors Bureau. 515 S. Main St.; (316) 265-2800; www.go wichita.com. Stop by for a visitors' guide and a coupon book for reduced admission to many of the museums.

Kansas Aviation Museum. 3350 S. George Washington Blvd.; (316) 683-9242; www .kansasaviationmuseum.org. At one point, more than 70 percent of all private aircraft in the world were made right here in Wichita, and this museum is located at the terminal of the former municipal airport. Check out the Kansas Aviation Hall of Fame, test your skills in a flight simulator, or test your strength with an old hand-crank inertia engine. But the best thing is to watch volunteers lovingly restore old planes and talk with them about their work and their love of aviation. Open daily. $.

Old Cowtown Museum. 1865 W. Museum Blvd.; (316) 219-1871; www.oldcowtown.org. This living history center is located on about 27 acres right off the Chisholm Trail. It contains a number of authentic buildings, including the first home building in Wichita in 1865. A chuck-wagon supper on Fri, Sat, and Sun nights includes music and a comedy routine. Reservations required for the supper. Closed Mon and Tues. $.

Wichita Art Museum. 1400 W. Museum Blvd.; (316) 268-4921; www.wichitaartmuseum .org. This little gem has been a part of the Wichita landscape for more than 75 years, highlighting the works of American artists, such as Charles Russell, Winslow Homer, and the Wyeth family. The Muse Cafe is a nice bright spot for a light lunch. Closed Mon. $.

where to eat

Hangar One Steakhouse. 5925 W. Kellogg Ave.; (316) 941-4900; hangaronesteakhouse .com. The nose of an old C-45 is the prime seating spot in this restaurant located adjacent to the airport in what looks like a hangar with a control tower sticking out of the top. That control tower is a cigar bar with perhaps the most fabulous view anywhere in Wichita—looking right down the runway of the municipal airport. Some of the tables are built on top of a Pratt & Whitney engine. The bar has runway lights down the middle of the bar. The patio is called "the crash pad" and all the airplane decor items are from airplanes that crashed. Open for lunch and dinner. Reservations suggested on Fri and Sat nights. $$.

where to stay

The Castle Inn at Riverside. 1155 N. River Blvd.; (316) 263-9300; www.castleinnriverside .com. Built in 1888, this home is modeled after a castle in Scotland and has a number of architectural elements brought from Europe that are several hundred years old. One fireplace from Greece is 650 years old. The woodwork is magnificent, as is the stained glass, the fireplaces, and decorative accents. Each of the 14 guest rooms has a distinct theme or decor. For example, in the Native American room, the bed is located in a teepee. Reservations require a 2-night stay. $$–$$$.

The Hotel at Old Town. 830 E. First St.; (316) 267-4800; www.hotelatoldtown.com. Exhibits of Wichita history fill the lobby of this hotel that dates to 1900. Rooms are all generous in size, many with balconies, hot tubs, and numerous amenities. Each room has a kitchenette and a cupboard downstairs provides all you'll need to prepare a nice breakfast. It's a great place to stay if you plan on visiting the Saturday farmers' market. $$.

west

day trip 01

west

>>> **history, culture & agriculture:**
bonner springs, ks; lawrence, ks

bonner springs, ks

Bonner Springs is home to the renowned Renaissance Festival held here in fall. For information: Bonner Springs/Edwardsville Chamber of Commerce, 129 N. Nettleton; (913) 422-5044; www.lifeisbetter.org.

getting there

Bonner Springs is a short 18-mile drive west from Kansas City on I-70.

where to go

Grinter House. 1420 S. Seventy-eighth St.; (Seventy-eighth Street and KS 32), Kansas City; (913) 299-0373; www.kshs.org/places/grinter/index.htm. Located 8 miles east of Bonner Springs, this house stands on the site of the first ferry across the Kansas River. The 2-story brick structure was built by Moses R. Grinter in 1857. Today it is a historic site and museum open to tour. Closed Dec through Feb, and on Mon the remainder of the year. Admission fee.

Holy-Field Vineyard & Winery. 18807 158th St., Basehor; (913) 724-9463; www.holy fieldwinery.com. This family-owned winery currently produces about 15 varieties of wine from a 12-acre vineyard, which is open for tour. The tasting room is also the site of such

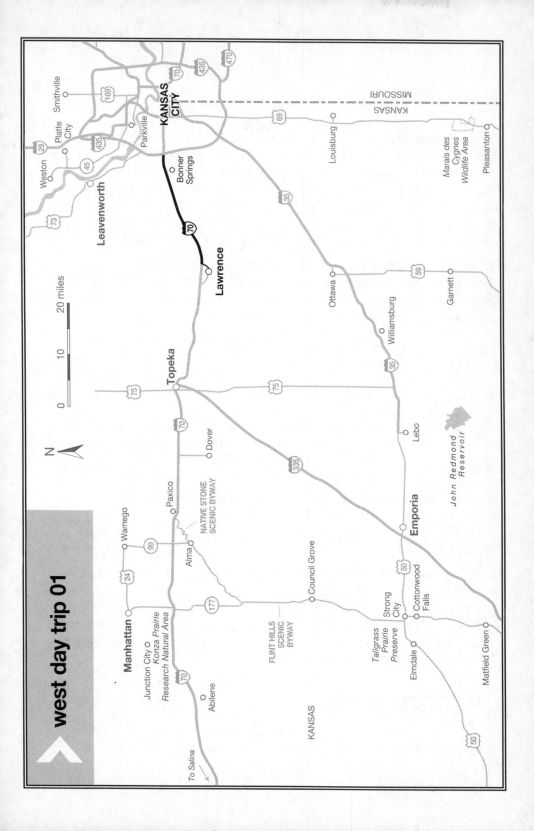

fun events as murder mysteries, jazz concerts, and holiday celebrations. Check out the gift shop for the wine-filled chocolates.

The National Agricultural Center and Hall of Fame. 630 Hall of Fame Dr. (North 126th Street, northeast of I-70 at K–7); (913) 721-1075; www.aghalloffame.com. Visitors can view 30,000 historic agricultural museum exhibits at the National Farmers Memorials located on the premises. There are a turn-of-the-20th-century home and farm implements, a century-old railroad depot, a blacksmith shop, a one-room schoolhouse, and a mile-long nature trail with 89 marked and identified specimens. A mini-train ride is fun for the kids in warm weather months. Tour guides are available. Open daily Mar through Nov. Admission fee.

Wyandotte County Bonner Springs Park. 3488 West Dr. (office), Bonner Springs; (913) 299-0550. This 640-acre park is adjacent to the National Agricultural Center and Hall of Fame and features ball fields, tennis courts, shelter houses, a radio-controlled airplane flying field (permit required), and the Wyandotte County Museum. Open daily. Free.

The Wyandotte County Historical Society and Museum. 631 N. 126th St., inside Wyandotte County Bonner Springs Park; (913) 721-1078. The museum tells the history of Wyandotte County through exhibits that cover 350 million years of development, spanning a period from the Stone Age to today. Displays document the immigrant cultures who settled Kansas, from the native Kanza Indians to the pioneers who came from around the world to live and work in the area. A scale model keelboat as used by the Lewis and Clark Expedition introduces an exhibit on the Corps of Discovery's experiences in Kansas. Photographs and artifacts relating to Wyandotte County's industrial heritage and multicultural background can be found throughout the exhibit gallery and archives. Newspapers, county records, books, maps, and other materials offer a wealth of information for those interested in the early settlement of the state. Closed Mon. Free.

where to stay

Back N Thyme Guest House and Herb Garden. 1100 S. 130th St.; (913) 422-5207; www.backnthyme.com. This charming Victorian retreat features a hearty breakfast buffet in a sunny room overlooking the kitchen herb garden. The bed-and-breakfast offers 4 guest rooms, all with spacious private baths and one with a Jacuzzi and double vanity. Rates also include evening hors d'oeuvres and dessert. Young children can be accommodated if families wish to reserve the entire second floor. $$–$$$.

lawrence, ks

In 1863, when William Quantrill and his raiders burned Lawrence to the ground in the name of pro-slavery, who could know that the town would bounce back and become the foodie hangout and cultural mecca that it is today?

With a long tradition of supporting the arts, the University of Kansas, or KU for short, offers one of the finest art museums in the Midwest, a theater that features 12 productions annually, and a School of Fine Arts that produces more than 400 events each year.

The university's diverse student mix has brought innovation and energy to the unusually stable local economy. On a hill where pioneers once paused along the Oregon Trail, KU's limestone buildings play host to scholars who come to study and learn on the beautiful, user-friendly campus. And, of course, KU sports and its connection to basketball history are legendary.

Lawrence today offers plenty of attractions and a downtown filled with boutiques, galleries, and gourmet restaurants, yet it also has a history behind it worth learning.

It's hard to forget that Lawrence was Indian country for more than 50 years after the 1803 Louisiana Purchase. Kansas itself was a territory opened for settlement in 1854. During this time, the issue of slavery in the soon-to-be-state dominated all aspects of life. A bitter struggle ensued for territorial control. Lawrence had Yankee blood, and pro-slavery neighbors in Missouri found that hard to bear. When the town became a center for free-state activity, trouble soon brewed between the abolitionists and the pro-slavers. Quantrill's morning raid on August 21, 1863, left Lawrence a shambles, with hundreds reported dead or missing and homes and businesses destroyed.

And as much as officials at the University of Kansas and University of Missouri would like the term "border wars" to disappear from local parlance, each time the two rival sports teams meet in competition, the days of the Civil War in this region are remembered in a healthy sporting event.

When the Civil War ended, Lawrence's economy grew. The Kansas Pacific Railroad reached Lawrence in 1864, bringing new businesses and industry. In 1866 KU held its first session; Haskell Indian Nations University, now a registered National Historic Landmark, opened in 1884.

Today Lawrence, with its 19th-century Victorian homes and ornate downtown landmarks, has an identity all its own.

getting there

From Bonner Springs, travel west 25 miles on I-70, remembering to have change for the toll booths.

where to go

Lawrence Visitors' Center. 402 N. Second St.; (785) 865-4411; www.visitlawrence.com. Located in a restored Union Pacific depot, this visitor center includes a film on Quantrill's Raid, as well as exhibits on other parts of Lawrence history.

Clinton Lake. US Army Corps of Engineers, 872 N. 1402nd Rd.; (785) 842-8562; www .kdwp.state.ks.us. Located 3 miles southwest of Lawrence, off Clinton Parkway (West

Twenty-third Street), the lake provides 7,000 surface acres for boating, fishing, and swimming. Excellent opportunities for bicycling and for viewing wildlife abound. There are more than 70 miles of hiking trails, plus camping and picnicking areas. The Clinton Lake Museum is open weekends during the summer and houses artifacts and exhibits on local history. Free.

Haskell Indian Nations University. 155 Indian Ave.; (785) 749-8404; www.haskell.edu. This is one of the oldest educational institutions for Native Americans and Alaska Natives supported by the federal government. Founded in 1884, Haskell has evolved from an elementary school to a university offering a baccalaureate in elementary teacher education. Open only to members of federally recognized Indian nations, enrollment averages 1,000 students a semester.

The Haskell Cultural Center and Museum houses exhibits on the history of the university and the Native American experience in Kansas. Cultural performances are held at the adjacent outdoor amphitheater. The grounds include a memorial to Native Americans who have served in the United States military. Walking-tour brochures that explain the history and significance of buildings on campus are available at the center. The museum is closed on Sat.

In the fall Haskell hosts an outdoor Indian Art Market in conjunction with Lawrence's annual Indian Arts Show. In the spring an outdoor powwow attracts hundreds of Native American and Alaska Native dancers and singers from across the United States.

Freedom's Frontier National Heritage Area. 200 W. Ninth St.; (785) 856-5300; www.freedomsfrontier.org. The headquarters for the Freedom's Frontier is located here in the Carnegie Building, and rotating exhibits explain the struggle for freedom that took place in 29 eastern Kansas and 12 western Missouri counties prior to, during, and immediately following the Civil War. Closed Mon and Tues. Free.

Lawrence Arts Center. 940 New Hampshire; (785) 843-2787; www.lawrenceartscenter.com. The Lawrence Arts Center is designed specifically for art education. Two visual arts galleries showcase area artists' works, and a gallery gift shop offers additional items for sale. Performing arts presentations are scheduled regularly in the theater. Open 7 days a week. Free.

Old West Lawrence Historic District. From Sixth to Ninth Streets between Tennessee and Illinois Streets; (785) 865-4499; www.visitlawrence.com. The impressive 19th-century architecture here is listed on the National Register of Historic Places. Drive by the Plymouth Congregational Church, 925 Vermont St., for a vision of spires, buttresses, and stained glass.

University of Kansas. Mount Oread Campus. The 1,000-acre campus is one of the prettiest in the country and features a pond called Potter Lake at the bottom of a grassy wooded knoll between the Campanile and Memorial Stadium. From the stop sign at the west end of Memorial Drive, you can turn left onto West Campus Road, where there are some sorority and fraternity houses. This leads to the Chi Omega Fountain. At the south side of the intersection is a large rock marking the site of many Oregon Trail campfires. If you go around the fountain, you'll wind up making a left turn onto Jayhawk Boulevard, the main drag of the campus. If school is in session, you'll need to stop and get a visitor's pass at the booth. Jayhawk Boulevard has some wonderful old buildings, including Strong Hall, Watson Library, and others. Detailed information and a map of the campus can be found at www.ku.edu. Some stops on your itinerary might include these:

Booth Hall of Athletics. Adjacent to Allen Fieldhouse; (785) 864-7050. If you'd like to get a firsthand look at the original rules of basketball, visit this museum-like facility adjacent to the sports center where some of the country's best basketball is played. But all KU sports are honored here in 6 different exhibit rooms. Free. Closed Sun.

Helen Foresman Spencer Museum of Art. 1301 Mississippi St. (behind the Kansas Union); (785) 864-4710; www.spencerart.ku.edu. This gem of a place houses one of the finest university art museums in the country. Eleven galleries offer changing exhibitions and art from the museum's collections that represent more than 4,000 years of world art history and include wonderful European and American paintings, sculpture, and photography. Japanese Edo-period painting and 20th-century Chinese painting are of particular interest. The Spencer also affords art lovers a chance to experience touring exhibitions of remarkable works not found elsewhere in the area. Closed Mon. Free.

KU Natural History Museum. Dyche Hall, 1345 Jayhawk Blvd.; (785) 864-4450; http://naturalhistory.ku.edu. Listed on the National Register of Historic Places, the museum holds exhibits of Kansas and Great Plains animals and offers a historic panorama of North American plants and animals. On display are live bees, fish, snakes, and minerals. Open daily. Donations suggested.

The Lied Center. 1600 Stewart Dr.; (785) 864-2787; www.lied.ku.edu. Located on the highest ridge on campus, this is the home for KU's Concert, Chamber Music, Broadway, and New Directions series. The lobbies here offer a magnificent view of the rolling hills and the Wakarusa Valley. The Lied Center provides a state-of-the-art setting for music, dance, theater, lectures, films, and convocations. Visitors are welcome to view the building during business hours Mon through Fri. Tickets to events can be purchased at the box office.

Robert J. Dole Institute of Public Policy. 2350 Petefish Dr.; (785) 864-4900; www.doleinstitute.org. Adjacent to the Lied Center is the newest addition to the University of Kansas campus honoring the public service of Kansas senator Bob Dole. The interactive exhibits here chronicle the life of the senator who served Kansas for 46 years and ran three times for president of the United States. The state-of-the-art presentations on this history of Kansas, the soaring stained-glass windows, and the Memory Wall honoring World War II veterans make the center worthy of a visit, no matter what your politics. The center hosts political presentations and historic discussions throughout the year. Open daily. Free.

where to shop

Community Mercantile. 901 Iowa St.; (785) 843-8544. "The Merc" has been serving the Lawrence community since 1974. It is cooperatively owned and offers a full selection of organic and local produce in season. It has an extensive bulk department, with an excellent selection of coffees and teas, herbs, dairy products, and more. There are books and housewares, plus a meat department that features locally raised beef and poultry. Freshly baked goods, crafts by area artists, and a deli department round out the fare. Member benefits include special discounts and a monthly newsletter. Open daily.

mustard madness

March is always a frenzied time in Lawrence thanks to March Madness—that hysterical time of year when college basketball fans overdose on their favorite sport via televised tournaments across the country night and day. The pack of 65 NCAA teams becomes the Sweet Sixteen, which is then pared to the Final Four. And more times than not, the Jayhawks are in that final number.

At the Free State Brewery, which is always packed with red and blue Jayhawk fans on game day, March Madness is not so much about basketball as it is mustard. You have to know Free State Brewery proprietor Chuck Magerl to truly understand the connection between basketball and mustard, and even then, it doesn't make much sense. After seeing a program on public television about the Mustard Museum in Mount Horeb, Wisconsin, Chuck decided to combine mustard tastings at his restaurant with the tournament brackets for basketball, allowing guests to sample 65 flavors, then 16, then select a Final Four of mustards.

(Note: Mount Horeb, Wisconsin, is about 20 miles west/southwest of Madison. The Mustard Museum tells the exciting story of this condiment and displays more than 4,000 containers of historic, thought-provoking mustard. The museum gift shop and catalog carry 400 varieties for sale.)

Each February the phone calls and e-mails fly fast and furious between Lawrence and Mount Horeb, scientifically identifying the precise varieties of mustards that will fill in the tournament brackets. All told, about 200 containers of Wisconsin mustard make their way to the Free State Brewery, a little more or a little less, based on how well the Jayhawks perform.

Farmers Market. 1000 block of Vermont Street; (785) 865-4499. This is the largest and oldest farmers' market in the state. Local growers and farm producers offer products and produce ranging from fresh fruits and veggies to baked goods, herbs, and homemade condiments. Open Sat morning and Tues and Thurs afternoon, May to Nov.

Phoenix Gallery. 825 Massachusetts St.; (785) 843-0080; www.phoenixgallery.biz. Works by local and regional artisans are represented here and include pottery, blown glass, jewelry, weaving, paintings, prints, and textiles. Open daily.

The Raven Bookstore. 6 E. Seventh St.; (785) 749-3300; www.ravenbookstore.com. This bookstore specializes primarily in mysteries and hosts 2 mystery reading groups a month for customers. It also offers a British-import mystery section for many titles that are hard to find in this country. Fiction, history and regional studies, travel, nature, and other works of literature also fill the shelves. Open daily.

Waxman Candles. 609 Massachusetts St.; (785) 843-8593; www.waxmancandles.com. Situated at the northern end of Historic Downtown Lawrence, this unique shop produces handmade candles, including the one-of-a-kind "Silhouette," which has a backlit effect as it burns and is quite a showstopper. Three tons of candles wait to be sold here, including clean-burning beeswax and soy candles. A product catalog is also available. Open daily.

where to eat

Free State Brewing Co. 636 Massachusetts St.; (785) 843-4555; www.freestatebrewing .com. This is the first brewery to operate in Kansas since the state passed a prohibition law more than a century ago. Located inside a renovated trolley barn, this combination brewery-restaurant produces a small variety of high-quality beer, using fresh, natural ingredients. The restaurant offers an interesting menu that includes everything from stir-fried veggies to fresh fish and steak. Brewery tours are offered Sat at 2 p.m. Open daily. $–$$.

Pachamama's. 800 New Hampshire St.; (785) 841-0990. This restaurant features an international menu that changes monthly. The uniquely inspired cuisine features everything from fish to wild-game entrees. Come for the wine tastings on Fri evenings. Open daily at 5 p.m. $$–$$$.

Paisano's. 2112 W. Twenty-fifth St.; (785) 838-3500. Like its sister restaurant in Topeka, Kansas, this bistro serves excellent Italian-inspired food. Entrees range from veal and chicken dishes to pasta dishes redolent with delectable sauces. The portions are large and the prices reasonable. Open daily for lunch and dinner. $$.

Sylas and Maddy's Homemade Ice Cream. 1014 Massachusetts St.; (785) 832-8323. This is the place to come for banana splits, sundaes, malts, milk shakes, sodas, and homemade waffle cones filled to the brim with fantastically rich and creamy ice cream made on the premises. Choose from 130 rotating flavors that include Da Bomb (Oreos, chocolate chips, and cookie dough), prairie pumpkin nut, and pineapple cheesecake, or try the choco-late chip and peanut butter chocolate chip made with superior chunks of chocolate. Take a cooler so that you can pack a pint or a quart to go. Yum! Open daily. $.

Teller's Restaurant. 746 Massachusetts St.; (785) 843-4111; www.746mass.com. Located in a historic 1877 bank building, Teller's features Italian cuisine, including pasta, chicken, lamb, and wood-fired brick-oven pizza, all of which should be enjoyed with a selec-tion from Teller's award-winning wine list. A contemporary blend of works by Kansas artists Stan Herd and Jon Havener complements original bank fixtures, such as the 20,000-pound safe door securing the restrooms. Open daily. $$.

Wheatfield's Bakery and Cafe. 904 Vermont St.; (785) 841-5553. This delightful place features fresh-baked breads made with Kansas wheat. Everything from traditional favorites like sourdough and raisin breads to cookies and truffles are made on the premises, along with soups, sandwiches, and stuffed pastries. Open daily for lunch and dinner; a full break-fast is served until 2 p.m. on Sun and until 11 a.m. on weekdays. $–$$.

where to stay

Circle S Guest Ranch & Country Inn. 3325 Circle S Ln.; (785) 843-4124 or (800) 625-2839; www.circlesranch.com. This charming retreat has been continuously owned and operated through five generations since the late 1800s. The ranch spans more than 1,200 acres and includes more than 400 head of cattle. More than 20 ponds dot the surroundings and there is abundant wildlife. The inn itself was built to resemble a Kansas barn. Twelve spacious guest rooms offer private baths and views. Some feature claw-foot or whirlpool baths and fireplaces. Breakfast is included in the price of the room. Dinner is available on Sat night by request. $$$.

The Eldridge Hotel. 701 Massachusetts St.; (785) 749-5011 or (800) 527-0909; www .eldridgehotel.com. This downtown hotel is the only hotel in Lawrence listed as an official Historic Hotel of America. Completely destroyed during Quantrill's Raid in 1863, the struc-ture was promptly rebuilt and named the Hotel Eldridge. After a period of decline in the mid-20th century, the hotel was renovated and reopened in 1986. All 48 rooms are suites, and the hotel restaurant serves a great Sunday brunch. $$.

Halcyon House Bed and Breakfast. 1000 Ohio St.; (785) 841-0314; www.thehalcyon house.com. A century-old restored home, Halcyon House offers a living room, 2 patios, and a lovely glass-enclosed kitchen. Nine uniquely styled and furnished bedrooms include a master suite with a king-size bed and private bath and a suite with 2 double beds, private bath, and fireplace. A complete breakfast is served daily and features homemade muffins, omelets, fresh fruit, and coffee. $$.

day trip 02

west

state capital:
topeka, ks

topeka, ks

The capital of Kansas, Topeka lies on rich, sandy river-bottom land where Indians lived for many years using the Kansas (Kaw) River for navigation. Each year Topeka celebrates its Native American heritage with the Shawnee Country Allied Tribes All Nations Powwow, held Labor Day weekend.

The Kaw River also drew to it three French Canadian brothers who started a ferry service across the river in 1842. They married three Kanza (Kansas) Indian sisters whose tribe had lived in the area for many years. Thus marked the beginnings of Topeka as a stopping point on the Oregon Trail. Years later one of the couples celebrated the election of their grandson, Charles Curtis, as vice president of the United States—the only US vice president of Native American descent.

Topeka has a rich abundance of attractions, including one of the most extensive rose gardens in the country, a tropical rain forest, an international raceway offering top-flight motor sports events, and several interesting museums. Springtime is especially beautiful in downtown Topeka. About 60 tulips beds with more than 35,000 tulip bulbs line Kansas Avenue and Topeka Boulevard. For more information: Topeka Convention and Visitors Bureau, 1275 SW Topeka Blvd.; (785) 234-1030; www.visittopeka.us.

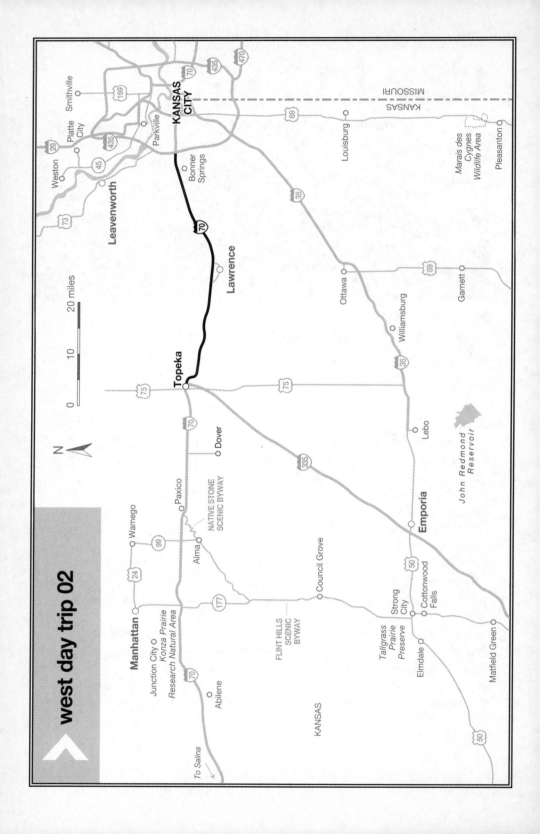

west day trip 02

getting there

From downtown, take I-70 west for 65 miles to exits for Topeka.

where to go

Brown v. Board of Education National Historic Site. 1515 SE Monroe St.; (785) 354-4273; www.nps.gov/brvb. Located in the former Monroe School, one of four African-American schools in the Topeka School District prior to 1954, this site represents the segregation of publicly funded schools, the Civil Rights movement of the time, and the landmark Supreme Court ruling on May 17, 1954, that ended segregation. Oliver Brown, a Topeka minister, was the first of 13 parents in Topeka to file suit on behalf of 20 children; thus, the name Brown on the case. However, the case represents similar lawsuits filed in five states at that time on behalf of more than 150 children. Today the building has been restored to its condition of the early 1950s. Numerous interactive exhibits encourage visitors to explore the concept of racial segregation and record their feelings at the conclusion of the tour. Free.

Cedar Crest. Located off I-70 and Fairlawn Road; (785) 296-3636. The home has been the official residence of the Kansas governor since 1962. Built in 1928, this 12-room French Norman–style home overlooks the Kansas River Valley. It was designed by W. D. Wight of Kansas City and was named for the numerous cedar trees on the property. The home is nestled on 244 acres that include hiking trails, fishing ponds, and nature areas open to the public. Public tours are offered on Mon between 1 and 4 p.m. Groups of 8 or more require reservations. Free.

Combat Air Museum. Forbes Field, Hangar 602, at exit 177 off I-70; (785) 862-3303; www.combatairmuseum.org. Dedicated to restoring, preserving, and displaying aircraft and artifacts, this museum is the only one in the world to display operational aircraft from every armed conflict utilizing powered aircraft. Housed here are surveillance aircraft fighters, missiles, and other military pieces dating to 1917. Visitors can walk through one of the early 1950 radar planes and browse through the many exhibits that include the Women Air Service Pilots, major battles fought by air, and information on other nations' air force programs. Open daily. Admission fee.

Gage Park. 635 SW Gage Blvd.; (785) 368-3838. Topeka's 160-acre Gage Park features many attractions, including the following:

> **Carousel in the Park.** The antique carousel was built around 1908 by New York's Herschell-Spillman Company. It was purchased by the city of Topeka in 1986 and totally restored for the public to enjoy and ride. Open daily in warm weather. Admission fee.

> **Reinisch Rose Garden.** (785) 272-6150. This is one of the most extensive rose gardens in the country, with more than 400 varieties and 7,000 bushes. It is one

of 23 test gardens in the nation for hybridizers and has one of the most complete displays of All-American Winners selected since 1940 on public view. Internationally famous for its beauty, the Reinisch Rose Garden was founded in 1931 and named after Topeka's first park superintendent. Today the roses grow in a lovely setting of rock gardens and pools. The red Topeka Rose stands majestically in the center of the garden. Blooming season normally is June through Oct; peak time, early June and mid-Sept. Open daily. Free.

Topeka Zoological Park. 635 SW Gage Blvd.; (785) 368-9180; http://topekazoo .org. Exhibits include the Tropical Rain Forest (see below) and "Gorilla Encounter," which allows visitors to view the creatures in an open environment from a glass-enclosed area. African lions, Japanese macaques, and Chinese muntjac deer are part of the displays. Warm weather makes the Water Bird Lagoon a pleasant place for bird-watching. There are many attractions to visit, including the Children's Zoo; it features a traditional red barn and a series of wooden corrals that create a farm-like setting for visitor-friendly animals. Another nice attraction is Black Bear Woods. A large wood ramp and deck provide viewing areas of the bears' home. There are a pool, tall trees for them to climb, natural berries to eat, and a large area for playing, sleeping, and just being bears. Open daily. Admission fee.

The Tropical Rain Forest. Located inside Topeka Zoo. The damp, pungent smell mingles with the sweet odor of rare flowers and plants; coupled with the cries of exotic birds, the rain forest is a rare experience to savor. Housed in a 30-foot-high geodesic dome, 100 feet in diameter, the Tropical Rain Forest supports some of the rarest and most exotic plant and animal life in the world. This is a bird lover's paradise. The feathered creatures here are so lavishly colored that they look as though they have been dipped in richly textured paints. Many of the other inhabitants are so well camouflaged that most visitors miss them. Many are nocturnal and quite a few move freely about the dome, so be careful not to step on anybody's toes! Exhibits are open daily. Admission fee.

Great Overland Station. 701 N. Kansas Ave.; (785) 232-5533; www.greatoverlandstation .com. Topeka's proximity to the Oregon and Santa Fe Trails and the railroads played a key role in the city's development. The museum is housed in a former Union Pacific depot and helps tell the story of life on the rails and how those rails brought Topeka to life. The site now includes a Veteran's Memorial and avenue of 50 American flags. Closed Mon. Admission fee.

Heartland Park Topeka. 7530 SW Topeka Blvd.; (785) 862-4781; www.hpt.com. All the state-of-the-art elements found here are designed with the spectator in mind, from the 2.5-mile road-race course to the 0.25-mile drag strip—one of the fastest in the world. The viewing berms afford spectators an excellent view of the Grand Prix road-race course, while the modern grandstands offer onlookers a look at the pit-stop action. Open for seasonal events. Admission fee.

Kansas Museum of History. 6425 SW Sixth St.; (785) 272-8681; www.kshs.org. Located on the historic Oregon Trail, the museum holds one of the country's largest prairie collections of memorabilia and historic objects. In the permanent gallery, "Voices from the Heartland: A Kansas Legacy" tells the story of Kansas, from its first inhabitants to modern-day culture. The past comes alive through interactive video displays and exhibits that feature an 1866 log house; a Southern Cheyenne buffalo-hide tepee; a locomotive with coal, dining, and sleeping cars attached; and more. You can catch the pioneer spirit as you browse through special areas, such as a children's Discovery Place, where hands-on discovery is encouraged. Closed Mon. Admission fee.

Kansas State Capitol Building. Tenth and Jackson Streets; (785) 296-3966; www.kshs .org. Original construction of the building began in 1861 but wasn't completed until 1903. The grounds surrounding the building contain monuments of interest, including a statue of Abraham Lincoln located southeast of the capitol. In 1915 Robert Merrell Gage was just out of school and living with his parents when he completed the figure of Lincoln in the barn adjacent to his parents' home.

Southwest of the capitol is another monument by Gage, dedicated to the pioneer women of Kansas. A bronze replica of the Statue of Liberty, at the northwest section of Capitol Square, and a replica of the Liberty Bell, at the east side of Capitol Square, complete the grouping.

Inside the building, murals by John Steuart Curry and David Overmyer tell an unusual pioneer story. Check out the huge panel of a furious John Brown on the second floor. Guided tours are offered daily Mon through Fri. The building is also open on weekends just to look around. Free.

Mulvane Art Museum. 1700 SW Jewell St. on the Washburn University campus; (785) 231-1124; www.washburn.edu. Built in 1922, this is the oldest visual-arts museum in the state. It offers changing exhibits from its permanent collection and focuses on contemporary art from the Mountain-Plains region. The exterior courtyard features sculptures and fountains, along with native wildflowers. Closed Mon. Free.

Old Prairie Town. 124 NW Fillmore St.; (785) 368-3888. Old-fashioned fun can be had at this unusual city park. It features 5.5 acres of living history that includes a restored 1870 Victorian mansion, a log cabin, a train depot, a one-room schoolhouse, a stone barn, a drugstore, and botanical gardens.

The Potwin Drug Store is worth seeing. A 1920s-style building was designed to house fixtures that were once part of Edelblute's Drug Store in Potwin, Kansas. There is a superb back bar and marble counter perfect for sipping sodas. On the second floor of the Potwin Drug Store, professional, medical, and dental offices appear as they would have a century ago. Also on the park premises is the Mulvane General Store, featuring yesteryear decor and gift items for sale.

Staffed by volunteers, the park offers special meals for groups and organizations. One of the most popular and original dinners is served at fireside tables in the Ward Cabin. The hearthside-cooked food includes ham or smoked turkey, sweet potatoes, Irish potatoes, spiced fruit, baked biscuits, and cookies; homemade ice cream is served as well. The family-style fare is offered from Oct 15 through Mar 15. Reservations are required. Old Prairie Town also features an elegant Victorian dinner, served buffet-style in the dining room of the mansion. You get a choice of entree, salad, and vegetable, plus homemade scones and ice cream for dessert. A minimum of 25 persons is required, as are reservations. Admission fee. Open daily.

where to eat

Annie's Place. Gage Shopping Center, 4014 Gage Center Dr.; (785) 273-0848.This family-owned restaurant bakes its buns fresh daily, along with dinner rolls, cinnamon rolls, and desserts. The baker is visible through a "showroom" in the restaurant. Annie's also grinds prime beef to make its famous gourmet burgers. Don't forget to try the renowned "hot air fries," cooked without grease. Ask for a side order of chicken gravy, which is served with chunks of white-meat chicken. $$.

Paisano's Ristorante. Fleming Place, 4043 SW Tenth St.; (785) 273-0100. Like its Lawrence, Kansas, counterpart, Paisano's serves superior Italian food. Appetizers include tasty mushroom caps stuffed with sausage and baked in white wine cream sauce. Entrees include veal and chicken dishes, Pesce al Vino Bianco (lobster, shrimp, scallops, crab, and whitefish in a sage and garlic cream sauce), and penne primavera (penne pasta sautéed in extra-virgin olive oil, garlic, and fresh basil sauce, then tossed with vegetables and topped with crumbled Gorgonzola cheese). The portions are large and the prices reasonable. Early-bird lunch special: Entrees are half-price before 11:30 a.m. Open daily for lunch and dinner. $$.

The Plantation Steak House. 6646 N. Topeka Blvd.; (785) 246-1933. A longtime favorite in Topeka, The Plantation recently closed, remodeled, and reopened under new owners. With a fresh atmosphere, it's still one of the best steak options in the state of Kansas. Open for dinner only. Closed Sun. $$.

where to stay

Brickyard Barn Inn. 4020 NW Twenty-fifth St.; (785) 235-0057; www.brickyardbarninn .com. This 1927 dairy barn has been converted into an elegant country inn with an inviting pool and hot tub. The 3 guest rooms are furnished with antiques and have private baths. A good choice for business travel and romantic getaways, the Brickyard Barn Inn features a full or continental breakfast served in relaxing surroundings. As a "private party facility," it is also available for corporate entertaining, weddings, luncheons, cocktail parties, and dinners. $$.

Senate Luxury Suites. 900 SW Tyler St.; (800) 488-3188 or (785) 233-5050; www.senate suites.com. As intimate as a bed-and-breakfast and as grand as a first-class hotel, the Senate Luxury Suites was originally built in the 1920s as an elegant apartment building. Today, the location appeals to business and leisure travelers alike, with 52 elegantly furnished suites, some with kitchenettes, some with hot tubs and fireplaces. Guests are treated to a complimentary breakfast. $$–$$$.

day trip 03

west

native stone scenic byway:
wamego, ks; alma, ks

The scene is miles of rolling hills and prairie under a sweeping sky. Native bluestem prairie grass follows vast stretches of virgin land in a seemingly endless vista. At times the expanse is so immense that one can see the curve of the earth. Sky and land merge as one. It takes the breath away.

Where is this? Surely not Kansas. It's supposed to be flat. It shouldn't look like New Mexico or Montana. But it does along Skyline–Mill Creek Drive, an offshoot of the Native Stone Scenic Byway. The drive is clearly marked, and the byway takes you past land covered with stone fences. A historical marker tells you that the 1867 law abolishing open range provided payment to landowners for building and maintaining the venerable stone fences that still stand today. The only sound is your car as it hums along the road, and if you stop along the way and sit quietly, you can almost feel the 1800s surround you: The buffalo, the Indians, the pioneers—they were here, and it's hard to tell where the past stops and the present begins.

wamego, ks

A small community of 4,000, the town is located on the Vermillion River, where Louis Vieux, a Potawatomie Indian, operated the first ferry along the Oregon Trail. Wamego is also the birthplace of Walter P. Chrysler, who built the car named after him. The annual Tulip Festival, held in April at the city park, offers a beautiful floral display, along with entertainment and

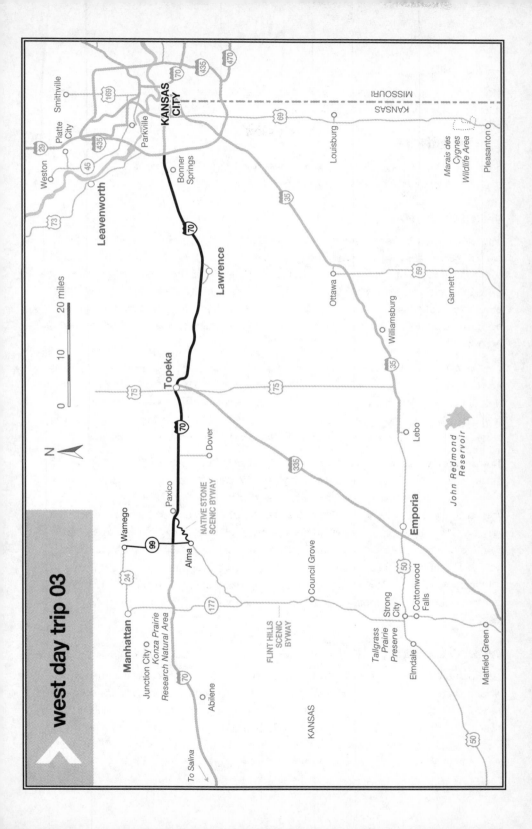

west day trip 03

food. For more information: Wamego Area Chamber of Commerce, 529 Lincoln Ave.; (785) 456-7849; www.wamegochamber.com.

getting there

From downtown Kansas City, drive west on I-70 about 90 miles to the exit 328 for Wamego and Alma. Head north on KS 99 to Wamego.

where to go

The Columbian Theatre Museum and Art Center. 521 Lincoln Ave.; (800) 899-1893 or (785) 456-2029; www.columbiantheatre.com. In 1994 a $1.8-million renovation restored the luster and elegance to this century-old theater. Rare 1893 murals, the only remaining set of decorative art from the 1893 Chicago World's Fair, grace the walls of the 250-seat theater, which features a guest-artist series, musical concerts, drama and dance productions, educational programs, and regional art exhibits. Docent-guided tours are by appointment. Admission fee (for events).

Dutch Mill. East side of City Park, Fourth Street; (785) 456-2040 or (785) 456-9119.This is Kansas's only authentic operating stone Dutch mill. Built in 1879 and listed on the National Register of Historic Places, the mill overlooks the beautiful city park—a perfect place for picnicking. The mill grinds wheat to flour while you watch, and you can purchase products to take back home. An adjacent museum contains historical and American Indian artifacts.

The Marvelous Land of Oz Museum. 511 Lincoln Ave.; (866) 458-TOTO; www.oz museum.com. A Wamego native began collecting *Wizard of Oz* items as a child and has now donated more than 2,000 pieces to this magical museum. As you enter, you find yourself in the Gale barnyard looking at the weathered farmhouse Dorothy flew in over the rainbow. The museum progresses chronologically through both the movie and the books by L. Frank Baum, taking visitors through Munchkinland, the Haunted Forest, and Emerald City. An in-house theater runs original black-and-white silent *Wizard of Oz* movies. A gift shop should satisfy any cravings you have for *Wizard of Oz* memorabilia. If not, an Oz festival in October brings remaining actors from the movie to sign autographs. Admission fee. Open daily.

where to eat

Friendship House. 507 Ash St.; (785) 456-9616. The bakery items sold here use stone-ground flour from the Dutch Mill and are made from scratch each day along with tasty sandwiches, homemade soups, breads, and pastries that include cookies, muffins, and sweet rolls. Weekly menu items include bread pudding, fresh-baked pie (Fri), and honey wheat bierocks, unique hamburger and cabbage pocket sandwiches. Work by local artists and crafters is also on display and for sale. Open for lunch Tues through Sat. $.

alma, ks

Alma is considered the heart of the Native Stone region and here you can see numerous buildings, fences, and natural formations made out of the limestone. KS 99 and KS 4 are the key routes to follow, but feel free to explore along any public roads to appreciate this region's natural beauty. For information about the Native Stone Scenic Byway, call (785) 765-4655 or visit www.ksbyways.org.

getting there

From Wamego, head south on KS 99 toward Alma and you will access the Native Stone Scenic Byway, clearly marked by signs.

where to go

Alma Creamery. 509 E. Third St.; (785) 765-3522; www.almacreamery.com. For more than 60 years, the Alma Creamery has been making cheese by hand, the old-fashioned way. Today people call it "artisan cheese." The gift shop sells the cheese, along with Kansas wines and other treats appropriate for a picnic at several area locations. Tours are offered, but advanced notice is requested. Closed Sun.

Grandma Hoerner's Foods. 31862 Thompson Rd.; (785) 765-2300; www.grandmahoerners .com. You've probably seen the Grandma Hoerner's label in area grocery stores and specialty food shops, but here you can see how the applesauce and other goodies are bottled from all-natural, organic ingredients. Or you can simply pick up some of your favorite items in the outlet store for prices better than you'll find elsewhere. And for the record, there was a real Grandma Hoerner. Just ask her grandson Duane McCoy who owns the family business. Closed Sun.

Echo Cliff Park. Between Eskridge and Dover on KS 4—watch for signs; (785) 256-6050. Plan a picnic at this beautiful park, and don't forget to pack your camera. You'll feel like you are in Colorado or places more renowned for their natural beauty than Kansas. An old iron bridge crosses Mission Creek, and of course, shout or yodel to hear your own echo. Open daily. Free.

where to stay

1878 Sage Inn and Stagecoach Stop. 13553 SW KS 4, Dover; (785) 256-6050 or (800) 466-6736; www.historicsageinn.com. History surrounds you at this historic stagecoach stop that shows exterior scars from numerous gunfights and attacks by Indians more than 125 years ago when this was the wild, wild West. As you climb the narrow, original stairs to the second floor, it's easy to imagine the weary travelers who made this climb before. However, the surroundings provided to you by owners Ken and Joan Benjamin are certainly more comfortable than those of the late 1800s. Joan's stuffed French toast for breakfast will fill you up for the rest of the day. A gift shop on the property also carries a few antiques. $$.

day trip 04

west

the little apple:
manhattan, ks

manhattan, ks

Touting itself as the "Little Apple," this thriving college town has a charm all its own, and quite different from its sunflower rival in Lawrence.

Kansas State University and the K-State Wildcat football team are located here, and home games are held on "Wildcat Weekends," drawing thousands of fans who converge on the city wearing purple to participate in numerous events and activities that are part of the fun.

The university also boasts scientific research that is on the cutting edge of agricultural technology. Thanks to techniques instituted here, K-State has produced great-tasting hormone- and antibiotic-free beef, poultry, pork, bread, pasta, pastry, milk, eggs, and ice cream.

Manhattan is a pretty place to visit. The streets are filled with lovely homes and venerable shade trees that offer respite on a hot Kansas day. Just a short drive from here is the Konza Prairie, a Nature Conservancy Preserve that features a pristine and beautiful landscape with a hiking trail open to the public. Manhattan is also the starting point for one of the most gorgeous scenic drives in America, according to *National Geographic's Guide to Scenic Highways and Byways*.

You'll want to spend more than a day here, so it's fortunate that the city has plenty of good restaurants, shops, and places to stay. For more information: Manhattan Convention and Visitors Bureau, 501 Poyntz Ave.; (785) 776-8829; www.manhattancvb.org.

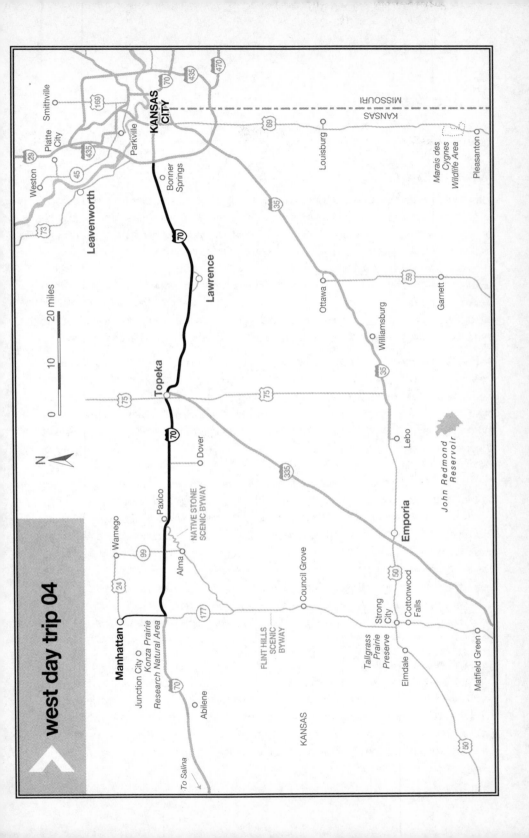

getting there

Manhattan is located about 120 miles west of Kansas City, a straight 2-hour drive on I-70. Remember the change for the toll booths.

where to go

Flint Hills Discovery Center. 315 S. Third St.; (785) 587-2726; www.flinthillsdiscovery .org. One of the most exciting developments in Manhattan, KS, since the color purple, this brand, spankin' new facility is 35,000 square feet dedicated to understanding and appreciating the Flint Hills region. Focusing on 22 counties in central Kansas, the center encompasses the geology and soil science of the Flint Hills. Walk underground under the tall grass prairie to see the root systems of prairie wildflowers and witness the prairie on fire in order to understand how important such destruction is for the health of the prairie. Numerous hands-on, interactive exhibits help children and adults appreciate the impact of the Flint Hills and the tall grass prairie on the much larger global environment. Open daily. Admission fee.

Fort Riley. Located 10 miles west of Manhattan at exit 301 on I-70; (785) 239-2737; www .riley.army.mil. The grounds of historic Fort Riley hold colorful exhibits that showcase the history of the Great Plains. The beautifully restored Custer House stands as the only set of surviving officers' quarters from the fort's early history. Built in 1855 of native limestone, the quarters are nearly identical to the house that George Armstrong Custer and his wife occupied while residing at the fort. The Custer House also depicts military and family life on the western frontier during the Indian wars.

The US Cavalry and First Infantry Division Museums are housed in separate buildings on the Main Post. The US Cavalry Museum, located in Building 205 on Custer Avenue, houses displays that chronicle the years of the American mounted horse soldier from the Revolutionary War to 1950. Adjacent to the US Cavalry Museum, the First Infantry Division Museum offers the history of this decorated division in life-size dioramas that portray the trenches and battlefields of both World War I and World War II, as well as the jungles of Vietnam and the sands of Desert Storm. Buffalo are still kept in a nearby corral as a further reminder of the history of America before fast-food franchises and tract housing bulldozed away much of the tallgrass prairie. Open daily. Free. Be prepared to show photo ID when entering the military base.

Kansas State University. 1700 Anderson Ave.; (785) 532-6011; www.k-state.edu. The 668-acre campus is located throughout Manhattan. Founded in 1863, K-State has a number of internationally recognized programs that attract teachers and students from around the globe. Its College of Agriculture offers the only worldwide programs in grain, milling, baking, and feed science and management. Its College of Architecture, Planning, and Design, where all programs are professionally accredited, is one of only five public, comprehensive design schools in the nation.

The College of Veterinary Medicine is internationally recognized as a center for the study of livestock diseases. It has a top-notch veterinary medicine program and hospital—complete with emergency rooms for both large and small animals—that is considered to be one of the finest in the country. (It's not unusual to find a trio of doctors simultaneously performing eye surgery on a cat, leg surgery on a llama, and something you don't want to know about on a cow.)

As far as cutting-edge research goes, the Department of Animal Sciences and Industry has invented a new steam process to kill those nasty bacteria that thrive on uncooked meat and has also created a way to produce hormone- and antibiotic-free dairy products.

K-State's campus holds several attractions, including the following:

Aggieville. Located on the southeast edge of the K-State campus. This full-service shopping area is a center for student activity and is the oldest shopping center of its kind in Kansas.

Marianna Kistler Beach Museum of Art. 701 Beach Ln.; (785) 532-7718; http://beach.k-state.edu. A 17,000-square-foot-expansion in 2007 added 2 galleries, bringing the museum's capacity to 6 galleries. The museum promotes appreciation of the fine arts through exhibitions of works by popular regional artists and through various educational and outreach programs. It also offers displays held in conjunction with other museums of art around the country. As a Lending Affiliate for the National Gallery of Art in Washington, D.C., the museum enables teachers to borrow educational resource materials developed by the National Gallery. Closed Mon and during school breaks. Free.

University Gardens, Butterfly Conservatory, and Insect Zoo. (785) 532-2122; www.k-state.edu/butterfly. Located at Denison Avenue, north of Claflin Road, the University Gardens is a work-in-progress that, when completed, will be 19 acres of hardscape and tested ornamental plant material in different aesthetic settings. Included in the garden is a visitor information center with computers and other resource materials for public use. Located in an old dairy barn is the Butterfly Conservatory, which houses about 50 species of tropical plants that are home to dozens of species of butterflies. The best time to see butterflies in action is between 10 a.m. and noon. Maybe not as beautiful, but certainly as interesting, is the Insect Zoo, where you'll see many exhibits of live insects and their relatives, as well as displays featuring preserved specimens of exotic butterflies, moths, beetles, and other arthropods. The Butterfly Conservancy is open 7 days a week. The Insect Zoo is open Mon, Wed, Fri, and Sat. Free.

Milford Lake. Located 4 miles northwest of Junction City, c/o Milford State Park, 8811 State Park Rd., Milford; (785) 238-3014; www.kdwp.state.ks.us/milford. Kansas's largest reservoir is one of the state's most productive for anglers. Walleye, crappie, smallmouth bass, and wiper—a hybrid between white and striped bass—abound in the lake waters. Weighing 6 to 8 pounds, they join up with white bass and cruise together in the early summer to the main part of Milford to search for their favorite food of shad. According to experts, that's the time the wipers and white bass are easy to catch. With more than 16,000 surface acres and 163 miles of shoreline, there are plenty of fish around for the eating. Milford Lake and its surrounding 21,000 acres make up one of Kansas's prime outdoor habitats, and the body of water is one of the more scenic lakes in the area.

The Milford Nature Center/Fish Hatchery is located at the base of Milford Dam and offers displays and exhibits that explore the surrounding natural area. Free.

Strecker-Nelson Gallery. 406½ Poyntz Ave.; (785) 537-2099; www.strecker-nelson gallery.com. This upstairs gallery highlights the work of about 40 local artists whose media include ceramics, silk, and oil. If you enjoy the beauty of the Flint Hills, you will find many of those images reflected in the work here. Closed Sun.

Sunset Zoo. 2333 Oak St.; (785) 587-2737; www.sunsetzoo.com. This 56-acre zoo may be small, but it is one of the most romantic zoos in the Midwest. That's because love is always in bloom here and lots of animals grow up healthy thanks to the zoo's excellent breeding program. There are 13 endangered species in the zoo, including snow leopards and red pandas that have managed to thrive in captivity.

Other zoos, including the famed San Diego Zoo, send their animals here for breeding purposes because of the zoo's spectacular success rate at producing healthy zoo babies. The medical care for animals is unique. With K-State's renowned veterinary medical school and exotic medicine program available at all times, two K-State vets are employed by the zoo to monitor and care for the animals and their offspring. Open daily. Admission fee.

Tuttle Creek Lake. 5020–B Tuttle Creek Blvd.,15 miles north of I-70 on KS 177; (785) 539-7941; www.kdwp.state.ks.us. The 12,500-acre lake is surrounded by 104 miles of irregular, wooded shoreline, and its wildlife, water, and climate make it a good spot for outdoor recreation. White bass, crappie, channel catfish, and spawn fishing draw anglers, who come in spring and summer to drop a line in any of the numerous sites around the lake that are available for fishing. Other activities include boating, waterskiing, swimming, hunting, picnicking, camping, and other outdoor sports. Pontoon and fishing boat rentals, fishing supplies, fuel, boat-slip rentals, and concessions are available at the marina. Dinner cruises aboard a houseboat are offered for small groups. Free.

where to shop

Aggieville. Southeast of the K-State campus, Manhattan; (785) 776-8050; www.aggieville .org. The first shopping center in Kansas is named for the former K-State Aggies. Today it is a pre- and postgame host to Wildcat sporting events. Aggieville offers more than 100 businesses that feature shopping, dining, dancing, and nightlife, all within walking distance of K-State and concentrated in a little over 4 blocks. Everything from barbecue to women's clothing can be found here. Part of the fun is trying out the food, which ranges from cappuccino and croissants to Cajun jambalaya and gumbo.

where to eat

Call Hall. Dairy and Poultry Science Building, Claflin and Mid-Campus Road, on the K-State campus; (785) 532-1292. Although the locals know about it, newcomers seldom realize that a place like this could actually exist outside a health food store. Thanks to the scientific laboratories in the Dairy and Poultry Science Building, all the superb-tasting milk, butter, cheese, and ice cream comes straight from the cow to your mouth, hormone-free with no antibiotics. There are 40 flavors of ice cream that change daily, and each one is better than the one before it. You might want to bring a cooler and plenty of ice to take back some of the terrific cheese and butter sold here. Closed Sun. $.

Harry's. 418 Poyntz Ave., inside the Wareham Hotel; (785) 537-1300; www.harrysmanhattan.com. Turn-of-the-20th-century elegance, complete with wingback chairs, crystal chandeliers, and cloth-covered tables, highlights the ambience at this establishment. The wine list is extensive, and the menu features hand-cut Kansas choice beef, fresh seafood, chicken, and pasta. The raspberry cheesecake is delightful and so is the apple pie. Closed Sun. $$–$$$.

Hibachi Hut. 608 N. Twelfth St.; (785) 539-9393; www.hibachihut.com. The Cajun-inspired menu offers everything from boudin (rice and pork Cajun sausage) to red beans and rice, jambalaya, and bayou catfish served with jambalaya on the side. The Cajun Feast includes gumbo to red beans and rice, and choice of blackened catfish fillet or top sirloin, served with cornbread, plus homemade bread pudding with whiskey sauce. $–$$.

Little Apple Brewing Company. 1110 Westloop Shopping Center; (785) 539-5500. Five refreshing handcrafted brews and certified Angus beef steaks are the claim to fame at this friendly restaurant and pub that caters to football lovers. $–$$.

The Chef Cafe. 111 S. Fourth St.; (785) 537-6843, www.thechefcafe.com. Voted the Best Breakfast in Kansas, the Chef has been a presence in Manhattan since shortly after World War II. Despite being closed for a few years, the Chef still draws crowds, particularly for breakfast. The signature item is the Fajita Scramble, but the Stacked French Toach with Caramel Cream Cheese is a reason to come back for breakfast again the next day. Open daily for breakfast and lunch. $.

Cox Brothers Barbecue. 223 McCall Rd.; (785) 539-0770; www.coxbbq.com. A little bit Texas, a little bit Carolina and Memphis, but a whole lotta Kansas City influences the barbecue here. Seriously, barbecue is made to satisfy all taste buds here. The coleslaw is creamy and the turkey legs are Manhattan-style. You'll just have to ask about that. Open daily. $$.

where to stay

Guest Haus Bed-and-Breakfast. 1724 Sheffield Circle; (785) 776-6543; www.guesthaus .com. A Flint Hills view, a fish pond, and a cedar-lined walking path are part of the amenities here. Two antiques-filled guest rooms share a bath in the upstairs loft area. A continental breakfast is offered with your choice of room. $$ (no cards).

Morning Star. 617 Houston St.; (785) 587-9703; www.morningstaronthepark.com. Within just blocks of the K-State campus, Morning Star features large windows and an expansive front porch for watching the comings and goings around town or spending some quality time with Ginger and Lucy, the two resident Boston terriers. Each of the 5 guest rooms is a corner room with private bath and in-room whirlpool. Are you familiar with Greek omelets? If not, you'll be delighted when breakfast is served. No children. $$.

day trip 05

west

flint hills scenic byway:
konza prairie research natural area;
council grove, ks; tallgrass prairie
national preserve; cottonwood falls, ks

Flint Hills Scenic Byway (KS 177) runs for 84 miles meandering from Manhattan to Cassoday, through a region of rounded limestone hills covered with bluestem prairie. Along the way you'll reach the eastern segment of the Konza Prairie Research Natural Area, and from there you can visit the Tallgrass Prairie National Preserve, Kansas's first national park. Keep traveling south and you'll come to the bed-and-breakfast country of Council Grove and Cottonwood Falls. For more information on all eight Kansas scenic byways, visit www .ksbyways.org.

konza prairie research natural area

Owned by the Nature Conservancy and managed by Kansas State University for the purpose of scientific study of this natural ecosystem, the Konza Prairie is the most intensively studied grassland on earth.

getting there

Just south of Manhattan, the Konza Prairie Research Natural Area is easily viewed from adjacent highways. KS 177 parallels the eastern segment of the preserve, and I-70 runs

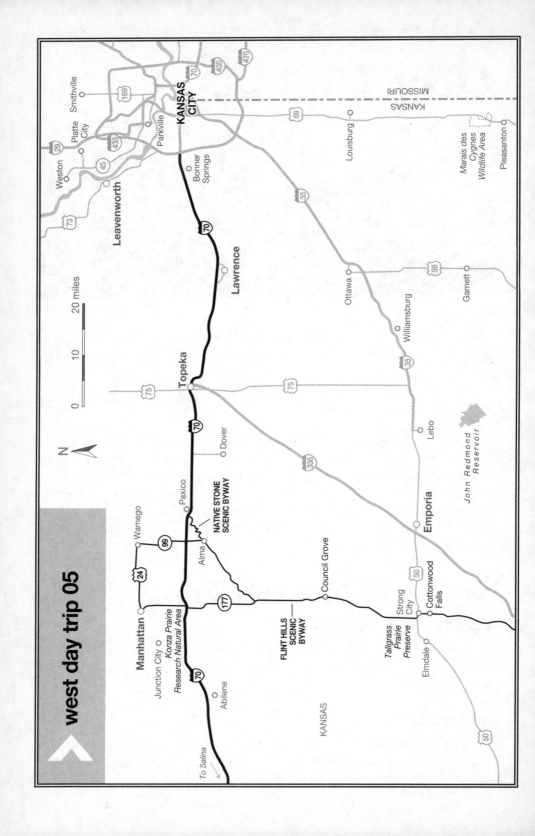

west day trip 05

along most of its southern border. To reach the Konza Prairie entrance from KS 177, drive to the east end of the Kansas River Bridge and turn onto McDowell Creek Road (County Road 901S). The entrance is about 6 miles down the road on the left. (From I-70 take exit 307 and drive northeast on McDowell Creek Road. The entrance is approximately 5 miles on your right.)

where to go

Konza Prairie Research Natural Area. (785) 587-0441; www.konza.k-state.edu. This scenic area, named for the Kanza Indians who once roamed here, covers more than 8,600 acres of unplowed, uncultivated land filled with 70 species of dominant grasses and more than 500 species of wildflowers, shrubs, and trees.

The bison herd that lives here is part of a scientific effort to study the effect of these native grazers upon the grasslands. Fire, along with innumerable animals who grazed here, shaped the landscape, and it is here at Konza that the effects of both are being investigated.

Most of the Konza Prairie Research Natural Area is closed to the public. However, a self-guided nature trail is open daily and trail maps are available at the front gate.

The Fall Visitors Day, offered every other year on even-numbered years, is filled with special tours and presentations. Tour guides are available with advance reservations. Pack

defining the flint hills

Draped in bluestem grasses and colorful wildflowers during warm weather, the Flint Hills are an ancient reminder of our planet's ecological history. This represents the largest tract of tallgrass prairie in North America that has never been broken by a plow or other man-made efforts. The surface of the Flint Hills is composed of lime- stone sediment and thin layers of chert (commonly known as flint) that were depos- ited by inland seas more than 200 million years ago.

Centuries of erosion formed the rugged, high escarpments and gently rolling landforms found in Chase County. Woodland Indians once roamed the area, and archaeological digs at Eldorado and Council Grove have unearthed many prehistoric campsites.

The early settlers in the area found that a combination of farming and ranching was not only possible in this region but often necessary for survival. Today's suc- cessful farmer-stockman must also use the rich bottomland soil for growing crops such as wheat, soybeans, corn, milo, and alfalfa, while employing the upland prairie, with its wonderful native grasses, for grazing cattle.

your binoculars, since deer and hawk sightings are a common occurrence. Open from dawn to dusk year-round. Free.

council grove, ks

The historic town of Council Grove got its name from a negotiated treaty between US commissioners and the Osage Indian chiefs in 1825, an agreement that granted whites safe passage along the Santa Fe Trail.

A camping and meeting place for explorers, soldiers, traders, and Native Americans, Council Grove offered ample water, grass, and abundant wood, making it a rendezvous point for wagon trains heading west.

John Fremont's expedition of 1845 and Colonel A. W. Doniphan's troops bound for Mexico in 1846 camped on this site. In 1849 the Overland Mail was established with the supply headquarters at Council Grove, followed the next year by monthly coach service.

Council Grove today offers a quaint shopping district, restaurants, and lodging.

The town offers an informative self-guided walking-tour brochure, filled with historic things to see that include the wheel ruts left by the wagon trains heading west; the Custer Elm, where George Armstrong Custer camped; and the Council Oak, named for the treaty signed beneath the tree by the Osage Indians and the US commissioners. For more information: Council Grove/Morris County Visitors Bureau, 207 W. Main St.; (620) 767-5413; www.councilgrove.com.

getting there

From Manhattan, follow KS 177 south 35 miles to Council Grove.

where to shop

The Apothecary Shops. 115–119 West Main St.; (800) 499-9747 or (620) 767-6731; www.aldrichapothecary.com. The Canopy, Aldrich Apothecary, and Santa Fe T-Shirt Shop constitute a grouping of stores that feature a pharmacy, a boutique, and one of the last remaining soda fountains in Kansas. The soda fountain was installed in the 1920s and is marked by distinctive tile that adorns the fountain front, an original back bar, and a brass foot rail. In addition to cherry phosphates, sodas, sundaes, and shakes, you can order a cup of gourmet coffee or some frozen yogurt to go.

The adjacent full-line pharmacy opened in 1892 and has been refurbished with a nostalgic charm highlighted by a restored pressed-tin ceiling and antique fixtures. The soda fountain and pharmacy are connected with the Santa Fe T-shirt shop, which specializes in T-shirts, gifts, and collectibles.

where to eat

Hays House 1857 Restaurant and Tavern. 112 W. Main St.; (620) 767-5911; www
.hayshouse.com. This National Historic Landmark was built in 1857 by Seth Hays, great-
grandson of Daniel Boone and cousin of Kit Carson. As the oldest continuously operated
restaurant west of the Mississippi, the tavern is an attraction on the Santa Fe National Historic Trail tour. In its early days it was host to theatricals, court proceedings, mail distribution,
and church services, as well as serving good food to all.

Now a comfortable stop for modern-day travelers, the Hays House offers delicious
foods served in a relaxed atmosphere. Specialties include aged Kansas beef, homemade
breads, and desserts. The Victorian-inspired second floor houses the Hays Tavern, which
offers a fully stocked bar in the evening. The restaurant also features several private dining
rooms. Open 7 days a week. $$.

where to stay

The Cottage House Hotel. 25 N. Neosho St.; (800) 727-7903 or (620) 767-6828; www
.cottagehousehotel.com. This restored Victorian hotel is on the National Register of Historic
Places and has been serving travelers for more than a century. It features modern comforts
in nostalgic surroundings and offers a relaxing atmosphere, with gazebo-style porches, a
sauna, and period furnishings. Each of the 26 rooms in the main hotel has a distinctive style.
Stained glass and a brass-and-iron bed are featured in the bridal chamber. A continental
breakfast is served each morning. $$.

tallgrass prairie national preserve

This unique cooperative between the National Park Trust and the National Park Service
contains 10,894 acres of tallgrass prairie, which is leased to the National Park Service.
Expansive rolling hills and wide-open vistas greet you as you experience the beauty of this
quiet land. From Apr 10 through Oct 31, a 7-mile bus tour is available to take you through
the area. The natural prairie cycle of climate, fire, and animal grazing has sustained this
beautiful land, where nearly 400 species of plants, 150 kinds of birds, 31 species of mammals, and assorted reptiles and amphibians reside.

Also at the preserve is the Z-Bar/Spring Hill Ranch, home of the original owner, Ste-
phen F. Jones. The 11-room structure, built with hand-cut native limestone, is characteristic
of the Second Empire style of 19th-century architecture. Also on the premises is a massive
3-story barn and Lower Fox Creek School, a one-room schoolhouse located on a nearby
hilltop. Brochures are available for self-guided tours. Docent tours are given hourly between
Apr 10 and Oct 31. Admission fee. Call (620) 273-8494 or visit www.nps.gov/tapr.

getting there

From downtown Kansas City, follow I-35 south to Emporia approximately 110 miles. Turn west on US 50 and travel about 20 miles to the intersection of KS 177. Turn north and travel 2 miles.

where to stay

Clover Cliff Ranch. Rural Route 1, Box 30–1, Elmdale; (800) 457-7406 or (620) 273-6698; www.clovercliff.com. Bring your own horse along to ride the trail that runs along this 4,000-acre working cattle ranch located east of Strong City, off US 50. Hiking, fishing, and general all-purpose relaxing are other amenities found at the ranch, which is listed on the National Register of Historic Places. The main house offers 4 guest rooms, 2 with private baths. There are also adjacent guest houses that are truly "homes away from home." The larger one features 2 bedrooms, a loft area with twin beds, a sitting room, 2 baths, kitchen facilities, a fireplace, and a television. The smaller guest house has 2 bedrooms, a sleeper sofa, 1 bath, kitchen facilities, a fireplace, and a television. Breakfast is served in the main house. Meetings, receptions, luncheons, or a tour and tea can also be scheduled. $$–$$$ (no cards).

cottonwood falls, ks

The oldest settlement in Chase County, the tiny hamlet of Cottonwood Falls is located in the center of the picturesque Flint Hills. The best time to visit the area is spring, fall, or early summer, rather than during a hot summer scorcher. Don't be fooled by appearances; there are plenty of things to see and do around the town, provided you know where to go. And come on Friday nights for free music in the streets. Every Friday night, musicians from around the region simply gather for an impromptu jam session that goes on for hours. For more information: Chase County Chamber of Commerce, 318 Broadway; (800) 431-6344; www.chasecountychamber.org.

getting there

When leaving the Tallgrass Prairie, turn south on KS 177 and travel just 3 miles into Cottonwood Falls.

where to go

Chase County Courthouse. Broadway and Pearl Streets; (620) 273-8469. Built in 1872 of native limestone, the courthouse is an impressive structure. Listed on the National Register of Historic Places, it remains the oldest courthouse in continual use in Kansas. Each year more than 6,000 visitors from around the country visit the structure, marveling at the

symphony on the prairie

The best seat in the house for this performance is a hay bale, facing west.

In the most unlikely, but undeniably natural and appropriate setting, the Kansas City Symphony has found a new audience in the annual **Symphony on the Prairie**. *Begun in 2006 as a 10th anniversary tribute to the Tallgrass National Prairie, the symphony has become an immediate and sold-out hit.*

The Symphony on the Prairie is held the second weekend in June, while the nights are still cool. Eighty-five musicians from the Kansas City Symphony perform under the stars, accompanied by singing cicadas and crickets, as the sun sets dramatically beyond the Flint Hills. Before the performance, visitors can take part in guided nature walks through the prairie, horse-drawn wagon rides, and a musical-instrument petting zoo. The location moves each year, but note that tickets go on sale in March and sell out quickly. Call (620) 273-8955 or visit www.symphonyinthe flinthills.org.

architectural design, stonework, and spiral staircase. Guided tours of the courthouse can be arranged in advance. Admission fee.

Chase County Historical Society Museum. 301 Broadway; (620) 273-8500. The museum holds historic memorabilia and artifacts of the area, including information about the demise of Knute Rockne, the famous Notre Dame coach who was killed when his airplane crashed in heavy fog near here in 1931. Donation requested. Closed Sun and Mon.

where to shop

Fiber Factory. 209 Broadway; (620) 273-8686. Watch century-old looms in operation. Customers can make their own rope on an original old-time rope machine. You can purchase hand-woven rugs, placemats, blankets, and scarves to take home. There's also an unexpected, yet interesting, display of old camera equipment and other items used by the Kansas Bureau of Investigation in solving crimes in this area years ago. Open daily.

Flint Hills and Tallgrass Gallery. 321 Broadway; (620) 273-6454. The gallery features the paintings of Chase County artists, along with custom-made spurs, knives, belt buckles, and hat racks. The shop also sells jewelry, Indian baskets, drums, and stained glass. Closed Sun.

Jim Bell & Son. 322 Broadway; (620) 273-6381. If you're looking for a unique shopping experience, try this place. The restored building was opened in 1927 as a retail store for real cowboys. It still supplies any piece of custom-made tack the working cowboy needs, plus there's a boot and saddle repair shop located in the store's basement in case you decide to gallop into town on your horse. Even nonworking cowboys and cowgirls can find the latest styles in western and casual wear for the entire family, from boots and hats to outdoor wear, hunting apparel, and more. Open daily.

where to eat

Emma Chase Cafe. 317 Broadway; (620) 273-6020; www.emmachasecafe.com. The restaurant serves delightful sandwiches, entrees, ice cream, and desserts in a laid-back setting. If you choose to fly early into Cottonwood Falls the fourth Sunday of the month, owner Sue Smith will pick you up at the airport for breakfast. Call before you go. Visit on the first Friday of the month for catfish and music by local performers. $.

Grand Central Hotel and Grill. 215 Broadway; (800) 951-6763; www.grandcentralhotel .com. Looking for a little espresso, Asti Spumante, champagne, or Carmel Valley sauvignon blanc to perk up your day? What better place to find it than smack in the middle of a vast Midwestern plain.

Located in the center of the Flint Hills, along the one and only main thoroughfare of town, this restaurant specializes in Sterling Silver, a line of Certified Premium USDA Choice steaks so terrific that you'll think you've died and gone to Kansas.

Entrees are served with salad, choice of potato or vegetable, and fresh bread and butter. Dessert can be Grand Central cheesecake topped with cherries or almond amaretto or homemade bread pudding with New Orleans bourbon sauce. The full-service restaurant offers lunch and dinner to the public and an elegant continental breakfast daily to hotel guests. Closed Sun. $$–$$$.

where to stay

Grand Central Hotel. 215 Broadway; (800) 951-6763 or (620) 273-8381; www.grand centralhotel.com. Definitely not your little roadside prairie motel, the Grand Central Hotel is a must-stop on your way through Kansas. The AAA 4-diamond hotel and restaurant opened in 1884 and reopened in 1995; the hotel has been restored beyond its original elegance. Located 2 miles from the Tallgrass Prairie National Preserve and 1 block west of scenic KS 177, the Grand Central offers 10 beautifully appointed rooms, all designed with a western flair. Its full-service restaurant offers lunch and dinner to the public and an elegant continental breakfast daily to hotel guests.

For starters, there are queen- and king-size beds draped with Egyptian cotton duvets and sheets purchased in Paris. Plush VIP robes, Jacuzzi showers, full concierge service, complimentary continental breakfast, and meeting rooms for private dining and corporate retreats are offered. A very nice wheelchair-accessible room on the first floor has its own outdoor porch. The hotel is happy to provide guests with a variety of outdoor experiences that include nature hiking, horseback riding, and fishing. $$.

day trip 06

west

presidential town:
abilene, ks

abilene, ks

The name Abilene immediately conjures up images of the wild, wild West, with cowboys, cattle herds, and Main Street shootouts at the end of the Chisholm Trail. Although that image was certainly true in the mid-1800s, Abilene is now a quiet town that gave birth to one of the United States' most decorated military officers and beloved presidents.

Abilene comes from a Bible scripture that means "city of the plains," and although "city" may be a stretch, it is certainly a pleasant community on plains worthy of exploration. Too often, Kansas Citians blow through Abilene on I-70 on their way to more glamorous destinations at the other end of the interstate. However, those who stop for just a few moments or a few days will find a town void of many chain restaurants and commercial establishments, but with a vibrant downtown, lovely neighborhoods of historic homes, and a gentler pace of life.

Founded in a small dug-out homestead and stagecoach stop in 1857, Abilene had grown only slightly when the railroads began to reach across the Plains after the Civil War. The railroads meant a way to move cattle to market on the East Coast, and the Chisholm Trail brought cattle and cowboys from southern Texas by the millions beginning in 1867. For the next five years, more than three million cattle arrived in Abilene before being shipped east by rail. Some days as many as 5,000 cowboys received their pay for moving the cattle along the trail, so undoubtedly, things got a little rowdy downtown.

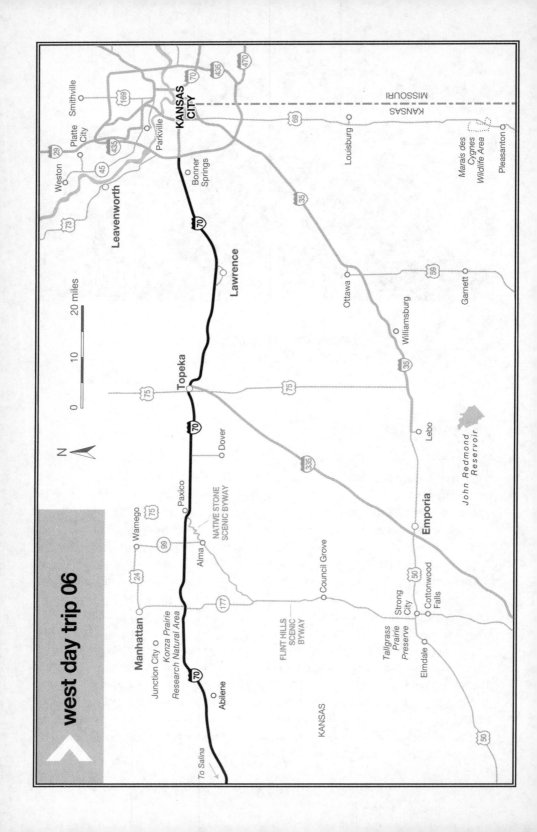

west day trip 06

Today you can learn much of the history of Abilene via a trolley ride that departs from the restored train depot. The influx of wealth at the end of the 19th century resulted in several elegant homes, two of which have been restored and are open to tour today. However, Abilene is perhaps best known as the home of Dwight D. Eisenhower, the leader of Allied Forces in Europe during World War II, who became the 34th president of the United States. He and his five brothers were raised here, and a tour of the presidential library and grounds is a must for anyone visiting the community.

Several other museums, restaurants, and a professional theater company provide plenty of activity for a few hours or a few days.

getting there

From Kansas City, take I-70 west 150 miles to exit 275.

where to go

Abilene Convention and Visitors Bureau. 201 NW Second St.; (800) 569-5915; www .abilenekansas.org. Located in the historic Union Pacific Depot, this where to find out the latest developments in town, as well as take one of the Trolley Rides through Historic Downtown.

Abilene Smoke Valley Excursion Train. 200 SE Fifth St.; (785) 263-1077; www.asvrr .org. Enjoy the Kansas countryside as you ride in a century-old dining car or open-air gondola car, or, for a special fare, you can ride in the caboose or the engine. The train is powered by a 1945 ALCO S–1 engine originally designed for World War II submarines. A gift shop in the depot carries all sorts of train memorabilia. Closed Nov through Apr.

American Indian Art Center. 206 S. Buckeye Ave.; (785) 263-0090. This unassuming facility showcases the artwork of nearly 100 American Indian artisans, representing 30 tribes from the region. American Indian history books, music, and weaponry are also for sale, but the good-natured humor from owner Patt Murphy, a member of the Ioway-Sauk Tribe, is free. Closed Wed. Free.

Bow Studio and Gallery. 921 S. Buckeye Ave.; (785) 263-7166; www.bowsart.com. Take a piece of native Kansas home with you after a visit to the studio of Inga and Bob Bow. The wildflower garden that fills their property is for more than show. This is where Inga gathers ideas and materials for her work. You'll find leaves, flowers, wheat, and other designs of nature pressed and painted into original clay designs and fired on site. Open daily.

Heritage Center of Dickinson County. 412 S. Campbell St.; (785) 263-2681; www .heritagecenterdk.com. Here's where you can learn about the wicked history of Abilene in the days when it was known as one of the wickedest towns in the West. From jail records to antique guns confiscated from rowdy cowboys, the artifacts here tell the story of the conflicts between American Indians, white settlers, the military, and cattle herders more than a century ago. Within the museum is the Museum of Independent Telephony, which chronicles the early days of telephone service in small, rural towns like Abilene. In a separate building behind the museum is an operating C. W. Parker Carousel, one of the original hand-carved track-operated machines created by the Abilene-based entertainment company in the early 1900s. Open daily. Admission fee.

Eisenhower Center. 200 SE Fourth St.; (785) 263-4751 or (877) RING-IKE; www.eisenhower.archives.gov. This complex tells the remarkable life story of native son Dwight D. Eisenhower, one of America's most honored military leaders and the 34th president of the United States. Historians of all genres and generations will appreciate the details presented from World War II and the D-day invasion led by then-General Eisenhower, as well as the global conflicts that followed World War II. Plan on spending several hours here touring the Eisenhower home, library, museum, and memorial chapel, where the former President and First Lady are buried. Fee for those 16 and older for the museum only. Open daily.

Greyhound Hall of Fame. 407 S. Buckeye Ave.; (785) 263-3000; www.greyhoundhalloffame.com. Sharon and Chig, two retired racing dogs, will greet you before you begin a self-guided tour, which showcases the "Sport of Queens." You may pet greyhounds and learn about the history of the world's fastest dogs all the way back to prehistoric times. Races and auctions of these animals are held here each Apr and Oct. Free. Open daily.

Seelye Mansion. 1105 N. Buckeye Ave.; (785) 263-1084; www.seeleyemansion.org. Step back in time as you are guided through this 1905 Georgian-style mansion built by Dr. and Mrs. A. B. Seelye, the name that for years was associated with rural medical care and patent medicines. Stroll through the gardens and learn about the patent medicine manufacturing business located in Abilene that once rivaled the names of Bayer and Eli Lilly. Built in the early years of the 20th century, the home contains many items and fixtures purchased at the 1904 World's Fair in St. Louis. Thomas Edison worked with the architect to bring lighting and other modern conveniences to the home. A basement-level bowling alley and a third-level ballroom speak to the opulence found on the Great Plains during this period. Christmas is an especially beautiful time to visit the Seelye Mansion to see the 40 decorated Christmas trees and more than 200 poinsettias throughout the home. Open for tours daily. Admission fee.

where to eat

Brookville Hotel. 105 E. Lafayette Ave.; (785) 263-2244; www.brookvillehotel.com. Since the 1870s, the Brookville Hotel, once located in the little town of Brookville, has been famous for its family-style fried-chicken dinners—the only thing on the menu here. Now the fourth generation of the Martin family continues the tradition in a replica of the original hotel from Brookville built in Abilene in 1999. Many of the furnishings are original to the old hotel. This Kansas institution received a 2007 James Beard Foundation America's Classics Award. Closed Mon and Tues. $$.

The Kirby House. 205 NE Third St.; (785) 263-7336. This elegantly restored home-turned-restaurant was built in 1885 by Thomas Kirby, a banker in early Abilene. Coconut walnut bread or a chilled strawberry soup are signature items here, but a little heartier fare is available with country-fried steak or a half-pound hamburger on sesame-seed bun. A Kirby House cookbook for sale on the premises has these recipes and other regional favorites. For special occasions, ask about dining in the cupola. Closed Sun and Mon. $.

Mr. K's Farmhouse. 407 S. Van Buren St.; (785) 263-7995; www.mrksfarmhouse.com. This rambling old farmhouse was a favorite of Dwight and Mamie Eisenhower when they lived in or returned to Abilene, and it's still popular today for homemade pies, roast beef, and huge pork chops. You may want to keep it quiet if you eat here on your birthday. You might just receive a paddling from one of the many wooden paddles hanging from the ceiling, a tradition that was begun when Dwight Eisenhower dined here on his 75th birthday. Closed Mon. $–$$.

where to stay

Abilene's Victorian Bed and Breakfast Inn. 820 NW Third St.; (785) 263-7774; www .abilenesvictorianinn.com. This home dates to 1900 and was once the family home of "Swede" Hazlett, a close, personal friend of President Eisenhower. Today the home has 6 spacious guest rooms across the street from Eisenhower Park and within walking distance of downtown. Homemade cookies await your check-in, as well as board games, a video library, and a spacious porch for relaxing. Jay and Adrian Potter keep everything here in tip-top condition, and Adrian, a trained chef, prepares a full breakfast to your liking each morning. $–$$.

worth more time:
salina, ks

As long as you are in Abilene, drive just another 25 miles west on I-70 to Salina. Or, on your next trip to Colorado, plan an overnight stop in Salina. Either way, make sure you're wearing your Lee jeans when you come to town. This is where Henry David Lee founded a mercantile company in the late 1800s that eventually became Lee Jeans, now based in Merriam, Kansas.

The **Historic Lee District** in downtown Salina is now a pedestrian-friendly shopping district with more than 300 businesses. A number of festivals and special events take place here throughout the year.

Salina is also home to the **Smoky Hill Vineyards and Winery,** a fabulous wildlife center, and NJCAA Women's Basketball Tournament each March that makes the hoops-lovers in Lawrence pause to take notice.

For more information, contact the **Salina Chamber of Commerce,** 120 W. Ash St.; (785) 827-9301; www.salinakansas.org.

northwest

day trip 01

northwest

military memorabilia, mansions, museums & memorials:
leavenworth, ks; atchison, ks; hiawatha, ks

leavenworth, ks

As the "First City of Kansas," Leavenworth was at the forefront of the transportation revolution. From boat to wagon to railroad, the town led the way in opening the vast resources of America. The Leavenworth Landing Park, located adjacent to the Missouri River, features exhibits that portray the town's part in forging a path through the American West.

All along the Overland Trails, US Cavalry fortifications such as Fort Leavenworth sprang up to defend western settlement. Between 1838 and 1845 a military road was constructed through the Indian Territory to connect Fort Leavenworth in Kansas and Fort Gibson in Oklahoma. Throughout the years the road was traveled by soldiers, immigrants, Indians, outlaws, and traders.

Today the old military road no longer exists, but modern US 69 and other connecting pathways located near its original route have been designated the Frontier Military Scenic Byway. Fort Leavenworth and Fort Scott, two of the remaining historic Kansas forts lying along that route, are open to tour today.

Established by Colonel Henry Leavenworth in 1827, Fort Leavenworth was a cantonment to protect wagon trains headed west and to help maintain peace with the Native Americans. Leavenworth was also the starting point for exploration parties. When travel to California began in the 1840s, thousands of prairie schooners passed through the posts.

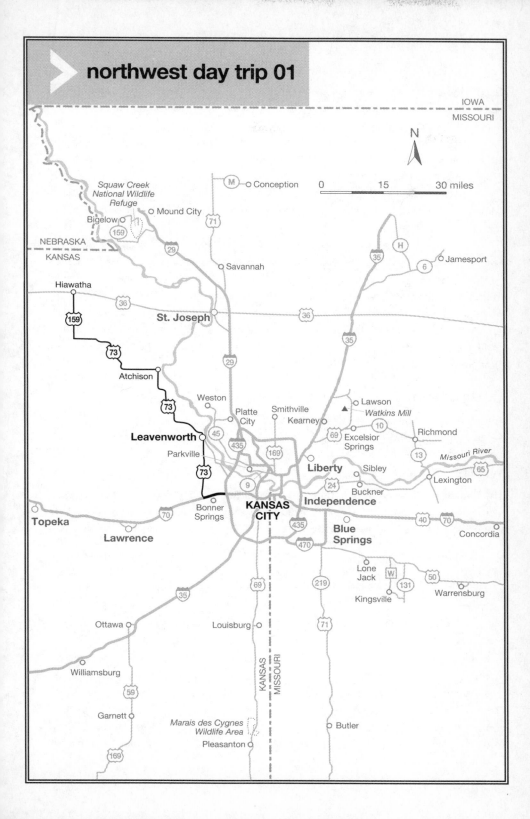

IOWA
MISSOURI

N

Squaw Creek
National Wildlife
Refuge

○ Conception

0   15   30 miles

Bigelow
(159)   ○ Mound City

NEBRASKA

KANSAS

(71)

(29)

(35)   (H)

○ Jamesport

6

Hiawatha

○ Savannah

(36)

(159)

(73)

St. Joseph

(36)

(35)

Atchison

(29)

Weston

Platte
City

Smithville

Lawson
▲ Watkins Mill

○ Richmond

Leavenworth   (45)

Kearney

(10)

(73)

Parkville

(435)

(169)

(69) Excelsior
Springs

(13)   Missouri River

(73)

(9)

Liberty   Sibley   (65)

Lexington

Topeka   ○

(70)

Bonner
Springs

KANSAS
CITY

(24)

Independence

Buckner

Lawrence

(435)

(40)   (70)

Blue
Springs

○ Concordia

(470)

Lone
Jack

(W)

(50)

(35)

(69)

(219)

Kingsville

(131)   ○ Warrensburg

Ottawa ○

Louisburg ○

(71)

Williamsburg

KANSAS

MISSOURI

(59)

Garnett ○

Marais des Cygnes
Wildlife Area

○ Butler

Pleasanton ○

(169)

Supplies to support the wagons flowed upriver in great quantities. The freight firm of Russell, Majors, and Waddell supplied 4,000 ox teams that hauled 16 million pounds of freight annually by wagon train.

Leavenworth has had its share of the famous and infamous. In 1895 the Fort Leavenworth Military Prison was transferred to the Department of Justice, and Congress authorized 1,000 acres of military reservation for a penitentiary.

The US Penitentiary at Leavenworth was completed in 1906 and has housed infamous criminals within its walls, including Al Capone, "Machine Gun" Kelly, and Robert Stroud, the "Birdman of Alcatraz."

Leavenworth has a long list of good guys, too. Civil War General William T. Sherman practiced law here, and restaurateur Fred Harvey built his magnificent home on one of the tree-shaded streets. William F. "Buffalo Bill" Cody, army scout and showman, came to Leavenworth in 1854 when he was 7 years old. Working for J. B. "Wild Bill" Hickok, he helped outfit trains with supplies for the Overland Stage Company. Leavenworth's US Army Command and General Staff College, on the post, educated such famous students as Douglas MacArthur, George Marshall, Black Jack Pershing, Dwight Eisenhower, and Colin Powell.

getting there

From downtown Kansas City, follow I-70 west to exit 224 and turn north. Follow US 73 for 15 miles into Leavenworth.

where to go

The Leavenworth Area Convention and Visitors Bureau. 518 Shawnee St.; (913) 682-4113; www.lvarea.com. The visitors bureau can supply you with brochures, self-guided-tour booklets, and other information on the city.

Carroll Mansion. 1128 Fifth Ave.; (913) 682-7759. More than a museum, this elegant 1882 Victorian home is a masterpiece of elaborately carved woodwork and stained-glass windows. You can feel the style and spirit of the age as you travel through this 16-room mansion. The parlor contains fine Sevres, Dresden, and Early American porcelain; Steuben glass; and lovely furniture. Elsewhere in the museum you'll see antiques from Leavenworth homes, some of them brought up the river by steamer in the past.

In the kitchen, along with the pitcher pump and woodstove, is a copper sink, a refinement of the period. The bathroom contains a lead tub that supplied both hot and cold water and a shower-bath, newfangled oddities that were probably among the first in the West. Old quilts and hand-loomed coverlets are displayed in the bedrooms, and a child's room contains a collection of antique toys. The museum is maintained by the Leavenworth County Historical Society. Closed on Sun and Mon. Admission fee. Group tours can be arranged by calling.

Chapel of the Veterans. Dwight D. Eisenhower VA Medical Center, 4101 Fourth St., Trafficway; 913-682-2000. The stained glass here will take your breath away, as will the Gothic architecture of the building. Constructed in 1893, the Chapel of Veterans was included in 1921's Ripley's Believe It or Not, which stated that this was the only chapel in the world where Catholic and Protestant services could be held simultaneously under one roof. The Catholic chapel is on the lower level, with the Protestant chapel above it. Open Mon through Fri 9 a.m. to 4 p.m.

Combined Arms Center & Fort Leavenworth. Seventh and Metropolitan Streets, Fort Leavenworth; (913) 684-5604; www.leavenworth.army.mil. Established in 1827, this is the oldest military installation in continuous service west of the Mississippi River. In the early part of the 19th century, it played an important role for settlers and wagon trains heading west. Generals George Custer, William Sherman, Robert E. Lee, Douglas MacArthur, Dwight D. Eisenhower, George S. Patton, Omar Bradley, "Stormin' Norman" Schwarzkopf, and Colin Powell were stationed here. Today it is home to the Combined Arms Center, the Command and General Staff College, and the US Disciplinary Barracks. A self-guided-tour booklet is available in the Frontier Army Museum Gift Shop on the premises. Visitors are welcome to drive through the fort year-round, but be prepared to present photo identification and have your vehicle searched upon entering the gates. The following on-site places are of note:

> **Berlin Wall Monument.** Three sections of the destroyed Berlin Wall were donated to Fort Leavenworth because of the worldwide influence of the US Army Command and General Staff College. The design of the memorial expresses three themes: a "falling position," representing the crumbling of the wall; a horizontal position, depicting the wall's destruction; and a vertical position, symbolizing democracy. Open daily. Free.

> **Buffalo Soldier Monument.** Grant Avenue and the south bank of Smith Lake, Fort Leavenworth. This monument, dedicated July 25, 1992, honors the African-American soldiers who served in the Ninth and Tenth Cavalry Regiments from 1866 until the armed services were integrated following World War II. Open daily. Free.

> **The Frontier Army Museum.** Off Reynolds Avenue, Fort Leavenworth; (913) 651-7440. The museum blends the history of Fort Leavenworth with that of the Frontier Army from 1817 to 1917. The outstanding exhibits graphically relate the history of the US Army and its role in western expansion beginning with the Lewis and Clark Expedition of 1804–1806. The carriage used by Abraham Lincoln on his visit to Kansas in December 1859 is displayed here. A special story hour about pioneer life is offered to elementary school children by appointment. Open daily. Free.

Fort Leavenworth National Cemetery. (913) 684-5604. More than 20,000 veterans representing every war since 1812 are buried here. The large monument near the flagpole marks the grave of Colonel Henry Leavenworth, for whom the fort and the city of Leavenworth are named. Captain Thomas West Custer, brother of General George A. Custer, is buried here beside other officers of the Seventh Cavalry who died at Little Bighorn. Open daily. Free.

Rookery. 12–14 Sumner Place, Fort Leavenworth. This was the temporary home of the first territorial governor of Kansas and is the oldest continuously occupied house in the state, built in 1834. A National Historic Landmark, it once housed First Lieutenant Douglas MacArthur, who lived here as a bachelor officer. The Rookery is not open to tour.

C. W. Parker Carousel Museum. 320 Esplanade St.; (913) 682-1866; www.firstcity museums.org. The C. W. Parker Amusement Company, which began in Abilene in 1896, later moved to Leavenworth, where it operated successfully until the start of the Great Depression. The museum to this amusement company houses a carousel from 1913 that is considered unique because of its 2 hand-carved rabbits used as a focal point. The carousel also has 24 hand-carved horses, 3 ponies, and a lovers' cup to ride in. A flying horse carousel from the 1850s also makes its home here. Open Thurs through Sat. Donations accepted.

First City Museum. 734 Delaware St.; (913) 682-1866; www.firstcitymuseums.org. Here you can find a collection of early frontier memorabilia and artifacts, including buggies and cutters that were manufactured in Leavenworth. Donations accepted.

glaciers & guitars

The latest addition to the Kansas Scenic Byway Program is located along KS 7 from Leavenworth, and north through Atchison, all the way to the Nebraska border. Also called the Glacial Hills Scenic Byway because of the region's glacier-created rolling hills and valleys, this part of Kansas looks more like "Little Switzer-land" than it does flatland.

In downtown Leavenworth, KS 7 is also known as Fourth Street, and it's where you'll find two guitar-shaped signs proclaiming Leavenworth to be the hometown of Melissa Etheridge. The Grammy award–winning singer was born here in 1961, graduated from Leavenworth High School in 1979, and returns often for benefit concerts and other events to support the community.

Leavenworth Landing Park. Missouri River and Esplanade; (913) 651-2132. This transportation-themed park is decorated with sculptures depicting different modes of transportation throughout Leavenworth's history. The Paddle Wheel Plaza is reminiscent of the actual riverboat landing located in this same area. The Roundhouse Plaza uses inlaid paving stones depicting the railroad roundhouse that was located at the eastern end of the downtown area. Another unique feature is a raised four-state map constructed of terrazzo and brass; it locates the rivers, trails, and railroads that were an important part of Kansas's history. A diorama explains the scientific value of plant specimens gathered during the Lewis and Clark Expedition. Open daily. Free.

National Fred Harvey Museum. 624 Olive St.; (913) 682-1866. In the early days of railroading, passengers on the Santa Fe stopped at Fred Harvey restaurants for good food. The Harvey waitresses were the subject of a 1946 movie (*The Harvey Girls*). Fred Harvey, founder of the chain, made a fortune on his restaurants. He lived in the house that later became this museum in the 19th century until his death in 1901. The home is filled with artifacts.

Performing Arts Center. 500 Delaware St.; (913) 682-7557. This 1938 theater is an interesting example of American art deco architecture. Now on the National Register of Historic Places, the structure was donated to the city by Durwood, Inc., and today hosts live performances by Leavenworth's River City Community Players. A schedule of performances is listed at www.lvarea.com under Arts & Culture.

Riverfront Community and Convention Center. 123 S. Esplanade St.; (800) 844-4114 or (913) 651-2132. The former 1888 Union Pacific Train Depot, now called the Riverfront Convention and Community Center, is now the city's multipurpose complex. It provides attractive, well-equipped meeting rooms, with on-site recreational opportunities and banquet service by the Harvey Girls upon request. Even if you don't have an event there, stick your head in and look around. Tours are free.

where to eat

The Corner Pharmacy. 429 Delaware St.; (913) 682-1602. The pharmacy has been around since 1871, and its old-fashioned soda fountain and lunch counter are a throwback to the days when you could get good food and medicine all in one trip. Breakfast and lunch are served at the Victorian-style soda fountain, which comes complete with mahogany bentwood swivel stools and a mirrored back bar. The shakes, malts, and sodas are served in glass containers with the cans from the mixer alongside. The Corner also features homemade chili and an assortment of sandwiches, plus terrific fresh-squeezed limeades and homemade lemonades. Closed Sun. $.

High Noon Saloon. 206 Choctaw St.; (913) 682-4876; www.thehighnoon.com. Housed in the old 1858 Great Western Manufacturing Company Building, the restaurant features good barbecue and the Frontier Prairie Brewing Company. Daily specials include meatloaf and mashed potatoes and roast beef sandwiches. The Leavenworth Players Group, a local acting company, stages monthly murder mystery dinners at the High Noon. $$.

Homer's Drive-In. 1320 S. Fourth St.; 913-651-3500. Homer's has been an institution in Leavenworth since just about the time the first automobile arrived on the streets here and needed someplace to drive. It's not quite that old, but it is a classic burger drive-in, with a nice dining area indoors as well. Old pictures on the walls document that Homer's has been here a long, long time. Open daily. $ (no cards).

Mama Mia's. 402 S. Twentieth St.; (913) 682-2131; www.eatatmamamias.com. During the summer months, enjoy the lovely landscaped backyard with a garden pool while you wait for your table. The menu features Italian dishes and hand-cut steaks. Open Tues through Fri for lunch and Tues through Sat for dinner. $$.

where to stay

The Prairie Queen Bed and Breakfast. 221 Arch St.; (913) 758-1959; www.prairiequeen .com. Named in honor of a Missouri riverboat that stopped in Leavenworth, this 1868 home has been restored to elegance. It features 3 bedrooms with king-size beds and private baths, and a full breakfast, afternoon tea, and evening snack of your choice. $$.

atchison, ks

It was here on July 4, 1804, that Lewis and Clark and the Corps of Discovery camped and celebrated the 28th birthday of the United States by firing their cannon. Independence Creek, the waterway that runs through Atchison into the Missouri River where Lewis and Clark camped, received its name that day. During the mid-19th century, Atchison was an important center of overland freighting. In 1859 the Atchison, Topeka, Santa Fe Railway Company was founded here. A renovated 1880s-era freight depot now houses the Santa Fe Depot Visitors Center, historical museum, and gift shop.

Atchison is filled with history, museums, antiques and specialty shops, and magnificent 19th-century mansions, many of which are located on the beautiful Missouri River bluffs.

getting there

From Leavenworth, follow US 73 north for a scenic 30 miles to Atchison.

where to go

Atchison Chamber of Commerce. 200 S. Tenth St.; (800) 234-1854 or (913) 367-2427; www.atchisonkansas.net. Located in the former Santa Fe Depot, this visitor center includes a nice exhibit on Amelia Earhart along with other aspects of the city's history. This is where the trolley tours start as well.

Amelia Earhart Birthplace Museum. 223 N. Terrace St.; (913) 367-4217; www.amelia earhartmuseum.org. This historic home, where Amelia Earhart was born in 1897, is listed on the National Register of Historic Places. Interpretive displays, newspaper and magazine clippings, and family belongings tell the story of the legendary aviatrix. Open daily Feb through mid-Dec, afternoons and by appointment from mid-Dec through Feb. Admission fee.

Amelia Earhart Earthwork. 17862 274th Rd., Warnock Lake; (800) 234-1854 or (913) 367-2427. This 1-acre portrait of Amelia Earhart is on a hillside near Warnock Lake on the city's south side. It comprises live plantings, stone, and other natural materials. It is the first perpetual crop artwork created by famed Kansas artist Stan Herd and was designed to commemorate Earhart's 100th birthday. A nearby viewing deck offers a good look at the earthwork and photographic displays that illustrate how the artist created his unusual portrait. Free.

Atchison County Historical Society. 200 S. Tenth St.; (913) 367-6238; www.atchison history.org. Located in a restored Santa Fe Depot, this museum hosts some interesting exhibits on Amelia Earhart, Lewis and Clark, and other events, large and small, in the area. It is also home to the Unofficial David Rice Atchison Presidential Library. (Atchison served as president for a 24-hour period in March 1849.)

Benedictine College. 1020 N. Second St.; (913) 367-5340; www.benedictine.edu. Founded more than 145 years ago by the joint Catholic communities of Mount St. Scholastica and St. Benedict's Abbey, the entire Second Street complex is listed on the National Register of Historic Places. Visitors can tour the campus, which is located above a river bluff affording a breathtaking autumn view. Tours are given through prior arrangement and are free.

International Forest of Friendship. South of Atchison on KS 7 near Warnock Lake; (913) 367-2427. Trees from all 50 states and from 30 countries grow here. Spend a pleasant afternoon walking along a path engraved with the names of famous aviators, and spend a minute or two reflecting at a memorial for the astronauts who died aboard the space shuttle *Challenger*. There's no charge here, but donations are welcome.

Muchnic Art Gallery. 704 N. Fourth St.; (913) 367-4278; www.atchison-art.org. Monthly displays by regional artists are exhibited amid the elegant furnishings of one of Atchison's most spectacular Victorian mansions. The interior features rich woodwork, fine hand-tooled leather, brilliant stained-glass windows, and elaborate fireplaces. Open Sat and Sun afternoon and 10 a.m. to 5 p.m. on Wed.

where to shop

Nell Hill's. 501 Commercial St.; (913) 367-1086; www.nellhills.com. This large, upscale store specializes in furniture, prints, pictures, and home accessories in an intimate setting. This is where designer Mary Carol Garrity began her career. Closed Sun.

Cottage of the Seasons. 507 Commercial St.; (913) 367-6171. Just around the corner from Nell Hill's, this garden shop features practical and whimsical items for your home and garden. From candles and stepping-stones to wind chimes and doormats, you'll find a delightful collection of indoor and outdoor art here. Closed Sun.

where to eat

Marigold Bakery and Cafe. 715 Commercial St.; (913) 367-3858. This European-style cafe serves fresh-baked breads and breakfast goods. Lunches feature specialty sand-wiches, soups, and salads, along with homemade pies, cakes, and cookies. Come Fri night for gourmet pizza. Closed Sun. $.

The River House Restaurant. 101 Commercial St.; (913) 367-3330. American fare is served in an open, airy atmosphere amid the charm of a restored 1870 building that was the former headquarters and business hotel of the Atchison & Nebraska Railroad. You may choose to dine on the outdoor patio during warm weather and enjoy a nice view of the Amelia Earhart Bridge, which spans the Missouri River. Open daily. $$.

where to stay

Glick Mansion Bed and Breakfast. 503 N. Second St.; (913) 367-9110; www.glickman sion.com. Listed on the National Register of Historic Places, the mansion was built in 1873 and named after its owner, Governor George Washington Glick. In 1913 the home under-went renovation by Kansas City's most innovative architect, Louis Curtiss, who converted it from a Victorian-style structure to a Tudor-Revival manor. Guest rooms feature private baths and queen-size beds. A full breakfast is served in the spacious dining room. Ask about the ghosts that haunt the neighborhood around Glick Mansion. $$–$$$.

St. Martin's Bed and Breakfast. 324 Santa Fe St.; (913) 367-4964; www.stmartinsbandb .com. Built in 1948, this yellow 2-story B&B's 5 individually decorated rooms have canopied beds, claw-foot tubs, and antiques. It's a great getaway for adults but not for kids under age 10. $$.

hiawatha, ks

The streets of little Hiawatha each fall host the oldest Halloween parade in the country. Started in 1914, the parade often calls for early dismissal from school. There's a Halloween queen. The governor is often in attendance. It's a big deal in Hiawatha. Join the parade! There is no entry fee and everyone is welcome! For more information: Hiawatha Chamber of Commerce, 413 Oregon St.; (913) 742-7136.

getting there

Head north on US 73 from Atchison to US 159 and on to Hiawatha.

where to go

The Davis Memorial. Mount Hope Cemetery, Hiawatha. From Horton take US 159/73 north to Hiawatha. Or if you're coming from St. Joseph, take US 36 West. It's worth the drive to see one of the most unusual monuments ever built. Each year thousands of people come to see the tomb and sign their names on the guest register mounted at the site of this strange rendering of love and loss.

When Sarah Davis of Hiawatha died in 1930, her husband, John M. Davis, perpetuated her memory by building a memorial that contains 11 life-size figures depicting the couple at various stages of their married life.

Davis spent a whopping sum of $500,000 to have the imported marble and granite figures carved by Italian craftsmen. He died penniless in a county home for the aged in 1947. A statue of Sarah, complete with angel wings, was positioned over the vault in which his coffin was placed, and her body rests in the crypt next to his. Atop that stone slab is a kneeling statue of Davis.

Although Davis's death and funeral were written up in *Life* magazine, few people attended the service. Only one man, Horace England, the tombstone salesman, seemed genuinely concerned by Davis's passing. Open daily. Free. No phone.

where to eat

Gus's Restaurant. 604 Oregon St.; (785) 742-4533. Here you'll find a basic country-style interior and an open kitchen area, so you'll have the opportunity to talk with Gus or the other cooks as they prepare hot beef sandwiches or pork tenderloin with a Greek flair, courtesy of Gus. $ (no cards).

day trip 02

northwest

history at the river's edge:
parkville, mo; weston, mo;
platte city, mo

parkville, mo

The land for the town of Parkville was purchased in 1840 by Colonel George S. Park, a veteran of Sam Houston's cavalry who recognized the value of riverfront land for steamboat trade. As trade and commerce grew along the river, so did Parkville.

Despite floods, tornadoes, and train derailments, the town of Parkville is alive and well. Downtown shops combine specialty items with antiques, crafts, clothing, home furnishings, and art. Remember to cross the railroad tracks to the shops and restaurants located there.

Park University, formerly Park College, was founded in 1875 and sits high on a bluff overlooking the town. It has always been an integral part of city activities, frequently opening its facilities to the community.

Getting to Parkville from Kansas City is easy. It's northwest of the city on MO 45 and is also accessible by I-435, I-70, and I-635. The town's amenities include English Landing Park, a short block from downtown. Although it was covered by flood waters for several months in 2011, the walking trail by the river, picnic facilities, basketball goals, and a volleyball court have all been restored as good as new. The unusual Waddell A-Frame Bridge, listed on the National Register of Historic Places, is located within the park. Parkville also boasts an unusual nature sanctuary that makes for a pleasant retreat, as well as a popular farmers' market on Wed afternoons and Sat mornings.

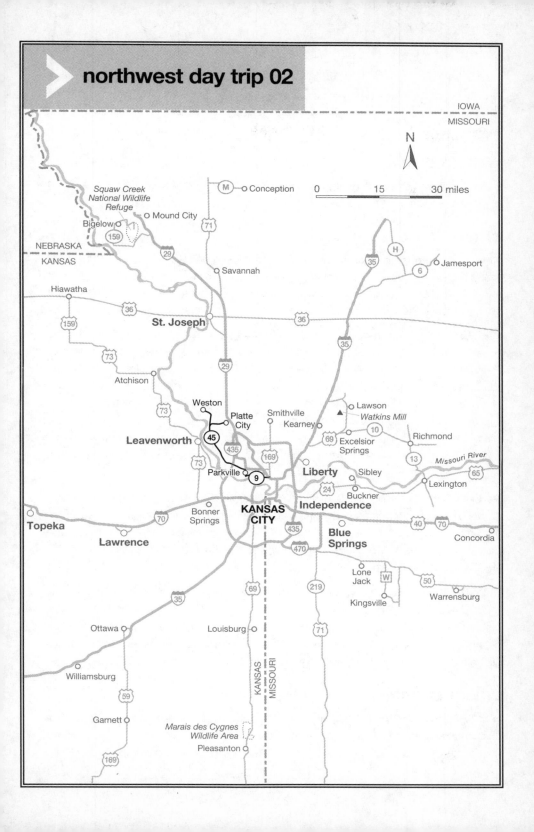

The city has a festival atmosphere year-round. There's a Parkville Jazz and Fine Arts River Jam in June and Christmas on the River in Dec. Information on Parkville, as well as a walking-tour brochure, can be obtained at the Chamber of Commerce office.

getting there

From downtown, cross the Broadway Bridge, or US 169, heading north and follow MO 9 about 8 miles into downtown Parkville.

where to go

Parkville Chamber of Commerce. 8701 NW River Park Dr.; (816) 587-2700; www .parkvillechamber.com. The Chamber of Commerce is located in the old train depot that dates to the 1850s and includes a small exhibit on the heritage of the Burlington Line that passes through Parkville.

Park University. 8700 NW River Park Dr.; (816) 741-2000, ext. 6211; www.park.edu. The university has a unique and contrasting campus that boasts buildings listed on the National Register of Historic Places. A variety of educational offerings is available to the public. Free tours are given Mon through Fri. Be sure to visit the underground library and the Campanella Gallery, which highlights the work of students, faculty, and some community members. The Jenkin and Barbara David Theatre hosts 6 impressive performances each year, and the Graham Tyler Memorial Chapel is home to musical performances by the Parkville Community Band and other community groups. Stop by for a soccer or volleyball game on the fields on the north side of town on MO 9.

Parkville Mini Golf. 7 Mill St.; (816) 505-9555; www.parkvilleminigolf.com. This challenging 18-hole miniature golf course is great for families with children. There is room for private parties and birthday groups. Located on the bluff overlooking downtown Parkville, the course offers an unbeatable view of the town below and a clubhouse that houses a full-service snack bar and video game entertainment. Hours change seasonally. Admission fee.

Parkville Nature Sanctuary. Main entrance behind Platte County Health Department, 1201 East St.; (816) 741-7676; www.parkvillemo.com. Featuring more than 110 acres of natural fields, woodlands, ponds, and small waterfalls, the sanctuary makes a wonderful getaway from the stress of the city. A picnic shelter is located along the trail. The volunteer staff offers guided nature hikes and special events. Open daily. Free.

where to shop

H.M.S. Beagle. 180 English Landing Dr.; (816) 587-9998; www.hms-beagle.com. Part museum, part retail center, this fun science store is owned by the family of an archeologist who is often away on assignment, digging for fossils and such around the world. Check out the remains of Polly, a 125-million-year-old dinosaur. Anything the aspiring astronomer or archeologist could want can be found here.

Northland Exposure Artists Cooperative Gallery. 104 Main St.; (816) 746-6300. If you're looking for one-of-a-kind finds, check out this artists' cooperative and gallery. The Northland Exposure Gallery is owned and operated by 50 regional artists from a 2-state area. Inside you'll find exceptional silver and glass jewelry designs and exciting works in watercolor, acrylic, oil, mixed media, pottery, and handcrafted paper. Closed Mon.

River's Bend Gallery. 102 Main St.; (816) 587-8070. This spacious gallery represents the work of about 100 artists from around the country and is known for high-end glass art. You'll also find a nice selection of wooden bowls, jewelry, and some hand-woven scarves. Closed Mon.

Wines by Jennifer. 405 Main St.; (816) 505-9463; www.winesbyjennifer.com. Located in a former residence on Main Street, Wines by Jennifer is as comfy/cozy as enjoying a glass of your favorite wine in your own living room. Wine tastings and pairings are often held on the back patio, also as casual as getting together with your favorite friends in your own backyard. Check the schedule of events or just drop in. Jennifer and gang will welcome you like family.

where to eat

Cafe des Amis. 112½ Main St.; (816) 587-3844. Fine French cuisine is available in the upper level of a building built in 1844. The restaurant is building a reputation for delicious crepes, but daily specials run the gamut of everything delectable from the French. $$.

Parkville Coffeehouse. 103 Main St.; (816) 216-6560. This wonderful old building has exposed stone walls that date to the earliest days of Parkville. A nice quiet spot to read or watch the foot traffic on Main Street, the coffeehouse offers multiple choices in coffee, tea, and snacks. $.

Piropos Argentinean Restaurant. (816) 741-3600; www.piroposkc.com. For more than a decade, Piropos has been one of the most talked about dining locations in the Kansas City area. Now with two locations just a few miles from each other, take care not to confuse one with the other. The original location at 1 W. First St. in Parkville is now known as Piropos Grille and is open for dinner Tues through Sat (816-741-9800). It's the location with a magnificent view of the Missouri River valley and includes a fabulous Happy Hour. The second location is just a few miles east on MO 9 in Briarcliff Village (4141 Mulberry Dr.). This location also has a magnificent view, but of the downtown skyline instead of the river. Both Piropos offer an expansive selection of South American and European wines with a lunch and dinner menu that highlights empanadas, Milanesa de Tilapia, and Argentinean beef. $$–$$$.

Stone Canyon Pizza Co. 15 Main St.; (816) 746-8686. Appetizers, pizza, pasta, salads, and sandwiches are served at this popular Parkville establishment. Clowns and magicians entertain kids on Fri night. Open for lunch and dinner. This is Parkville's only nonsmoking restaurant. $.

where to stay

Main Street Inn. 504 Main St.; (816) 272-9750; www.main-street-inn.com. Fans of Piropos Argentinean Restaurant will love a night at this historic inn, owned by the same Parkville couple who developed Piropos. This 1886 home, built from bricks kilned by Park College students in the 1880s, has 3 warm and cheery guest rooms named after various blends of wine, highlighted with intriguing stained glass and tastefully furnished with antiques and modern amenities. The Chardonnay Room overlooks Main Street, the Pinot Noir Room has a private entrance, and the Merlot Room has the easiest access to the centrally located coffee and refreshment bar. Your room rate also includes a bottle of wine and a $15 gift certificate toward dinner at either of the restaurants. Innkeeper Tiffany Miller offers a gourmet breakfast that may include ham strata or sticky bun French toast. $$–$$$.

Porch Swing Inn. 702 East St.; (816) 587-6282; www.theporchswinginn.com. Built in the 1890s for a Park College professor, this 3-story home overlooks the Park University soccer fields today and is 2 blocks from downtown shops. Each room is named for and themed around western characters, such as Jesse James and Calamity Jane. $$.

weston, mo

Founded in 1837, Weston still preserves its antebellum homes, which rest peacefully on hillsides and bluffs that once overlooked the Missouri River. It seems that the Missouri, mighty fickle lady that she is, decided to change her course after the flood of 1884. This left Weston drained of its bustling potential as a river town, with the river diverted to a channel 2 miles away. Long before that, the Lewis and Clark Expedition camped at what is now the foot of Main Street during the summer of 1804. A marker identifies the significance of the explorers' presence in Platte County.

Weston's many antiques shops contain a treasure trove of goodies. Everything from country primitives, antique dolls, and Depression glass to European furniture and country crafts can be found along Main Street.

getting there

From Parkville, follow MO 9 north 4 miles to the intersection of MO 45. Turn left or west and travel 22 miles into downtown Weston.

where to go

Weston Development Company. 502 Main St.; (816) 640-2909; www.westonmo.com. Stop in while exploring Main Street for a map of the walking and driving tours of the area.

National Silk Art Museum. 500 Main St., inside the St. George Hotel; (816) 640-2608. This unusual museum houses a collection of 150 silk tapestries dating to 1872. It's the largest private collection of such works in the world and is the result of John Pottie's fascination with the intricate art form. Open Thurs through Sun. Free.

Pirtle's Winery. 502 Spring St.; (816) 640-5728; www.pirtlewinery.com. Housed in a former church, this winery has vineyards in northern Platte County. Wine and cheese tastings are available for groups. Mead (honey wine) is a specialty here. On the premises is a wine garden where you can sip wine and enjoy sausage, cheese, Tuscan loaves, and fruit. Open daily.

Red Barn Farm. 16300 Wilkerson Rd.; (816) 386-5437; www.westonredbarnfarm.com. Get the kids and yourself into life on a real working farm. Turkeys, geese, and chickens roam the property along with goats, pigs, and cows in pens. Take a hayride through corn and soybean fields, or pick apples and pumpkins during the autumn months. Pick strawberries in May and June. There's a small gift shop in the big red barn. The farm is open daily Apr through Dec or by appointment. Admission fee.

Riverwood Winery. 22200 MO 45 North; (816) 579-9797; www.riverwoodwinery.com. Located in an old schoolhouse, Riverwood offers 9 varieties of dry and sweet wines. There's always something going on—from programs highlighting regional foods and cheeses, to book signings, to musical events. Open weekends from noon to 5 p.m.

Snow Creek, Inc. Snow Creek Drive, 5 miles north of Weston on MO 45. (816) 640-2200; www.peakresorts.com; Snow Report Line: (816) 589-SNOW. Kansas City's only downhill ski area includes intermediate trails, chairlifts, and beginner areas with rope tows. A day lodge features a cafeteria-style restaurant, a lounge, ski rentals, a ski school, and ticket sales. Open daily and at night from mid-Dec through Mar, depending on the weather. Admission fee.

Weston Historical Museum. 601 Main St.; (816) 386-2977. Located in the former Baptist Church, this museum offers displays depicting life in Platte County from prehistoric days through World War II. Exhibits include household items, tools, glassware, china, furniture, historic documents, and other items. Open afternoons; closed Mon and mid-Dec through mid-Mar. Free.

where to shop

Backroads Art Gallery. 416 Main St.; (816) 386-0140; www.backroadsartgallery.com. If you're looking to spruce up the outside of your home, you'll find lots of high quality metal and outdoor art here, as well as Native American and wildlife art indoors from talented artists around the country. Closed Mon through Wed.

Celtic Ranch. 404 Main St.; (816) 640-2881; www.celticranch.com. The Irish in all of us finds a voice in this shop that carries clothing imported directly from shops in the United Kingdom, along with teas, jewelry, and books. But mixed right in are a large number of items that satisfy the cowboy in us, such as leather vests, horsehair bracelets, and other treats. Open daily.

McCormick Distilling Company Country Store. 420 Main St.; (816) 640-3149. Founded in 1856, McCormick Distilling Company is best known for being the oldest continuously active distillery still operating on its original site. The store sells McCormick products and other Weston memorabilia. Closed Mon.

Missouri Bluffs Boutique. 512 Main St.; (816) 640-2770; www.missouribluffs.com. Clothes hounds looking for something nobody else has will love this place. You'll find a variety of styles here, from Native American, Asian, and African to vintage-inspired, contemporary, and locally made natural fiber garments. Like most other customers, you may wind up spending a lot of time trying on various ensembles and playing with the unusual baubles, so tell your significant other to bring along reading material while you shop. Open daily.

The Youngblood Gallery. 415 Main St.; (816) 640-2996. This gallery offers a wide variety of accessories for the home, including antique reproduction furniture, willow furniture, brass and pewter, home fragrances, and an interesting art collection by artists from across North America. Closed Mon.

where to eat

America Bowman Restaurant. Short and Welt Streets; (816) 640-5235. This is the place to find a fine home-cooked lunch and dinner, served in a pre–Civil War setting. Inside this restaurant is Pat O'Malley's Pub. It was patterned after Granary Tavern in Limerick, Ireland. Closed Mon. $$.

Avalon Cafe. 608 Main St.; (816) 640-2835. The restaurant is located inside an 1847 antebellum home and features Continental cuisine prepared by French-trained chefs and co-owners. Choose from beef tenderloin in Missouri bourbon sauce to American lamb chops in burgundy butter. Desserts are excellent. Closed Mon. $$.

The Vineyards. 505 Spring St.; (816) 640-5588. Local wines are served up in this 1845 antebellum structure, together with lamb, duck, beef tenderloin, and other house specialties. Closed Mon. $$–$$$.

where to stay

Benner House Bed-and-Breakfast. 645 Main St.; (816) 640-2616; www.bennerhouse .com. This beautiful Victorian home, overlooking downtown Weston, offers 4 guest rooms with 2 private baths. A main parlor, a sitting room, and a wraparound front porch are available for relaxing. $$.

The Hatchery House. 618 Short St.; (816) 640-5700; www.hatcherybb.com. This 1845 antebellum bed-and-breakfast has 4 guest rooms with queen-size beds, gas-burning fireplaces, and private baths. A large outside garden is available for teas and weddings. Ask innkeepers Jan and Larry Jabara where the name "The Hatchery House" comes from. You might be surprised. $$–$$$.

The Inn at Weston Landing. 526 Welt St.; (816) 640-5788; www.inatwestonlanding.com. Located at the end of a block lined with pre–Civil War homes, the inn offers deluxe accommodations with the ambience of a mid-19th-century Irish cottage. A high-pitched roof, low-set dormers, and gables define Celtic and rural British Isles influences. A full authentic Celtic breakfast features rashers, kippers, trifle cakes, and bramble jelly. An 1842 Irish pub is a favorite for private parties. $$.

Laurel Brooke Farm. 22520 Hwy. M; (816) 640-2525; www.laurelbrookefarm.com. Stay out in the country surrounded by apple trees, ponds, and the sweet sounds of birds calling on this acreage owned by Warren and Debra Keith. The couple renovated a historic barn for this bed-and-breakfast and filled it with antiques they purchased from estate sales around northwest Missouri. You'll enjoy an in-ground swimming pool in warm weather and freshly baked treats by Warren, the family chef. $$.

The St. George Hotel. 500 Main St.; (816) 640-9902; www.thesaintgeorgehotel.com. A fixture on Main Street Weston since 1845, this hotel has once again been renovated and returned to its original luxury. The hotel offers much more than overnight accommodations in one of its 26 boutique guest rooms. It is a destination in itself that includes fine dining at Charlemagne's Restaurant, a museum, a wine bar, and gift shop. $$$.

platte city, mo

The seat of Platte County has too often been overlooked as a destination for anyone other than those with business at the courthouse. The annual antiques show at Platte County R-3 High School each October is a good reason to head north to Platte City (816-858-3322).

However, recent additions to business and hospitality community require that day-trippers give Platte City another look.

getting there

From Weston, follow MO 92 to the east just about 10 miles into Platte City.

where to go

Ben Ferrel Platte County Museum. 220 Ferrel St.; (816) 431-5121. If this building looks familiar, that's because it is an 1881 replica of the Missouri Governor's Mansion in Jefferson City. As home to the Platte County Historical Society, it offers lots to learn about Platte County. The building is on the National Register of Historic Places.

where to eat

JRay's. 1302 Platte Falls Rd.; (816) 431-6855. Its location in a strip mall at first is not that impressive, but when you sit down and look at the menu, then taste some of those items, you'll realize that a great dining experience can finally be found in Platte City. Jeremy Ray specializes in made-from-scratch food. You'll often see Jeremy himself at local farmers' markets picking out the freshest produce. There's an outdoor patio and a well-stocked bar. It hosts quite easily the best happy hour in Platte County. Come on Thurs, Fri, and Sat nights for live blues and jazz. $–$$.

Suzie's Cafe. 1302-A Platte Falls Rd.; (816) 858-6050. For the best breakfast in Platte County, Suzie's is the place to go. Serving all-natural ingredients from local vendors, Suzie makes everything you eat in her restaurant. It's a great coffee shop, with more than 100 different types of drinks available. And if you're in a hurry, zip through the drive-thru window. $.

where to stay

Basswood Country Resort. 15880 Interurban Rd.; (816) 858-5556; www.basswood resort.com. Accommodations are available for just about all sizes and tastes here. This place started out as a very nice RV park and campground, but slowly over the years cabins have been added, as well as a fishing pond, swimming pool, playground, volleyball courts, walking trails. Oh, there's also a house with traditional guest rooms, each named for a celebrity that has actually stayed at the property. You'll find Bing Crosby, Harry Truman, Rudy Vallee, and Matthew McConaughey. A country store and pizza parlor leave you with no reason to leave this resort for quite a while. $–$$.

day trip 03

northwest

the start of snail mail:
st. joseph, mo; savannah, mo;
conception, mo

st. joseph, mo

When the Lewis and Clark Expedition camped here in 1804 and 1806, they named the area St. Michael's Prairie. You can pick up pieces of the past by strolling down streets lined with elegant mansions and restored buildings that were built at a time when raising hemp and selling supplies to wagon trains made fortunes.

Founded in 1826 by Joseph Robidoux as a fur-trading post located in the Blacksnake Hills along the Missouri River, the town later became the starting point for settlers heading west over the Oregon Trail. In 1843 the community was named St. Joseph in honor of Robidoux's patron saint. Five years later gold was discovered in California, and in 1849 more than 20,000 forty-niners migrated through St. Joseph, buying food and supplies to sustain them on their journey.

Steamboats made this an important river town, but with the coming of the railroad in 1859, St. Joseph became the farthest point west to be reached by rail. Trains eventually eclipsed steamboats as the prevailing mode of transportation, but still a fast mail service was needed to the West Coast. Thousands of people turned out to watch the first run of the Pony Express on April 3, 1860. St. Joseph's Golden Age began in 1875, after the Civil War. The Victorian years made fortunes for many that would last several generations. Many of the luxurious dwellings still stand and are on the National Register of Historic Places.

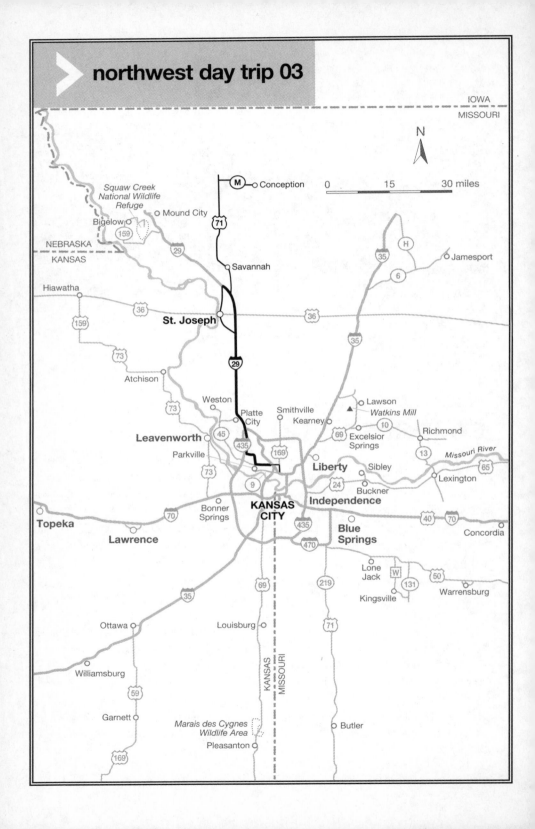

For many history buffs, St. Joseph will forever be associated with the infamous outlaw Jesse James, who was gunned down here by a member of his own gang in April 1882.

However, since the Kansas City Chiefs summer training camp moved to Missouri Western University, St. Jo is now better known as the August home of their favorite football team.

getting there

From downtown, head north across the Broadway Bridge, otherwise known as US 169, to I-29. Travel about 50 miles to the St. Jo area.

where to go

St. Joseph Visitors Center. 502 N. Woodbine St.; (816) 232-1839; www.stjomo.com. Located adjacent to the public library, this is a bit more than your average visitor center. Interactive maps allow you to track the trails that moved west from St. Joseph. Pick up maps of your own, or print them out from computers available to the public. And look closely at the backs of the chairs you're using. You'll see Walter Cronkite, Jesse James, Aunt Jemima, and other figures associated with St. Jo.

Albrecht-Kemper Museum of Art. 2818 Frederick Blvd.; (816) 233-7003; www.albrecht-kemper.org. The museum holds one of the finest and most comprehensive collections of 18th-, 19th-, and 20th-century American art in the Midwest. Included here are works by Thomas Hart Benton, Albert Bierstadt, George Caleb Bingham, George Catlin, and others. Since 1966 the museum has been housed in a 1935 Georgian-style mansion designed by architects Edward Buehler Delk and Eugene Meyer for William Albrecht, founder of the Western Tablet Company. For guided tours call in advance. Lunch is served on Wed and Thurs. Wine tastings are held on the third Thursday of each month. Closed Mon. Admission fee.

Glore Psychiatric Museum. 3406 Frederick St.; (816) 364-1209; www.gloremuseum.org. The permanent display covers 400 years of psychiatric history and includes exhibits such as the Bath of Surprise, O'Halloran's Swing, the Tranquilizer Chair, and the Hollow Wheel. There are also displays from St. Joseph State Hospital's history. However interesting this museum is, it is not necessarily for children or those easily upset by the human condition. Open daily. Admission fee.

Jesse James Home Museum. Twelfth and Penn Streets; (816) 232-8206. The outlaw Jesse James was only 34 when he was killed by Bob Ford, a member of the former James Gang. James was living in the house with his wife and two children, under the assumed name of Tom Howard. Ford shot him from behind while James stood on a chair to straighten a picture. The bullet passed through his head and entered the wall. Visitors today can still see the bullet hole. Exhibits include artifacts obtained from the outlaw's grave when he was exhumed in 1995 for DNA tests, which showed a 99.7 percent certainty that it was Jesse James who was killed in his home on April 3, 1882. Open daily. Admission fee.

Patee House Museum National Historic Landmark. Twelfth and Penn Streets; (816) 232-8206. Opened in 1858 by John Patee, this was a luxurious hotel built at a cost of $180,000, a substantial sum for that era. It contained 140 guest rooms. Later it served as headquarters for the Pony Express. Exhibits feature a restored 1860 Pony Express headquarters, a replica of the first railway mail car invented for the Pony Express, and other Pony Express memorabilia. Railroad displays include an 1860 Hannibal and St. Joseph locomotive. The 1854 Buffalo Saloon on the premises serves soft drinks and ice cream. Kids will also enjoy a ride on the Wild Things Carousel, a vintage 1941 merry-go-round. Open daily. Admission fee.

Paramount Theatre. 717 Edmond St.; (816) 271-4717; www.stjoearts.org. Built in 1927 by the Paramount Film Company, this 1,200-seat theater is one of only four remaining in the US from the glory days of Hollywood Oriental Theaters.

Although it is called an Oriental Theater, the building is very Middle Eastern in design with a Bedouin tent-style design hanging from the ceiling and marble carvings and gold features throughout. The theater served as a working movie theater until 1977, when it was closed and scheduled for demolition. However, the Allied Arts Organization rallied to save and restore it, and it reopened in 2002. Live performances continue to fill the stage today.

Pony Express Museum. 914 Penn St.; (816) 279-5059 or (800) 530-5930; www.pony express.org. On April 3, 1860, a lone rider on horseback left from this stable to begin his historic ride. Now on the National Register of Historic Places, the Pony Express National Memorial features state-of-the-art exhibits that tell the dramatic story of the creation and operation of the Pony Express. Visitors can take a walk along the 70-foot diorama of the Pony Express Trail. Among the many hands-on displays is the mochila (mailbag), which can be changed from one saddle to another. Visitors can also pump water from the original stable well. Open daily; closed holidays. Admission fee.

Remington Nature Center. 1502 MacArthur Dr.; (816) 271-5499; www.stjoenaturecenter .info. A monstrous woolly mammoth greets you at the door of this center located on the banks of the Missouri River. Dedicated to explaining the animal and plant life of this area, the center includes a 7,000-gallon fish tank and numerous hands-on exhibits that kids love. With both indoor and outdoor features, this center could keep any family entertained and better educated for hours. Admission fee.

St. Joseph Doll Museum. 1115 S. Twelfth St.; (816) 233-1420. Doll collectors will find happiness in this collection of more than 600 dolls, ranging from 1840s "covered wagon dolls" to Barbies and Cabbage Patch Kids. Tours are available. Open Tues through Sun or by appointment. Closed Nov through May. Admission fee.

St. Joseph Museum. 1100 Charles St.; (816) 232-8471 or (800) 530-8866; www.stjoseph museum.org. This 1879 Gothic-style mansion turned museum was copied after a castle on the Rhine and decorated later by the famed Tiffany Company of New York. The 5,000-piece Native American ethnographic collection is the largest in Missouri and represents more than 300 North American tribes. Items in the collection range from Pomo feather baskets to Haida copper masks. There are also local and natural history exhibits of interest. Open daily. Admission fee.

where to shop

Penn Street Square. Twelfth and Penn Streets; (816) 232-4626. Located in the heart of the city's historic museum area, Penn Street Square offers more than 20,000 square feet of antiques and collectibles.

Stetson Factory Outlet Store. 3601 S. Leonard Rd.; (816) 233-3286. Abraham Lincoln was the nation's president when John B. Stetson made his first western fur-felt hat. The St. Joseph–based company still makes a wide selection of world-famous western felt, straw, and dress hats at direct-from-the-manufacturer prices. This is the nation's only Stetson outlet store. Closed Sun.

where to eat

Boudreaux's Louisiana. 224 N. Fourth St.; (816) 387-9911; www.heybroudreax.com. Located in a beautiful old historic warehouse downtown, Boudreaux's celebrates Mardi Gras and all things Cajun 365 days a year. With creaky old wood floors and high ceilings, it gets a bit noisy when crowded, which is often, but with flat-screen TVs showing numerous sporting events and friends gathering with friends, yes, it's a lively place. Open for lunch and dinner. In addition to Cajun and seafood, you can find good pasta and bread pudding on the menu. $$.

The Old Hoof and Horn Steakhouse. 429 Illinois St.; (816) 238-0742. Located in the heart of the Stockyards, this venerable restaurant has been serving good prime rib, steaks, and seafood for more than a century. $$.

Galvins Dinner House. 6802 S. Twenty-second St.; (816) 238-0463; www.galvinsstjoe .com. A longtime St. Joseph staple in family dining and celebrations, the Galvins House specializes in fried chicken dinners served family-style. The place opened in 1940 as a gas station and the family that operated it had a little chicken operation. Mom would kill a few chickens each morning and fix fried chicken baskets for people who stopped at the gas sta-tion, particularly those traveling on buses. Slowly it became more and more of a restaurant and then the gas station operation just disappeared. Today, you can also enjoy steaks, trout and pork chops, but you must try the pure white French salad dressing. Closed Mon. $$.

J. C. Wyatt House. 1309 Felix St.; (816) 676-1004; www.jcwyatt.net. The beautiful home was built in 1891 by J. C. Wyatt, who was a principal in a major dry goods store of the city. It was a private home for many years, then an apartment building, and then sat empty for a long time waiting for the wrecking ball, until two guys from New York stepped in to save it. The house is fully restored and occasionally open for tour. Reservations are required for lunch and dinner, as well as the cooking classes that are offered seasonally. Closed Sun and Mon. $$.

savannah, mo

If you love animals, Kewpie dolls, or the family farm, you'll find a lot to love in Savannah. For more information: Savannah Chamber of Commerce, 411 Court St.; (816) 324-3976; www.savannahmochamber.com.

getting there

From St. Joseph, continue north on I-29 to US 71 just another 15 miles to Savannah.

where to go

Andrew County Museum. 202 E. Duncan Dr.; (816) 324-4720; www.andrewcounty museum.org. Explore an old-fashioned general store, a collection of Navajo rugs, and a larger collection of Kewpie dolls. This museum also provides a well-produced explanation of the value of the family farm, which dominates life in Andrew County. Closed Sun and Mon. Admission fee.

M'shoogy's Famous Emergency Animal Rescue World Headquarters. 11519 State Route C; (816) 324-5824; www.mshoogys.org. Nestled on 22 acres of hilly country, M'shoogy's is both an animal rescue facility and a veterinary clinic. More than 750 dogs, cats, and other assorted creatures are kept at this roadside haven, which is the largest no-kill animal shelter in the country. M'shoogy's compassionate owners, Gary and Lisa Silverglat, group all the dogs by temperament in well-maintained outdoor runs. Each animal gets its turn to play in a large fenced area that surrounds a pond. About 3,000 of M'shoogy's residents are adopted out each year, which evens the odds that they're going to live much happier lives. The Angels Vet Clinic is open to anyone, providing basic shots and other medical procedures at a fraction of the cost of most facilities in the metropolitan area. M'shoogy's is also a Federal Migratory Rehabilitation Center that attempts to restore injured birds to the wild. Open Sat for adoptions.

conception, mo

The village of Conception is really little more than that, barely a reduced speed sign on US 136 that many people associate with a trip to Maryville and Northeast Missouri State a little farther north. The primary attraction is the Abbey, a peaceful retreat in what is already a peaceful rural community of northwest Missouri.

getting there

From Savannah, continue north on US 71 23 miles to Highway M. You'll see a sign for Conception Abbey.

where to go

Conception Abbey. 37174 State Hwy. VV; (660) 944-3100; www.conceptionabbey.org. Located just south of Maryville off US 71, the monastery is an architectural masterpiece designed in the Romanesque style. Also on the premises is Conception Seminary College, a four-year seminary established in 1886.

Founded in 1873, Conception Abbey was dedicated in 1891 and was designated a Minor Basilica on its 50th anniversary by Pope Pius XII, becoming the fifth Minor Basilica in the country. The Basilica of the Immaculate Conception is breathtaking in design and, for those of any faith, represents a place to sit and contemplate.

The abbey has continued for years to open its doors to the public, inviting people in from the cold and often stressful environment around them. Many come here on weekend retreats to sit or walk the grounds in quiet meditation. The basilica is open each day to "pilgrims" for prayer and meditation and serves as a house of prayer for people of all faiths who enter its impressive wooden doors. It is open to the public during prayer services, including the evening vesper services, when the joyful and spirited harmony of the monks' voices becomes a welcome respite from the cacophony of the world.

Since hospitality is one of the defining characteristics of the Benedictine order, you can drop by any day for lunch at the abbey. The modestly priced, wholesome, and simple meal is served promptly at 12:35 p.m. and includes a salad, 2 main dishes, vegetable, dessert, and home-baked bread. Sunday dinner is also served here at 11:30 a.m.

Lodging rates are also inexpensive. The abbey is not a resort, so don't expect fancy rooms and amenities. Do expect shared baths, long walks, beautiful sunsets, and plenty of fresh air.

Visit the gift shop where you can buy unique cards and gifts from the abbey's Printery House. Art from the Holy Land, carved by artists from around the city of Bethlehem; porcelain and hand-carved nativity scenes; and limited offerings of gold-plated and polished bronze jewelry are also offered. Open daily. Fee for overnight accommodations and meals.

day trip 04

northwest

bird heaven & haven:
squaw creek national wildlife refuge

squaw creek national wildlife refuge

Established in 1935, Squaw Creek provides more than 7,000 acres of man-made marshes where waterfowl and other creatures can find food, water, and shelter. The refuge is located 5 miles south of Mound City, a town that gets its name from the loess mounds that bound Squaw Creek to the east. The loess bluffs are a rare geologic formation of wind-deposited soil from the past glacial period. The stuff is crumbly and falls apart in your fingers.

If you are making your first visit to Squaw Creek, you may want to ask some questions at the refuge headquarters, where you'll also find brochures about area wildlife. The refuge itself is open year-round from sunrise to sunset. Poaching has forced stricter adherence to the refuge's opening and closing hours. If you're found on the refuge after closing time, you risk receiving a stiff fine for trespassing.

getting there

You can reach the refuge by taking I-29 North to exit 79, then onto US 159. Follow US 159 West for 2.5 miles and it will take you in front of the refuge headquarters. The drive is about 90 miles and takes around 2 hours.

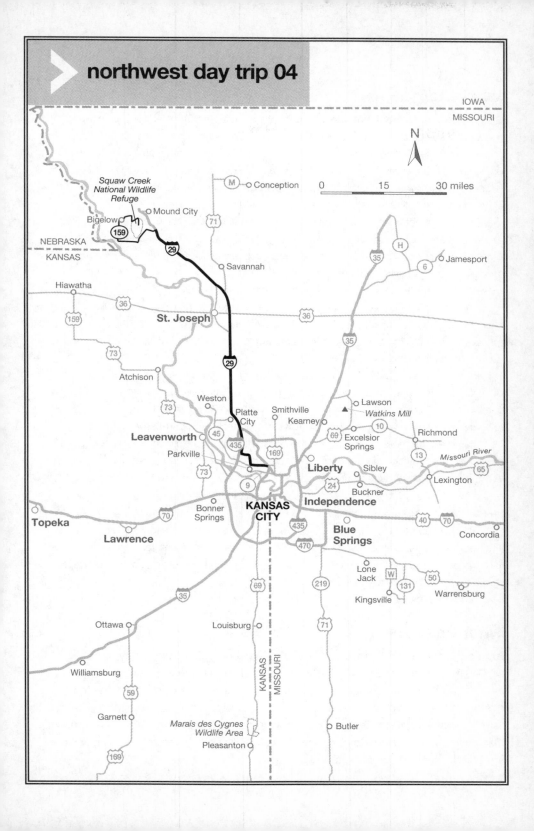

where to go

Squaw Creek National Wildlife Refuge. Mound City; (660) 442-3187; www.fws.gov/midwest/squawcreek. Birding is good year-round, although fall and spring are the most spectacular times. White pelicans are present during Sept and Apr. In Nov and Dec the refuge offers visitors a special treat when bald eagles migrate to the area. During winter Squaw Creek is said to have one of the highest concentrations of eagles in the United States, and eagle counts on the refuge have soared beyond 300 in the past.

The refuge holds an annual Eagle Days the first full weekend in December. The event includes a live eagle program, special viewing sites, an auto tour, handouts, and various other programs—every hour on the hour. Open-house weekends are held in spring and fall and center on the bird migrations.

After leaving the headquarters, take the bridge directly in front of it to the first observation tower you see, then turn left. An auto-tour route completes a 10-mile loop going through a variety of habitats. Follow the road around to Eagle Overlook, which is clearly marked on a sign. This is a split of land that extends into Eagle Pool, where you can mingle with the birds firsthand.

In warm weather look for red-tailed hawks, ring-necked pheasants, sandpipers, ring-billed gulls, terns, and owls. Fall and spring migrations often bring close to 200,000 snow geese, 150,000 ducks, and millions of blackbirds. Be sure to bring along a pair of binoculars to search for eagles, which perch along rows of high trees that border the water.

Mammals are more difficult to see than birds because of their nocturnal habits and the dense habitats they choose. But if you are patient and interested enough to wait and watch, you might observe white-tailed deer, opossums, raccoons, and coyotes along the roads. You don't have to be a Boy Scout to detect the presence of mammals; just look for their tracks in the snow, dust, or mud.

Hunting and camping aren't allowed. Bring your own snacks, especially energy foods and a thermos of something warm to drink on a cold day. The refuge temperature is about 10 degrees colder than it is in Kansas City and there's a wind-chill factor, so wear a sweater, plus a parka, hat, gloves, and boots in winter.

The refuge headquarters is open daily, except for federal holidays. Free.

where to stay

Big Lake State Park Resort. Located 11 miles northeast of Mound City, on MO 111 and US 159, Bigelow; (660) 442-5432; www.mostateparks.com/biglake.htm. Located on a natural oxbow lake, this lovely state park offers cabins with fireplaces, a meeting room, a dining room, and motel rooms and suites with kitchenettes. There's a swimming pool and fishing available as well. The resort is closed the end of Oct through the last weekend in Mar. A minimum of 2 nights' stay is required, but you'll want to spend at least that or more enjoying the tranquility of the area. $–$$.

 **regional information**

northeast

Excelsior Springs Chamber of Commerce, 461 S. Thompson, Excelsior Springs, MO 64024; (816) 630-6161; www.exspgschamber.com.

Jamesport Community Association, Jamesport, MO 64648; (660) 684-6146; www.jamesportmissouri.org.

Kearney Chamber of Commerce, PO Box 242, Kearney, MO 64060; (816) 628-4229; www.kearneymo.com.

Liberty Chamber of Commerce, 1170 W. Kansas St., # H, Liberty, MO 64068; (816) 781-5200; www.libertychamber.com.

Richmond Chamber of Commerce, 104 N. Main St., Richmond, MO 64085; (816) 776-6919; www.richmondchamber.org.

Smithville Chamber of Commerce, 105 W. Main St., Smithville, MO 64089; (816) 532-0946; www.smithvillechamber.org.

east

Friends of Arrow Rock, (660) 837-3305; www.friendsofarrowrock.org.

Boonville Chamber of Commerce, 320 First St., Boonville, MO 65233; (660) 882-2721; www.boonvillemochamberofcommerce.com.

City of Independence Tourism Department, 111 E. Maple St., Independence, MO 64050; (816) 325-7111; www.visitindependence.com.

Columbia Convention and Visitors Bureau, 300 S. Providence, Columbia, MO 65205; (800) 652-0987 or (573) 875-1231; www.visitcolumbiamo.com.

The Friends of Rocheport, 501 Third St., Rocheport, MO 65279; (573) 698-3207 or (573) 698-3210; www.rocheport.com.

Jefferson City Convention and Visitors Bureau, 100 E. High St., Jefferson City, MO 65101; (800) 769-4183 or (573) 632-2820; www.visitjeffersoncity.com.

Lexington Tourism Bureau, 1029 Franklin, Lexington, MO 64067; (660) 259-4711; www
.historiclexington.com.

New Franklin Chamber of Commerce, 130 E. Broadway, New Franklin, MO 65274;
(660) 848-2288; http://newfranklin.missouri.org.

Sedalia Chamber of Commerce, 600 E. Third St., Sedalia, MO 65301; (800) 827-5295;
www.visitsedaliamo.com.

Warrensburg Chamber of Commerce, 100 S. Holden St., Warrensburg, MO 64093;
(660) 747-3168; www.warrensburg.org.

southeast

Lake of the Ozarks Convention and Visitor Bureau, PO Box 1498, Osage Beach, MO
65065; (800) 386-5253; www.funlake.com.

south

Carthage Convention and Visitors Bureau, 402 S. Garrison St., Carthage, MO 64836;
(417) 359-8181 or (866) 357-8687; www.visit-carthage.com.

southwest

Chanute Chamber of Commerce, 21 N. Lincoln St., Chanute, KS 66720; (877) 431-3350
or (620) 431-3350; www.chanutechamber.com.

Crawford County Convention and Visitors Bureau, 117 W. Fourth St., Pittsburg, KS
66762; (800) 879-1112 or (620) 231-1212; www.visitcrawfordcounty.com.

Emporia County Convention and Visitors Bureau, 719 Commercial St., PO Box 703,
Emporia, KS 66801; (800) 279-3730 or (620) 342-1803; www.emporiakschamber.org.

Fort Scott Chamber of Commerce, 231 E. Wall St., Fort Scott, KS 66701; (800) 245-
FORT; www.fortscott.com.

Franklin County Convention and Tourism Bureau, 2011 E. Logan St., Ottawa, KS
66067; (785) 242-1411; www.visitottawakansas.com.

The Garnett Area Chamber of Commerce, 419 S. Oak St., Garnett, KS 66032; (785)
448-6767; www.garnettchamber.org.

Osawatomie Chamber of Commerce, 628 Main St., Osawatomie, KS 66064, (913) 755-
4114; www.osawatomiechamber.org.

Wichita Convention and Visitors Bureau, 515 S. Main St., Wichita, KS 67202; (316)
265-2800; www.gowichita.com.

west

Abilene Convention and Visitors Bureau, 201 NW Second St., Abilene, KS 67410; (800) 569-5915; www.abilenekansas.org.

Bonner Springs/Edwardsville Chamber of Commerce, 129 N. Nettleton, Bonner Springs, KS 66012; (913) 422-5044; www.lifeisbetter.org.

Chase County Chamber of Commerce, 318 Broadway, Cottonwood Falls, KS 66845; (800) 431-6344; www.chasecountyks.org.

Council Grove/Morris County Visitors Bureau, 207 W. Main St., Council Grove, KS 66846; (800) 732-9211 or (620) 767-5882; www.councilgrove.com.

Lawrence Convention and Visitors Bureau, 785 Vermont St., Ste. 101, Lawrence, KS 66044; (785) 865-4499; www.visitlawrence.com.

Manhattan Convention and Visitors Bureau, 501 Poyntz Ave., Manhattan, KS 66502; (785) 776-8829; www.manhattan.org.

Topeka Convention and Visitors Bureau, 1275 SW Topeka Blvd., Topeka, KS 66612; (785) 234-1030; www.visittopeka.us.

Wamego Area Chamber of Commerce, PO Box 34, Wamego, KS 66547; (785) 456-7849; www.wamego.org.

northwest

Atchison Chamber of Commerce, Santa Fe Depot Visitors Center, 200 S. Tenth St., Atchison, KS 66002; (800) 234-1854 or (913) 367-2427; www.atchisonkansas.net.

Hiawatha Chamber of Commerce, 701 Oregon St., Hiawatha, KS 66434; (913) 742-7136; www.cityofhiawatha.org.

Leavenworth Area Convention and Visitors Bureau, 518 Shawnee St., Leavenworth, KS 66048; (913) 682-4113; www.lvarea.com.

Parkville Chamber of Commerce, 8701 NW River Park Dr., Parkville, MO, 64152; (816) 587-2700, www.parkvillechamber.com.

Platte County Convention and Visitors Bureau, 11724 NW Plaza Circle, # 200, Kansas City, MO 64152; (816) 270-3979; www.visitplatte.com.

St. Joseph Visitors Center, 502 N. Woodbine, St. Joseph, MO 64502; (816) 232-1839; www.stjomo.com.

Savannah Chamber of Commerce, 411 Court St., (816) 324-3976; www.savannahmo chamber.com.

Weston Development Company, 502 Main St., Weston, MO 64098; (816) 640-2909; www.westonmo.com.

missouri wineries

Farhmeier Family Vineyards, 9364 Mitchell Trail, Lexington, MO; (816) 934-2472; www .ffvineyards.com.

Baltimore Bend Winery, 27150 US 24, Waverly, MO; (660) 493-0258; www.baltimore bend.com.

Belvoir Winery, 1325 Odd Fellows Rd., Liberty, MO; (816) 200-1811.

Bristle Ridge Vineyards, P Highway and US 50, Montserrat, MO; (660) 422-5646.

Bynum Winery, 13520 S. Sam Moore Rd., Lone Jack, MO; (816) 566-2240.

Casa de Loco Winery, 16952 N. MO 5, Sunrise Beach, MO; (573) 374-8801; www.casa delocowinery.com.

Les Bourgeois Vineyards, I-70 and Highway BB, Rocheport, MO; (573) 698-2133.

Montserrat Vineyards, 104 NE 641, Knob Noster, MO; (660) 747-9463.

Pirtle's Winery, 502 Spring St., Weston, MO; (816) 640-5728; www.pirtlewinery.com.

Riverwood Winery, 22200 MO 45 North, Weston, MO; (816) 579-9797; www.riverwood winery.com.

Seven Springs Winery, 846 Winery Hills Estates, Linn Creek, MO; (573) 317-0100; www .sevenspringswinery.com.

kansas wineries

Holy-Field Vineyard & Winery, 18807 158th St., Basehor, KS; (913) 724-9463; www .holyfieldwinery.com.

Somerset Ridge Vineyard, 29725 Somerset Rd., between Paolo and Louisburg, KS; (913) 491-0038; www.somersetridge.com.

festivals & celebrations

february

Step Back in Time Winter Festival, Jamesport, MO. First week of February. (816) 684-6146; www.jamesportmissouri.org.

march

True/False Film Festival, Columbia, MO. (573) 442-8783; www.truefalse.org.

Wurstfest, Hermann, MO. Annual mid-March event. (800) 932-8687; www.hermannmo.com.

april

Big Muddy Folk Festival, Boonville, MO. Two-day event in early April. (660) 882-2721; www.bigmuddy.org.

Dogwood Music Festival, Camdenton, MO. Annual mid-April event. (800) 769-1004; www.camdentonchamber.com.

Tulip Festival, Wamego, KS. Third Saturday and Sunday of April. (785) 456-7849; www.visitwamego.com.

may

Apple Blossom Festival and Parade, St. Joseph, MO. First weekend in May. (800) 785-0360; www.appleblossomparade.com.

Arrow Rock Annual Antique Show, Arrow Rock, MO. Third weekend in May. (816) 837-3470; www.arrowrock.org.

Civil War Reenactment, Carthage, MO. Mid-May event. (417) 358-2373; www.visit-carthage.com.

Fort Leavenworth Homes Tour and Frontier Army Encampment, Fort Leavenworth, KS. First Saturday in May. (800) 444-4114; www.lvarea.com.

Gatsby Days Festival, Excelsior Springs, MO. Second weekend in May. (816) 714-8585; www.gatsbydays.com

May Day Festival, Jamesport, MO. Early May event. (816) 684-6682; www.jamesport-mo
.com.

Mushroom Festival, Richmond, MO. First weekend in May. (816) 776-6916; www.rich
mondmissouri.com.

Spring on the Square, Liberty, MO. Early May event. (816) 781-5200; www.libertymo
.com.

Topeka Jazz Festival, Topeka, KS. Last weekend in May. (785) 234-2787; www.topeka
cvb.org.

june

Art in the Park, Columbia, MO. First weekend in June. (573) 443-8838; www.gocolumbia
mo.com.

Blind Boone Music Festival, Warrensburg, MO. Second weekend in June. (660) 747-
3268; www.blindboonepark.org.

Flint Hills Rodeo, Strong City, KS. (620) 273-6480; www.flintshillsrodeo.com.

Good Ol' Days, Fort Scott, KS. First weekend in June. (800) 245-FORT; www.fortscott
.com.

Heritage Days, Lexington, MO. Mid-June celebration. (660) 259-3082; www.historiclex
ington.com.

Parkville Jazz & Fine Arts River Jam, Parkville, MO. Third Friday and Saturday in June.
(816) 505-2227; www.parkvillemo.com.

Scott Joplin Ragtime Festival, Sedalia, MO. First week in June. (660) 826-2271; www
.scottjoplin.org.

Symphony on the Prairie, Flint Hills, KS. (620) 273-8955; www.symphonyintheflinthills
.org.

Wah-Shun-Gah Days, Council Grove, KS. Third weekend in June, in even numbered
years. (800) 732-9211 or (620) 767-5882; www.councilgrove.com.

Waterfest, Excelsior Springs, MO. Third weekend in June. (816) 630-6161; www.exspgs
chamber.com.

july

Amelia Earhart Festival, Atchison, KS. Annual festival in late July. (800) 234-1854; www
.atchisonkansas.net.

Fiesta Mexicana Week, Topeka, KS. Weeklong mid-July festival. (800) 235-1030; www .visittopeka.com.

Fort Osage Independence Day, Sibley, MO. July 4. (816) 650-3278.

Fourth of July Celebration, Wamego, KS. (785) 456-7849; www.wamego.org.

Kansas River Valley Art Fair, Topeka, KS. Last weekend in July. (785) 368-3888; www .visittopeka.com.

Kaw Valley Rodeo and Riley County Fair, Manhattan, KS. Last week in July. (785) 537-6350; www.manhattancvb.org.

Missouri State Powwow, Sedalia, MO. Mid-July event. (800) 827-5295; www.visitsedalia mo.com.

Missouri Town 1855 Independence Day, Fleming Park, Blue Springs, MO. July 4. (816) 795-8200, ext. 1260; www.co.jackson.mo.us.

Platte County Fair, Tracy, MO. Third weekend in July. (816) 431-3247; www.plattecofair .com.

Sunflower State Games, Lawrence, KS. Two weekends in late July. (785) 842-7774; www.sunflowergames.com.

Wild Bill Hickok Rodeo and Western Heritage Festival, Abilene, KS. Last weekend of July. (800) 569-5915; www.wildbillhickockrodeo.com

august

Gus Macker 3-on-3 Basketball Tournament, Jefferson City, MO. Third weekend in August. (573) 634-3616; www.jeffersoncity.org.

Missouri River Festival of the Arts, Boonville, MO. Second week of August. (660) 882-2721; www.goboonville.com.

Missouri State Fair, Sedalia, MO. (800) 422-FAIR; www.mostatefair.com.

Trails West, St. Joseph, MO. Third weekend in August. (800) 785-0360; www.stjoearts .org.

september

Annual Ciderfest, Louisburg Cider Mill, Louisburg, KS. Last week in September and first week in October. (913) 837-5202; www.louisburgcidermill.com.

Annual Lawrence Indian Arts Show, Lawrence, KS. September and October. (785) 864-4245; www.visitlawrence.com.

Apple Jubilee, Waverly, MO. Mid-September event. (660) 493-2616.

Boonslick Traditional Folk Music Festival, Arrow Rock, MO. Second Saturday in September. (660) 837-3335; www.arrowrock.org.

Capital Jazzfest/Balloon Race, Jefferson City, MO. (800)-CHILDREN; www.visitjefferson city.com.

Cider Days, Topeka, KS. Last weekend of September. (785) 230-5226; www.ciderdays topeka.com.

Columbia Festival of the Arts, Columbia, MO. Last weekend of September. (573) 874-6386; www.gocolumbiamo.com.

Roots n' Blues n' BBQ, Columbia, MO. Second weekend in September. (573) 442-5862; RootsnBluesnBBQ.com.

Fall Festival, Liberty, MO. (816) 781-5200; www.libertymo.com.

Fort Osage Rendezvous and Trade Fair, Sibley, MO. Second weekend in September. (816) 650-3278.

Heritage Day "Step Back in Time" Festival, Jamesport, MO. (660) 684-6682; www .jamesport-mo.com.

Jesse James Festival, Kearney, MO. Mid-September event. (816) 628-4229; www.jesse jamesfestival.com.

Leavenworth River Fest, Leavenworth, KS. Second weekend in September. (800) 844-4114; www.lvarea.com.

Little Balkans Days, Pittsburg, KS. Annual September event. (620) 704-7369; www.little balkans.com.

Ozark Ham and Turkey Festival, California, MO. Third Saturday in September. (573) 796-3040.

Power of the Past Antique Engine and Tractor Show, Ottawa, KS. Second weekend of September. (785) 242-1411; www.powerofthepast.net.

Renaissance Festival, Bonner Springs, KS. Weekends in September and October. (800) 373-0357 or (816) 561-8005; www.kcrenfest.com.

Santa-Cali-Gon Festival, Independence, MO. Labor Day weekend. (816) 325-7111; www .santacaligon.com.

october

Apple Fest, Weston, MO. Early October event. (816) 640-2909; www.westonmo.com.

Apple Festival, Topeka, KS. Early October celebration. (785) 368-3888; www.visittopeka .us.

Arrow Rock Craft Festival, Arrow Rock, MO. Second weekend in October. (660) 837-3335; www.arrowrock.org.

Chisholm Trail Day Festival, Abilene, KS. First Saturday of October. (785) 263-2681; www.abilenekansas.org.

Haunted Atchison Tours, Atchison, KS. Every night in September and October. (800) 234-1854; www.atchisonkansas.net.

Halloween Frolic, Hiawatha, KS. Halloween night. (913) 742-7136.

Maple Leaf Festival, Carthage, MO. Third weekend of the month. (417) 358-2373; www .visit-carthage.com.

Missouri Town 1855 Fall Festival, Fleming Park, Blue Springs, MO. First weekend in October. (816) 795-8200, ext. 1260; www.jacksongov.org.

Oktoberfest, Atchison, KS. First weekend of the month. (800) 234-1854; www.atchison .org.

OztoberFest, Wamego, KS. First Saturday of October. (866) 458-TOTO; www.oztoberfest .com.

Renaissance Festival, Bonner Springs, KS. Weekends in September and October. (800) 373-0357 or (816) 561-8005; www.kcrenfest.com.

november

Annual Christmas Lighting Ceremony, Carthage, MO. Mid-November event. (800) 543-7975; www.visit-carthage.com.

Annual Lake Lights Festival and Enchanted Holiday Park, Osage Beach, MO. Mid-November through January 1. (800) 386-5253; www.funlake.com.

Step Back in Time Christmas Festival, Jamesport, MO. Last week in November. (816) 684-6682; www.jamesport-mo.com.

Veterans Day Tribute, Emporia, KS. Early November. (800) 279-3730.

december

Christmas in Weston Candlelight Homes Tour, Weston, MO. First weekend in December. (816) 640-2909; www.westonmo.com.

Christmas on the River, Parkville, MO. First Thursday through Sunday in December. (816) 505-2227; www.parkvillemo.com.

Frontier Candlelight Tour, Fort Scott, KS. First weekend in December. (800) 245-FORT; www.fortscott.com.

Squaw Creek National Wildlife Refuge Eagle Days, Mound City, MO. First full weekend in December. (660) 442-3187; www.fws.gov/midwest.

index

Getaway ideas for the local traveler

Need a day away to relax, refresh, renew?
Just get in your car and go!